IMAGES
of America

HAMMOND

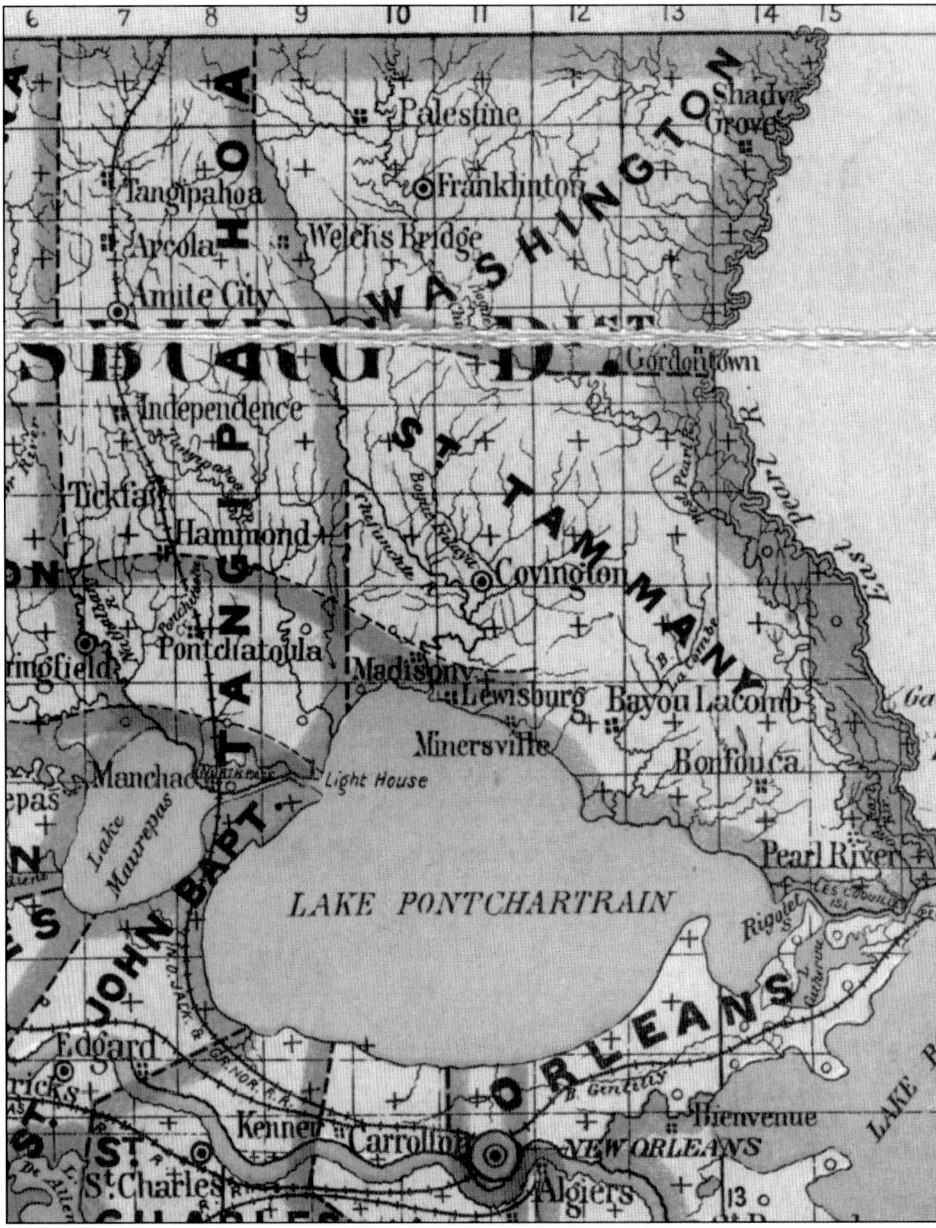

An early mention of Hammond appears on this 1876 US General Land Office map of Louisiana. The area, once referred to as Hammond's Crossing, is named for Peter Hammond, who settled there in the 1820s and sold timber and resin products. Hammond's property was situated in Livingston Parish until Tangipahoa Parish was created in 1869 from four existing parishes. Hammond's Crossing eventually became Hammond. (Courtesy of Library of Congress.)

On the Cover: Strawberries were being cultivated in the Greater Hammond area before 1847, and by the turn of the century the city had become a major shipping point for the fruit. Farmers would crowd the streets, bringing the berries into town for shipping by train. In this photograph, berry farmers line up in front of Neelis and Company Emporium, which sold, among other things, stencils and additional needs for the strawberry industry.

IMAGES
of America

HAMMOND

Eric W. Johnson and Catherine H. Tijerino

ARCADIA
PUBLISHING

ISBN 978-1-4671-1517-9

Published by Arcadia Publishing
Charleston, South Carolina

Printed in the United States of America

Library of Congress Control Number: 2015944263

For all general information, please contact Arcadia Publishing:
Telephone 843-853-2070
Fax 843-853-0044
E-mail sales@arcadiapublishing.com
For customer service and orders:
Toll-Free 1-888-313-2665

Visit us on the Internet at www.arcadiapublishing.com

This book is dedicated to three historians—the late Judge Leon Ford III, Tom Davidson, and C. Howard Nichols—and one journalist, Edna Campbell, whose photographs and local history acumen made this work possible; to Roger Tijerino for technical and editing support; to Roman Heleniak for instilling a love of history in one author; and to Al Hulett and Pat Forbes for patiently dealing with both authors' long hours of sleuthing, hunting, gathering, and writing.

Contents

ACKNOWLEDGMENTS

We are grateful to a number of people who assisted in the creation of this book. Please forgive us if we have overlooked anyone. Dr. Sam Hyde Jr. and Dr. Keith Finley of Southeastern Louisiana University's Center for Southeast Louisiana Studies allowed us access to the photographic and archival collections and provided suggestions and historical fact. Assistants Faith Allen, Megan Arledge, Sara Chauppette, Nicholas Heyd, Matt Jordan, and Chase Tomlin provided legwork and technical expertise. Roger Tijerino excelled in providing editing and technical support. Bill Dorman and Lenore Johnson at the Amite branch of the Tangipahoa Parish Library introduced us to their photographic collection. René Abadie and Randy Bergeron searched for Southeastern photographs. In addition to sharing photographs, Marion Ruth Chandler, Don Fellows Jr., H.P. Forbes, Cathy Martin, Helen Rownd, and H. Hall Starnes Jr. offered reminiscences that aided us greatly. Justice Jefferson D. Hughes III, Suzanne Barnes Graham, Cecilia Giannobile, Peggy Powell, Carlee White, Yolanda Robinson Cyprian, and Pat at Historic Opera provided photographs; Marjorie Morrison Raymond Pierce and Melanie Ricketts provided clarification; Timothy D. Hudson provided newspaper articles; Beth Stahr and Mary Lou Strong of Southeastern's Sims Memorial Library provided invaluable reference assistance; and library student workers Katy Clayton, Larsen Glover, and Kayla Scurich provided clerical support. Charlene Bonnette and the reference staff at the State Library of Louisiana helped us acquire needed photographs and information. Finally, C. Howard Nichols and Tom Davidson, who were already mentioned in the dedication, were extremely generous with their time, encouraging us in our efforts, sharing their extensive knowledge of local history, and helping us keep the information as accurate as possible. They, along with Leon Ford III and Citizens National Bank, were instrumental in the creation of earlier books, now long out of print, that included some of the images in this book. Any errors in the present book can be attributed solely to the authors.

Unless otherwise noted, images appear courtesy of the Center for Southeast Louisiana Studies at Southeastern Louisiana University. This key is used for other images: Don Fellows Jr. (DF), the Leon Ford III/Tom Davidson Collection (LF/TD); Roger Tijerino (RT).

Introduction

Hammond owes its existence to two men who played a huge part in its early settlement and development. The first, Peter Hammond, was a sailor born in 1798 in Hammerdal, Sweden, who was captured by the British during the War of 1812 while sailing to the United States. Fortunately, after a period of imprisonment, escape, and wandering, during which time he mastered the arts of making sails and rigging ships, he landed in New Orleans around 1820. He made his way across Lake Pontchartrain and up the local rivers to Wadesboro, a river shipping point near Ponchatoula. The rich pine forests would support his manufacturing of nautical goods, such as sail masts and charcoal, and after finding labor as a woodcutter, he became a homesteader, purchasing a large tract of land for pennies an acre. He began making kegs and processing turpentine, tar, pitch, and re-tarred coal, shipping the products to New Orleans for sale. He also cut pines and sold them for ship masts, hauling all of these products to Wadesboro and then sending them by flatboat to New Orleans.

Hammond built his business and a large log home and around 1830 married Caroline Tucker, a young woman from Ponchatoula with whom he had seven children. As the business grew, more people came to the area and stayed to raise families. Hammond, who built a store to sell his goods, granted the right-of-way to his land for the construction of a rail line from New Orleans to Jackson, Mississippi, and beyond; the line was completed in 1854. The New Orleans, Jackson & Great Northern Railroad brought more people to the stop that was known alternatively as Hammond's Crossing and Hammond Station, and the settlement began acquiring stores and other amenities.

Hammond began selling his land in 1859 to new settlers. Among them was the second man to vitalize the burgeoning community, Charles Emery Cate. Cate, an entrepreneur from New Hampshire operating a shoe business in New Orleans, had bought land from an estate and the State of Louisiana adjoining the railroad and moved his family to Hammond's Crossing, building a shoe factory, a sawmill, and a boardinghouse for his workers in 1861. Thus, Hammond's Crossing was well on its way to becoming the city of Hammond.

The Civil War brought destruction to Cate's enterprise when Union troops stationed in New Orleans burned his sawmill and destroyed the shoe factory equipment in April 1863, but he rebuilt the businesses and developed the area further by laying out streets and lots. The factory was subsequently turned into a hotel, more stores opened, oak trees were planted, a schoolroom was created, and a post office was built. Thanks to Cate's generosity, numerous churches and schools provided nourishment for the mind and spirit. Hammond, who died in 1870, lived long enough to see his settlement being galvanized into a growing and thriving community. Just 19 years later, Hammond's Crossing would incorporate as a city.

Meanwhile, the railroad began advertising the healthful pleasures of the warm climate, excellent spring waters, and the abundance of fruits and vegetables—especially strawberries, which would become a major industry within a decade or two. Northerners and Midwesterners hopped on the

Illinois Central Railroad trains, booked rooms at the Kidder or Oaks Hotel, liked the climate and the area, and stayed. New Orleanians, escaping the excessive heat and humidity of summers south of Lake Pontchartrain, refreshed themselves in Hammond on extended visits.

By the turn of the century, Hammond had developed a downtown area with shops to provide all manner of goods, restaurants, livery stables, and theaters. The city was electrified in 1894, and in the ensuing years paved roads and sewer pipes added to the convenience of living in town. Hammond had sent men to fight in the Spanish-American War, and patriotic parades would become a popular pastime. The lumber and strawberry industries kept the city financially solvent, and the establishment of more stores in safer buildings extended the downtown area and helped avoid the fires that had plagued the city in its early years. Houses sprang up around the downtown area, parks provided a respite from the rigors of daily life, and the population continued to grow.

The timber industry declined as forested areas were depleted and tastes in building materials changed, but the strawberry held sway for many years, enabling Hammond to call itself the "Strawberry Capital of the World." Tons of strawberries were auctioned off and shipped all over the country, even more so once the refrigerated train car was invented. Farms in Hammond and surrounding towns produced various varieties of berries, most notably the Klondyke, a large, juicy, hardy variety of strawberry cultivated by Robert L. Cloud that became the leading variety in the United States for 30 years. Strawberry harvest time would find the streets of Hammond teeming with wagons and later trucks full of berries; the city came alive with farmers, strawberry buyers, and their families. There were strawberry parades, strawberry festivals, and the crowning of a Strawberry Queen. The industry would peak and then decline, however, as other berries replaced Klondykes, farmers' children sought other livelihoods, labor and transportation problems increased, and changes in weather brought disaster to the crops. Hammond would eventually lose its strawberry crown to neighboring Ponchatoula, but the berry would always be associated with the city.

The decline in one industry would be accompanied by growth in others, such as banking, law, insurance, health care, and education. Hammond surged on through two World Wars, losing some of its finest young men to the battlefields. Early local heroes, such as Pulitzer Prize–winning editor Hodding Carter Jr. and Congressman Jimmy Morrison, worked to make sure Hammond and Louisiana stayed in the limelight while keeping to the straight and narrow. The emergence of a junior college by 1925, which evolved into four-year college and then a full-fledged university, produced such illustrious graduates as jazz great Bill Evans. By 1950, Hammond had a secure role in the development of south Louisiana, with residents enjoying the postwar industrial boom and its associated modern conveniences with few hints of the major changes that the Civil Rights Movement, Vietnam War, and counter-culture would bring in the ensuing decades.

While Hammond is not the parish seat, it is the business and cultural center of Tanghipahoa Parish and still enjoys the climate, natural beauty, and vivacity that generated its growth so many years ago. The descendants of Peter Hammond and Charles Emery Cate who still live in Hammond can be extremely proud of their ancestors' efforts in the creation and development of this vibrant Louisiana city.

One

History to 1950

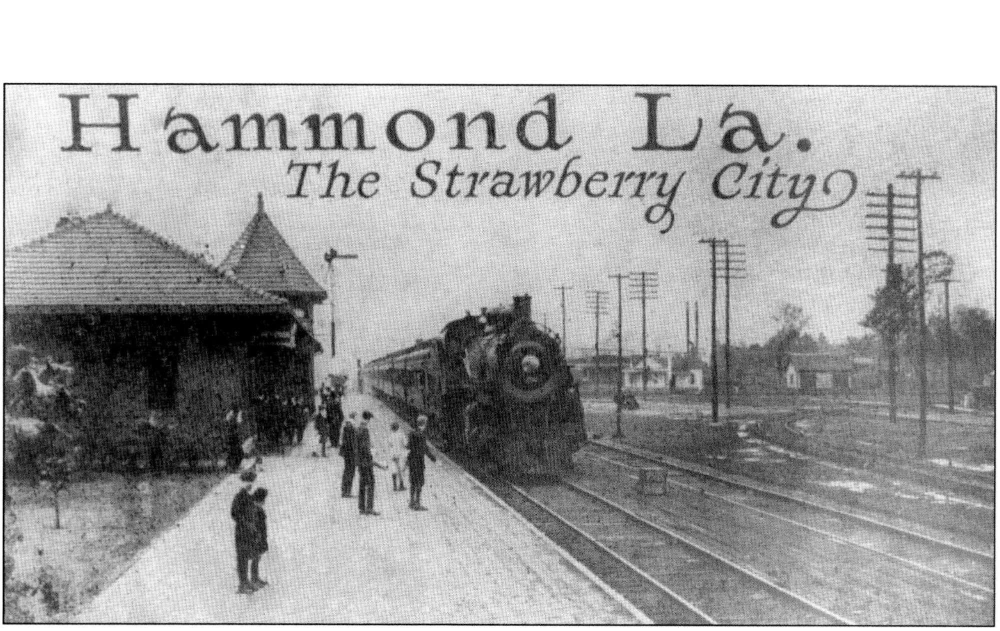

Many postcards from the turn of the century advertised Hammond by highlighting the railroad and the strawberry trade—two important industries that transformed the city from a sleepy logging town into an emerging community. As a train arrives at the depot, which was built in 1912, the text reminds the observer that Hammond is "The Strawberry City."

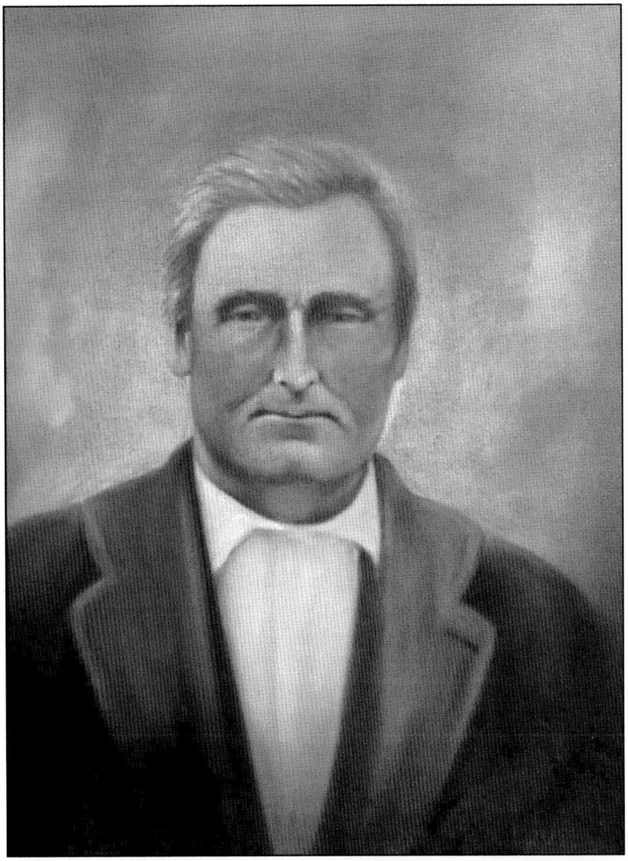

This 1968 oil painting by Isabel Lovel is based on a photograph presumed to be of Peter Hammond and his wife, Caroline Tucker. Hammond settled the area around 1830, buying land and building a log home near East Robert and Chestnut Streets, along with a warehouse and store. His provision of a right-of-way for the railroad resulted in greater accessibility to the area. (Courtesy of Jefferson D. Hughes III.)

The Hammond Oak stands on a plot of land on East Charles Street that is the site of the grave of Peter Hammond. The age of the tree is unknown, but it was already a landmark when this early postcard was printed. Also on-site are the graves of Hammond's wife Caroline, their daughter Maria, six other family members, and a favorite slave child, the first to be buried on the plot.

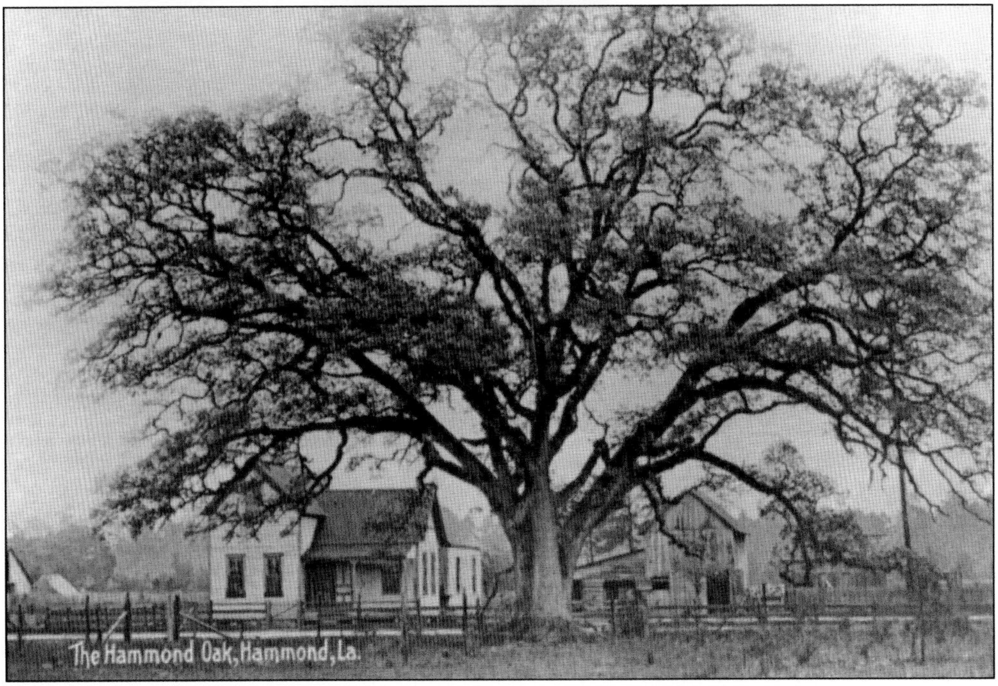

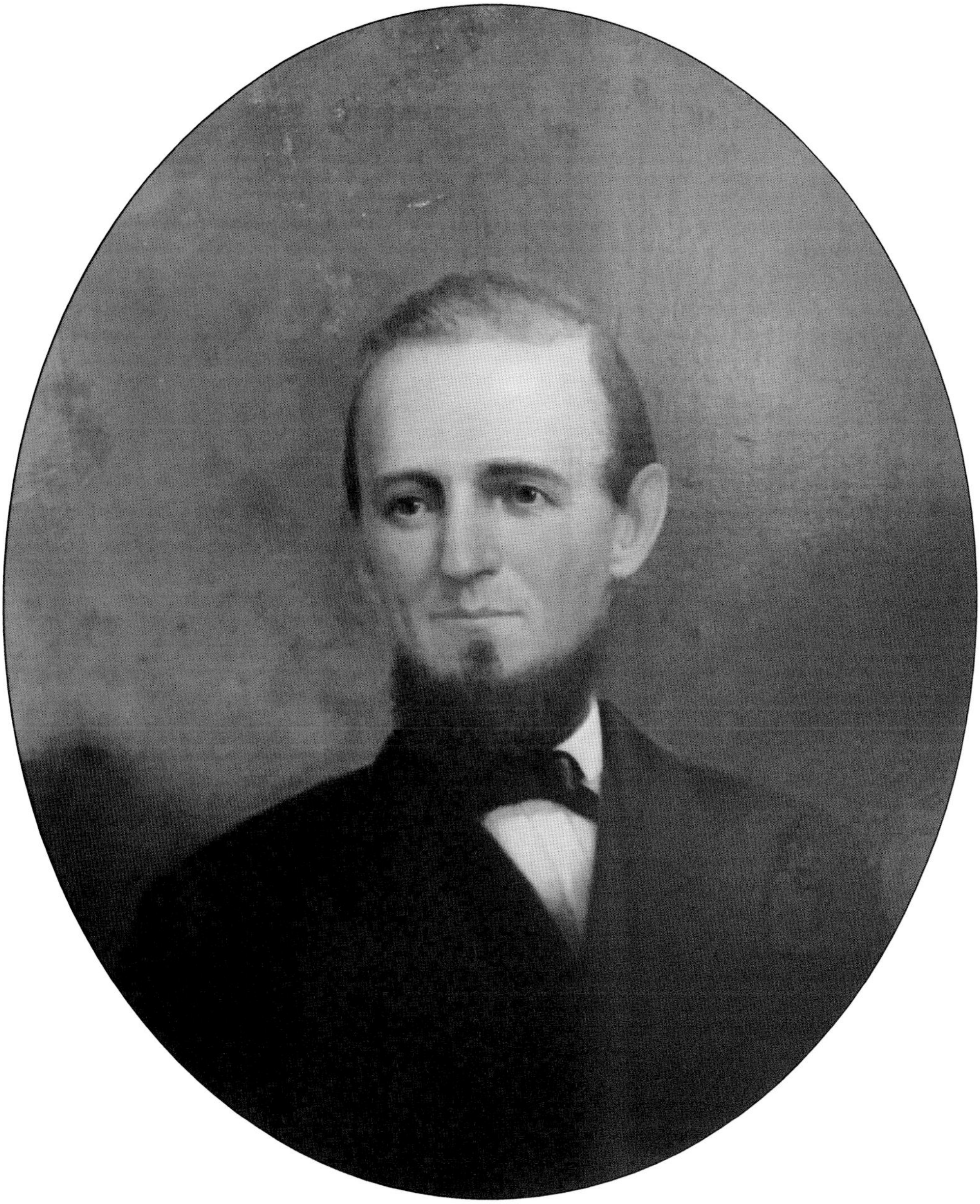

Born in New Hampshire in 1831, Charles Emery Cate moved to Hammond via New Orleans in the 1860s. While in New Orleans, he met and married Mercy "Mertie" Ann Waterman. Because of the Civil War, the Cates moved to the Hammond area in 1861 and established several businesses, including a lumber mill and a shoe factory that provided footwear to the Confederate army. Union troops destroyed the sawmill and part of the shoe factory in 1863. After the war, Cate focused on the reconstruction of "Hammond's Crossing," laying out and creating the city's street system. Short on cash, he sold his shoe business and commuted to New Orleans for 10 years. Eventually, he sold his New Orleans ventures and returned to Hammond and sawmilling. Cate began building houses and developed the first planned residential area. He offered land to the railroad to ensure a regular passenger stop and donated land for churches and schools. Cate died in 1916. (Courtesy of Suzanne Barnes Graham.)

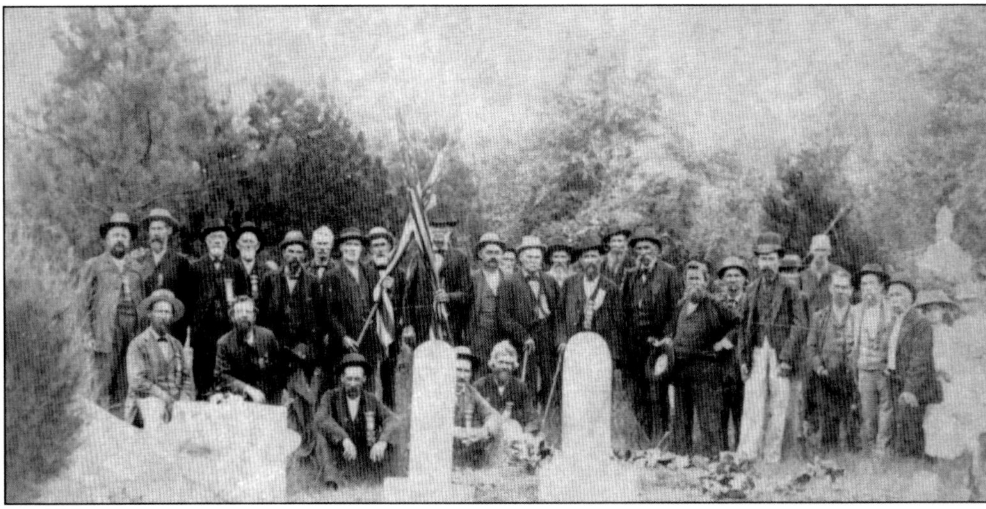

Many Union veterans settled in Hammond following the Civil War, the result of extensive advertising in the Midwest by the Illinois Central Railroad. Depicted is a Blue and Gray Memorial Day celebration in 1893, with veterans of both sides coming together. Mayor John W. Skinner (center left, with cane) lost his leg in the Battle of Manassas.

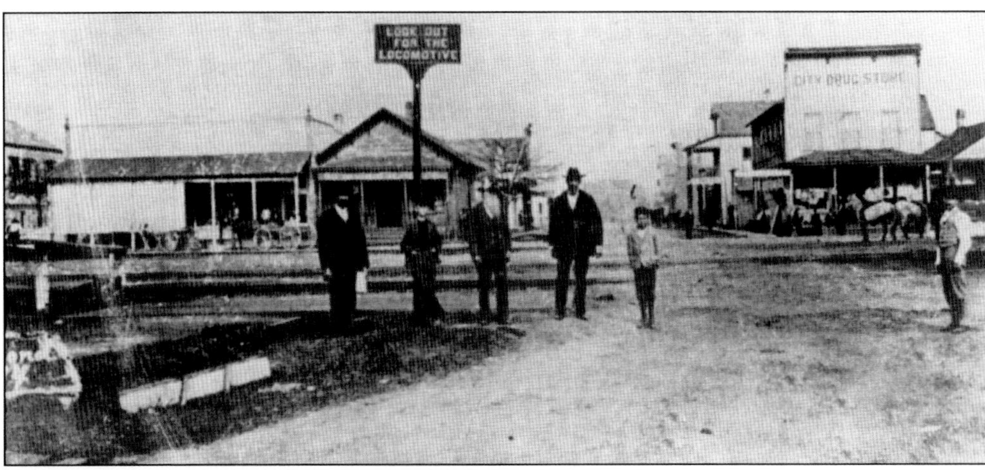

This 1894 photograph looks east on Thomas Street at the railroad crossing. The identified men are Willie Durkee (second from left), Mayor Urene Desouge (third from left), and Thomas G. Kidder (fifth from left). Note the warning sign that reads, "Look out for the locomotive." Many of the buildings in the photograph were destroyed by fire in 1896.

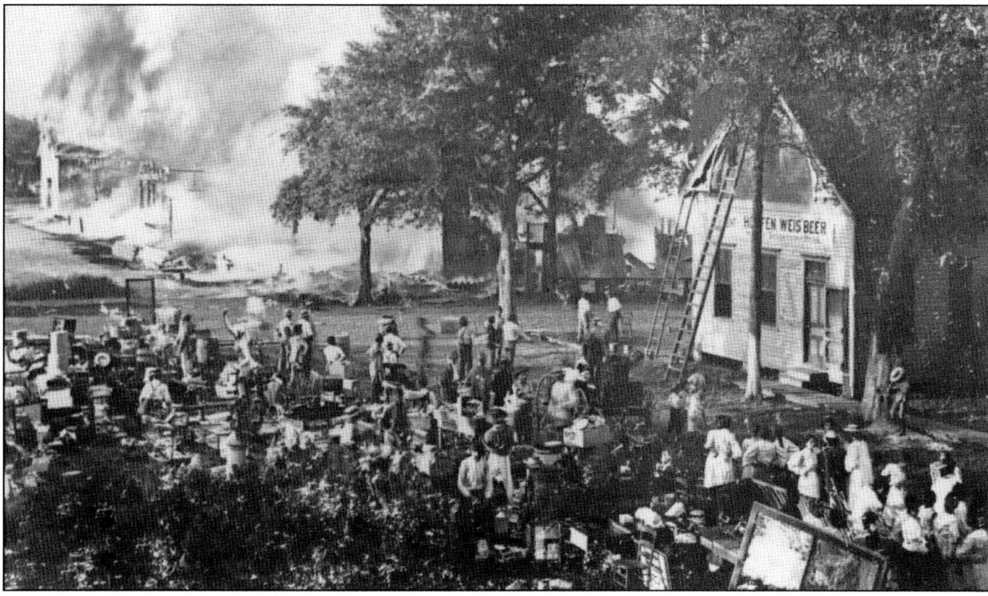

Downtown Hammond suffered two devastating fires in its first decade of incorporation. The first fire, which occurred September 8, 1895, destroyed the Northern Hotel and incinerated the first block of Southwestern Railroad Avenue. Since Hammond did not have organized fire protection, a special train left for Amite to secure assistance. Amite's Protection Fire Company No. 1 responded and fortunately succeeded in saving the rest of the downtown area.

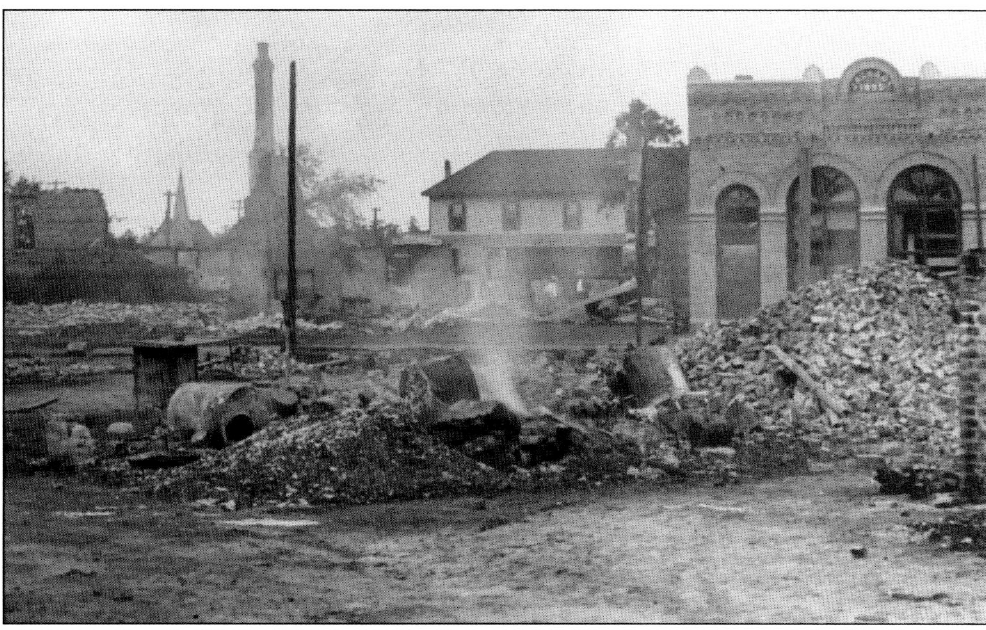

The second major fire occurred on July 24, 1896. The blaze started on East Railroad Avenue, destroying buildings along the street as well as structures on the north and south sides of East Thomas Street. The newly erected Jackson Building, which housed the Hammond Bank and the post office, was left standing. The fire prompted the city to establish a building code and organize a volunteer fire department.

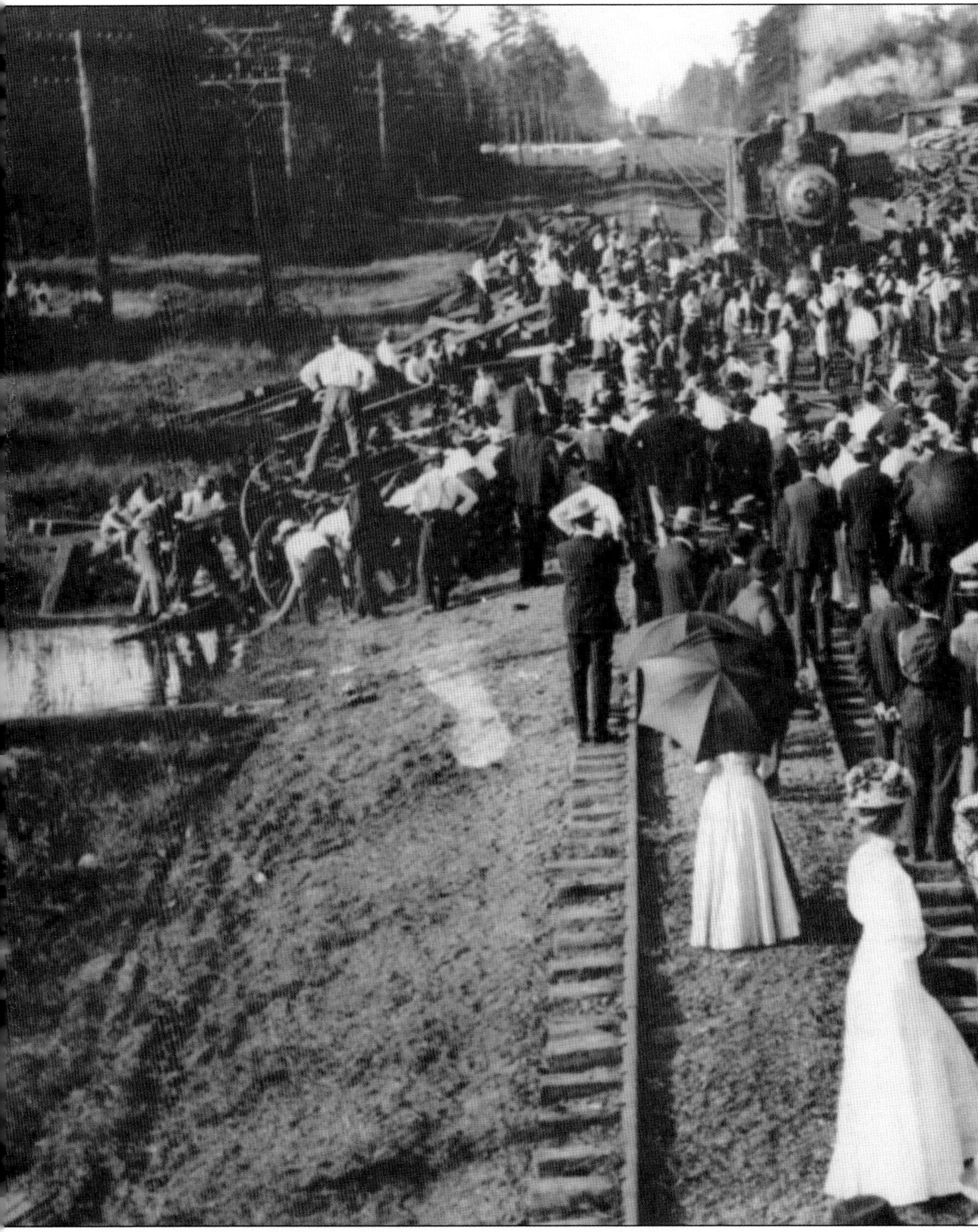

On October 27, 1907, Hammond citizens gathered north of the train depot, along the tracks, to watch firemen and their newly acquired fire truck battle flames emerging from a pile of railroad cross ties. The fire started around 3:00 p.m. that day and also ignited two train cars and burned telegraph wires on the east side of the tracks. The "fire truck"—in reality, a hand-operated water

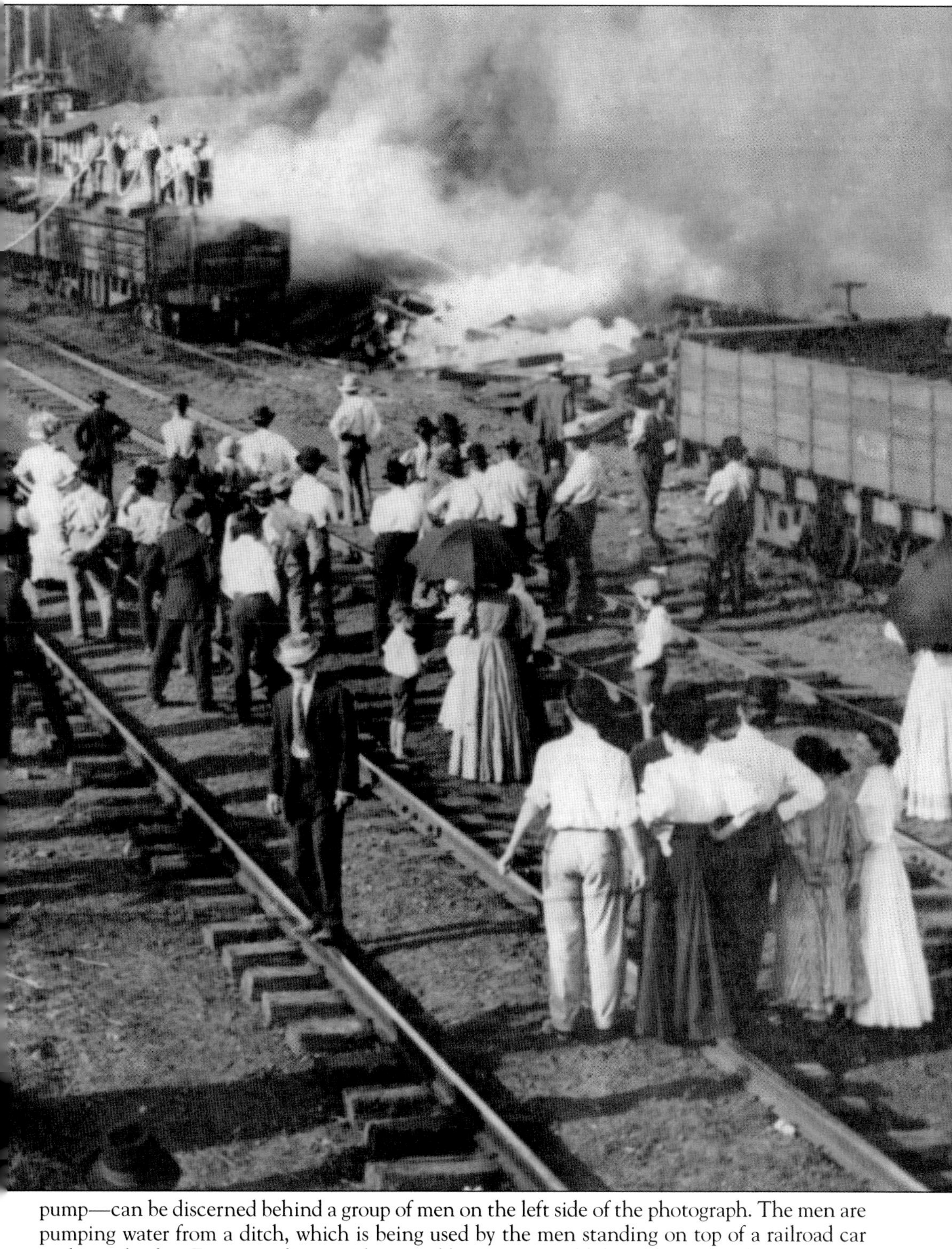

pump—can be discerned behind a group of men on the left side of the photograph. The men are pumping water from a ditch, which is being used by the men standing on top of a railroad car to douse the fire. For major fires, residents and businesses could depend on a combination of its volunteer fire department and assistance from nearby communities such as Amite.

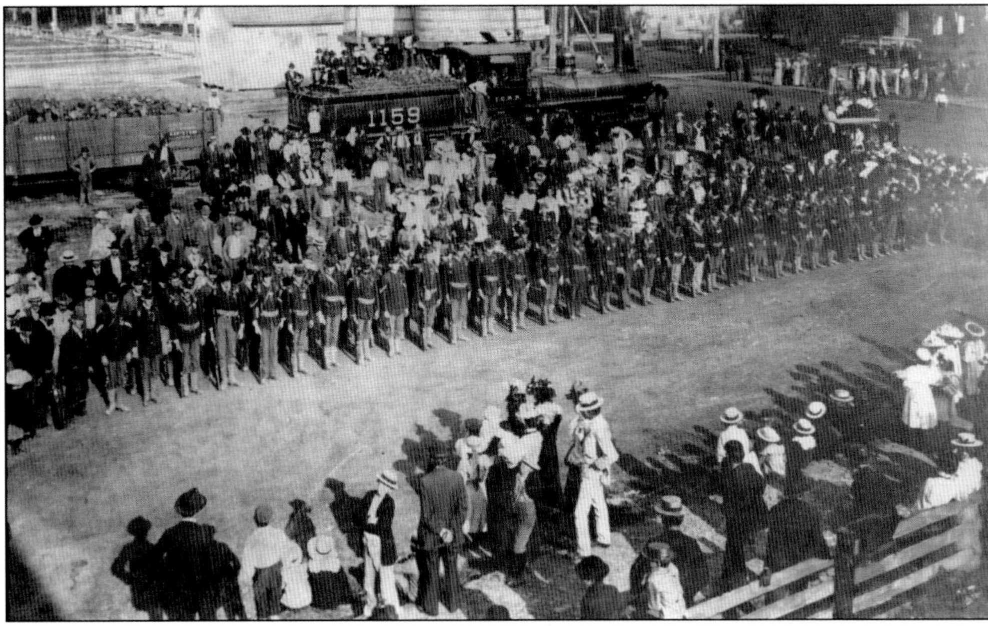

When Pres. William McKinley called for troops to fight in the Spanish-American War, Capt. Thomas W. Cate, son of Charles E. Cate, formed Company H of the 1st Infantry Regiment of Hammond. The regiment, known familiarly as the Hammond Light Guards, is seen in these May 1898 photographs. Above, the regiment is lined up outside the train, while below, the troops are seen waving from passenger cars, ready to report for duty while family and supporters cheer them on. Louisiana sent two regiments of infantry, three batteries of artillery, and a naval battalion. The 1st Louisiana Regiment never made it out of Jacksonville, Florida, mustered out of service on October 3, 1898.

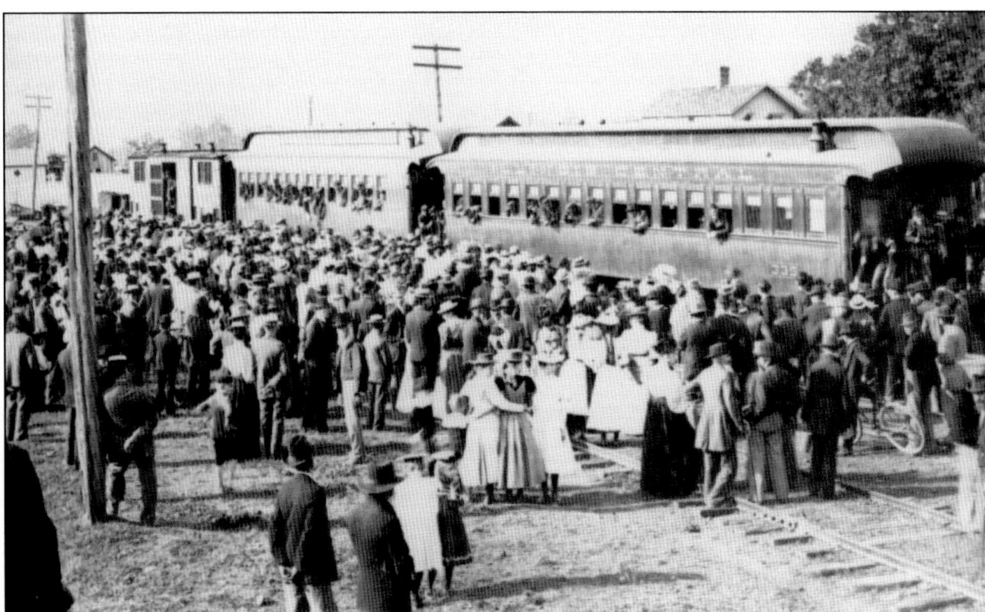

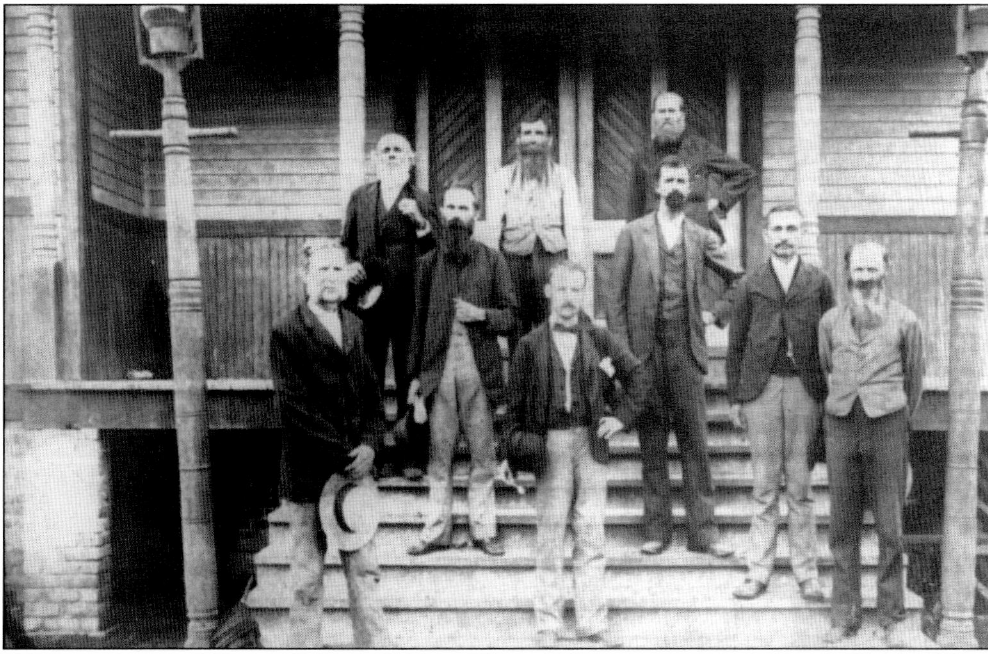

Hammond officials and aldermen are seen gathered on the steps of Hammond Hall in 1892. Situated on Cate property and designed to address a need for public gatherings, Hammond Hall was built with private funds. The large auditorium was located on the corner of East Robert Street and Northeast Railroad Avenue. Mayor Urene DeSouge is pictured in the back row, on the left, and merchant Frank Neelis is in the center of the first row.

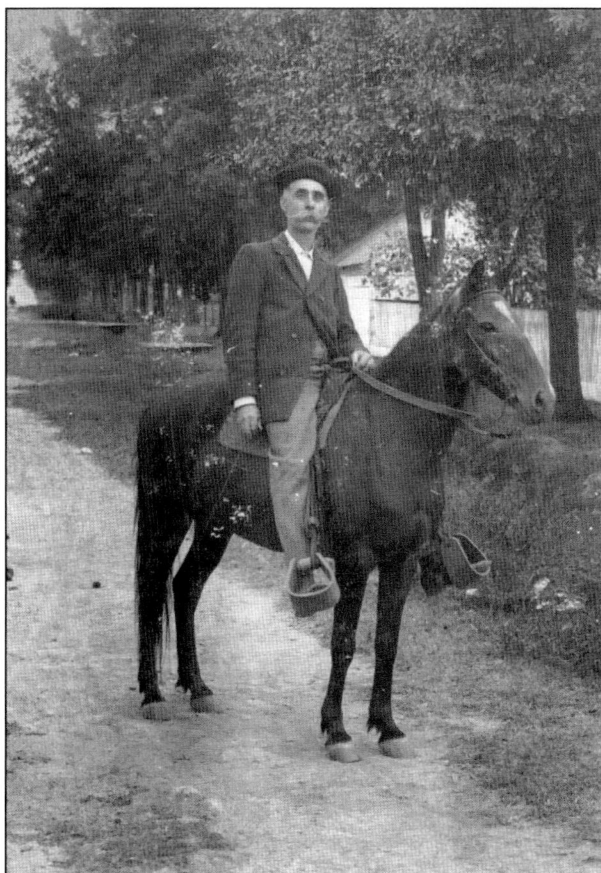

This 1896 photograph shows Norman R. Smith as he ventures out on one of the shady streets of early Hammond. Originally from Michigan, Smith was a timber estimator and businessman. Born in 1846, he arrived in Hammond in the late 1800s and was a Hammond resident until his death in 1928. His last-known residence was an undetermined address on Western Avenue.

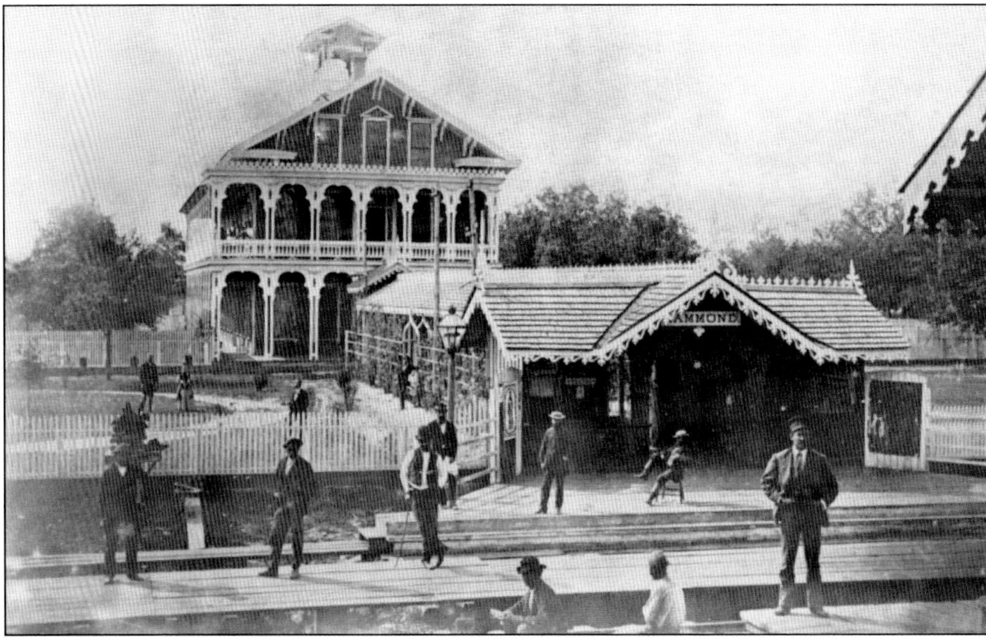

The Kidder Hotel on Northwest Railroad Avenue had a covered walkway from the railroad tracks. Originally built as a shoe factory by Charles E. Cate, it was commandeered as a hospital by the Union during the Civil War and later turned into a hotel. In 1881, Cate sold the hotel and its block of land to Thomas W. Kidder, who operated it until it burned in 1899.

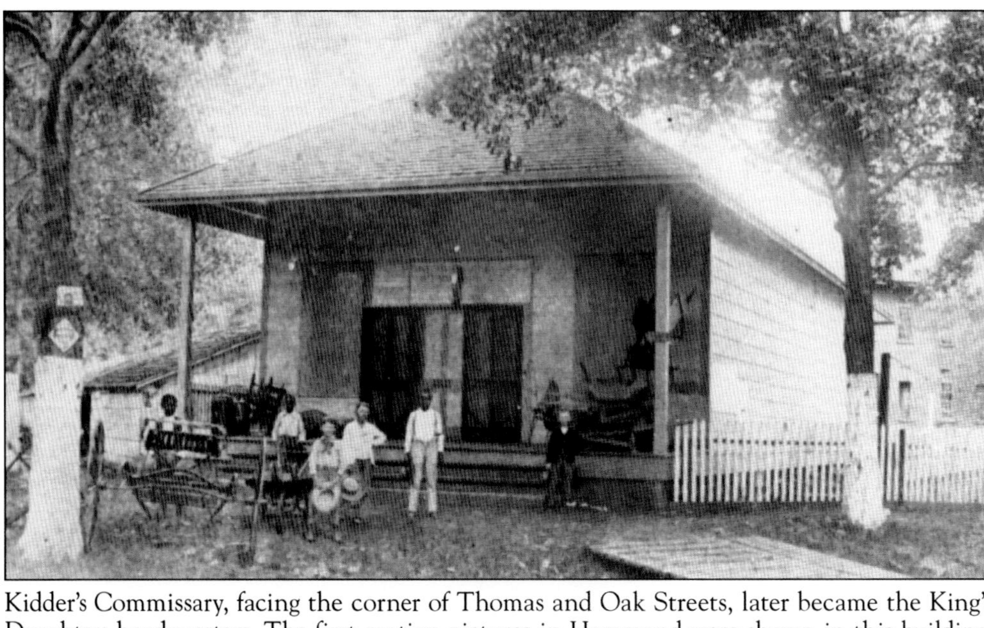

Kidder's Commissary, facing the corner of Thomas and Oak Streets, later became the King's Daughters headquarters. The first motion pictures in Hammond were shown in this building. It was later turned to face Thomas Street and used by merchant tailor Dan Fazekas. One of the oldest buildings in the city, it now houses a barbershop.

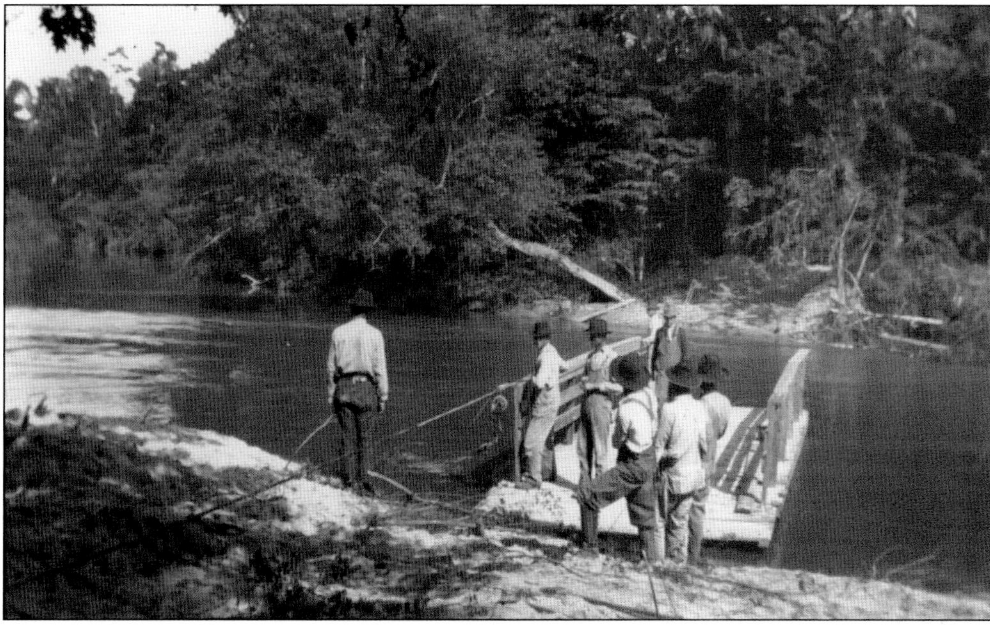

Since roadways and bridges were in their infancy, transporting goods by water was crucial. Located north of the Hammond Lumber Company's railroad bridge and almost at the end of Vineyard Road on the outskirts of town, the "Vineyard Ferry" operated on the Tangipahoa River. The ferry transported goods such as fruits, vegetables, and other products from farms located near the river.

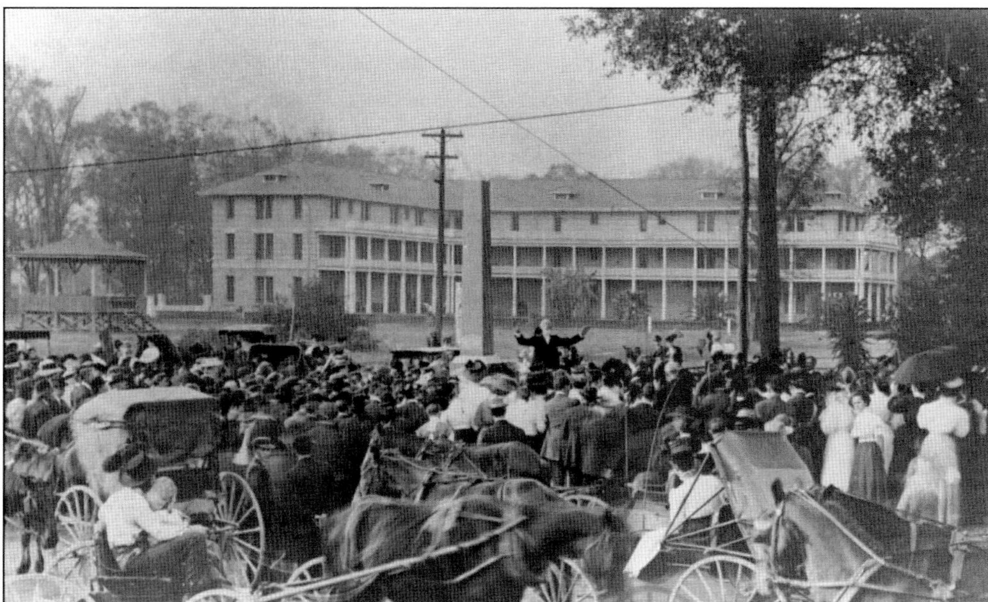

On August 5, 1908, a monument to hero Francis G. Stewart (1869–1908) was dedicated. Stewart, a watchman for the Illinois Central Railroad, saved schoolboy Gilbert "Gary" Bercaw from the path of an approaching train and died in the process. The Oaks Hotel is seen in the background, and the bandstand at left later became the site of the post office. The monument still stands behind the Downtown Development District office.

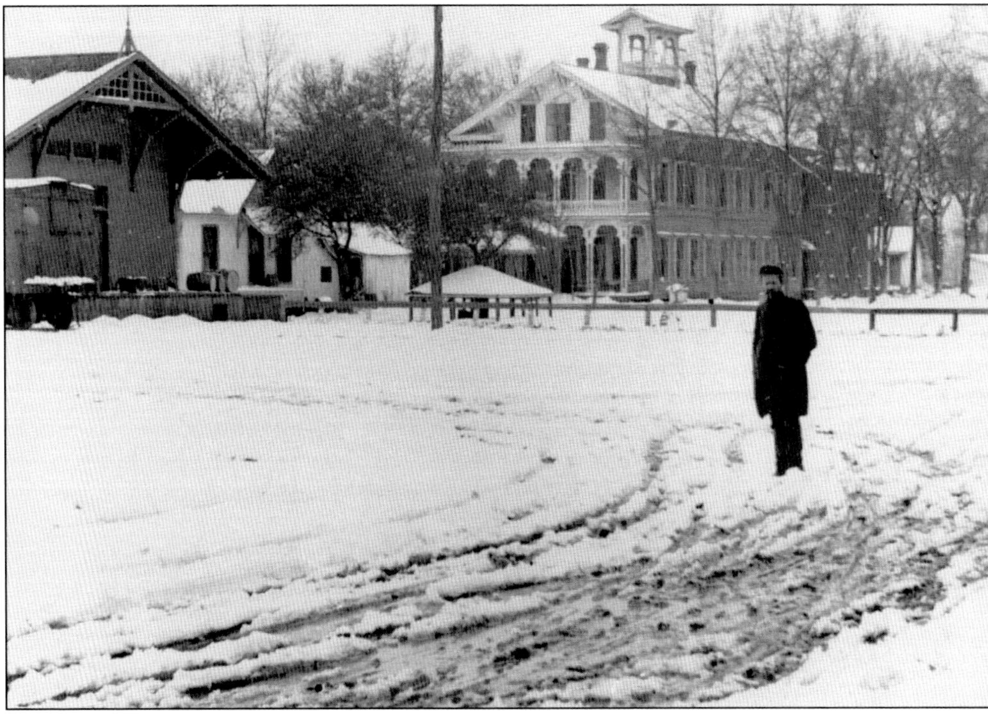

A man stands alone after a rare snowfall on February 15, 1895, blanketed Hammond. The Hammond Depot and the Kidder Hotel are shown from the corner of Charles Street. A bear named Betsy and an alligator lived on the hotel grounds. The hotel was destroyed by an arsonist on December 9, 1899.

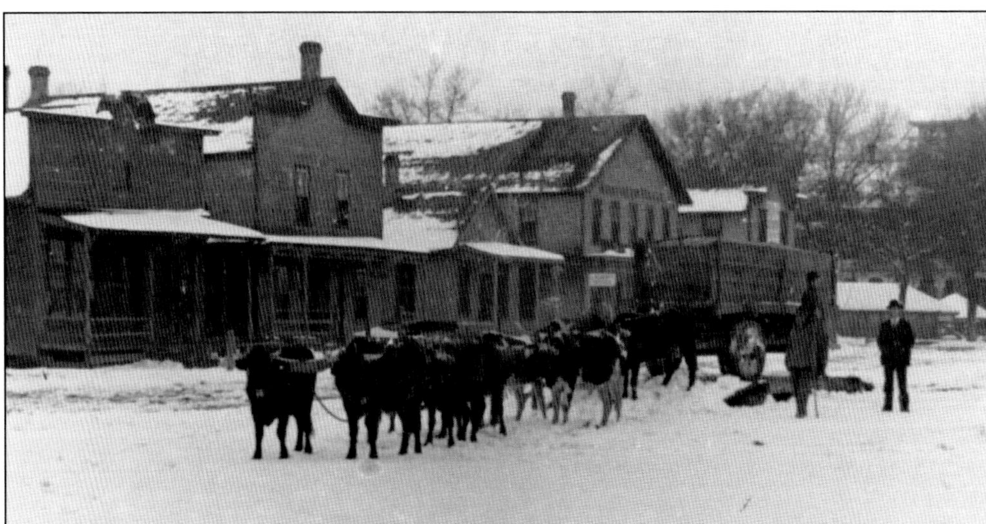

The 1895 snowfall prompted many photographs of Hammond. Here, a team of oxen is waiting near a wagon on the first block of Southwest Railroad Avenue. The Northern House Hotel is to the left of the wagon, and the Kidder Hotel is visible in the back. The Northern House Hotel was destroyed by fire several months later on September 8, 1895.

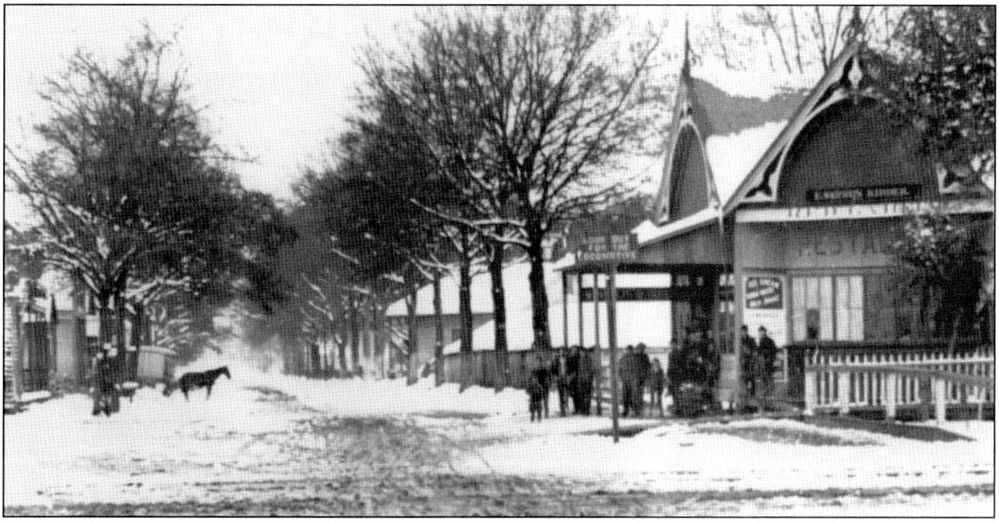

The Red Gables building, on West Thomas Street at the railroad crossing, housed a lunch stand that was operated by Warren Kidder. The building, which narrowly escaped destruction in the fire that leveled the nearby Kidder Hotel on December 9, 1899, later housed a variety of establishments, including a grocery store, a strawberry sales agency, and Western Union. The offices of Hammond's Downtown Development District currently occupy the site.

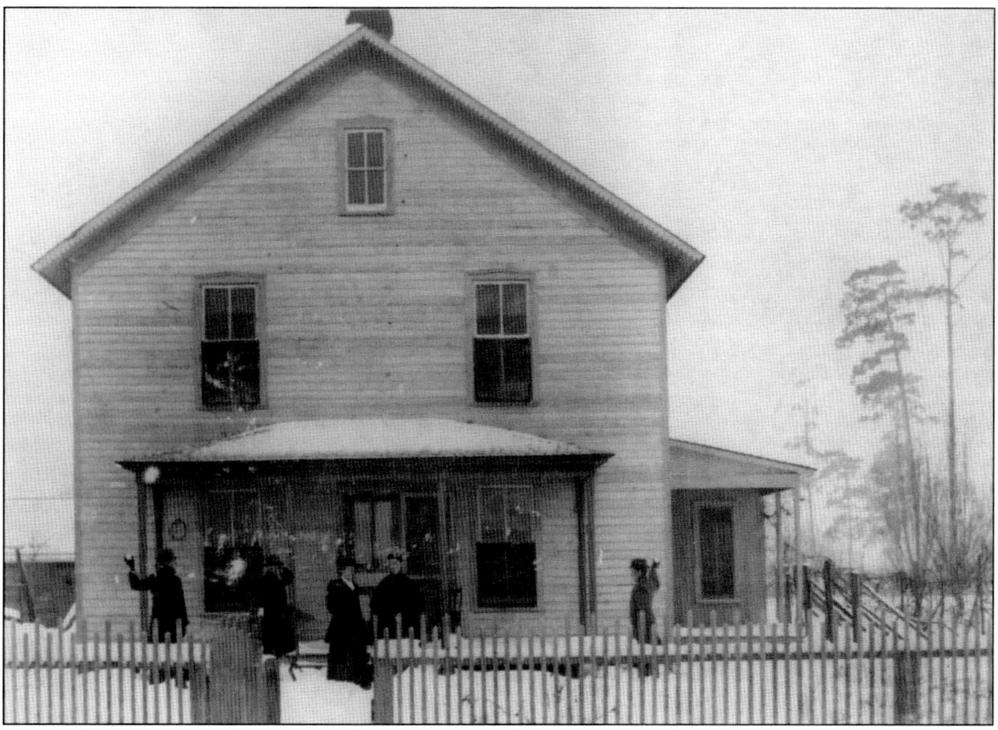

An unidentified group plays in what looks to be a substantial snowfall for Hammond, presumably the historic snowfall of February 15, 1895. While snow is very rare in south Louisiana, the *Hammond News* mentions two snowfalls during the previous winter, one occurring as late as March 1894. Snow in an area not used to it would cause giddy celebration as well as hardships in transportation and everyday life.

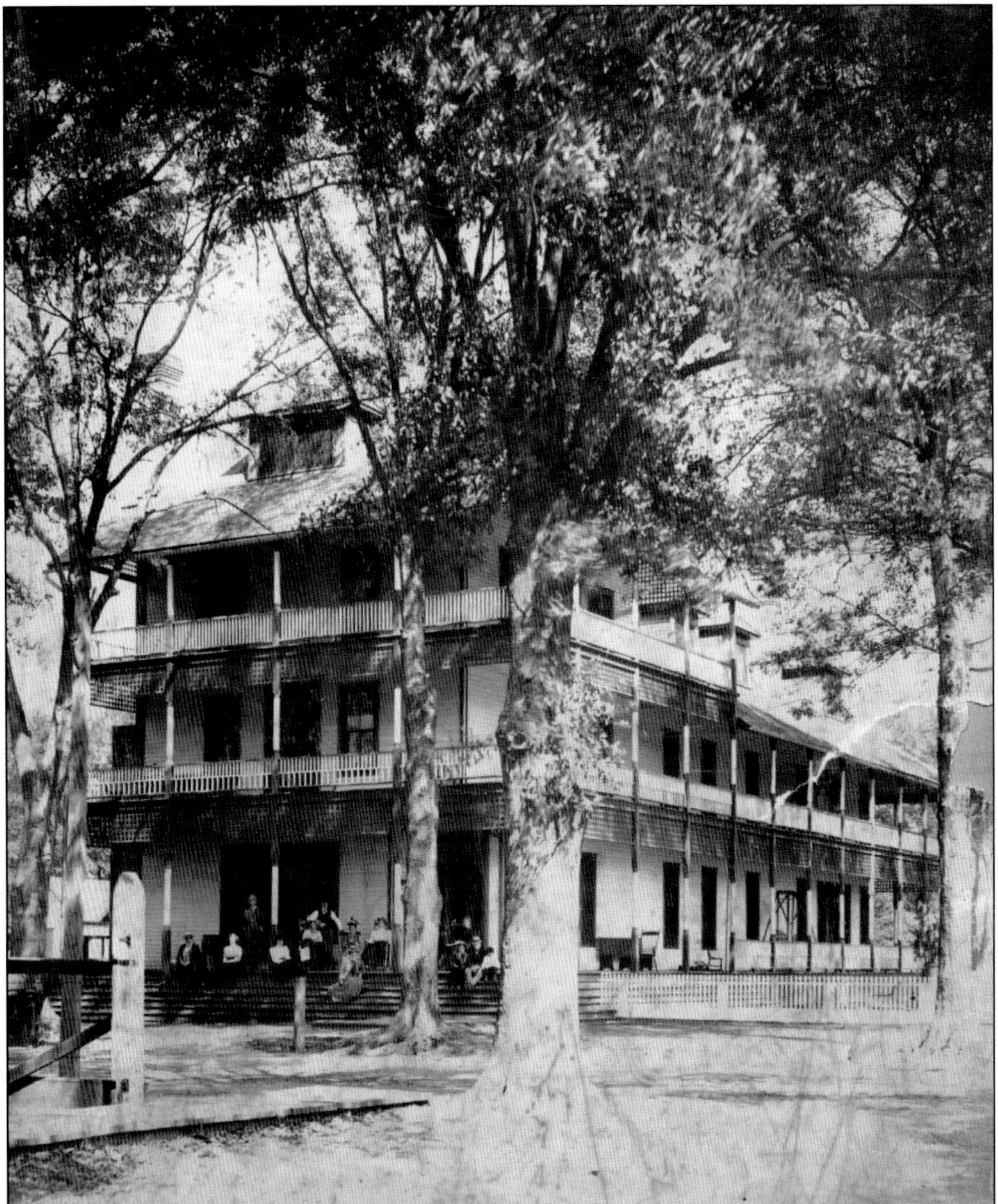

The Oaks Hotel was built by Iowans Col. Henry Robinson and his wife, Henrietta, in 1893 on the corner of West Charles Street and Railroad Avenue. Originally a three-story building with a two-story north wing, Robinson later added a west wing along Charles Street. The hotel was successful from the start, partially due to the engaging personalities of the Robinsons but also because it became a popular attraction for visitors from New Orleans and other places in the Mississippi River Valley who sought to escape the summer heat. Northern "snowbirds" also came south from the Midwest and North to enjoy the warmer winters, spurred by the advertisements of the Illinois Central Railroad. The surrounding oaks and landscaped grounds provided an idyllic setting for guests, who enjoyed lawn tennis and rocking on the large porches. The hotel was destroyed by fire on October 12, 1905, probably the result of a defective chimney flue at the north end of the building between the kitchen and dining room, but it was replaced with a new hotel.

Pictured is the sitting room of Col. Henry Robinson, owner of the Oaks Hotel, as it stood before the hotel burned in October 1905. Hammond enjoyed some level of electricity since 1894, as evidenced by the lightbulb in the hanging lamp featured in the foreground. Also of interest are the electrical wires on the ceiling behind the lamp and along the ceiling on the right in the back room.

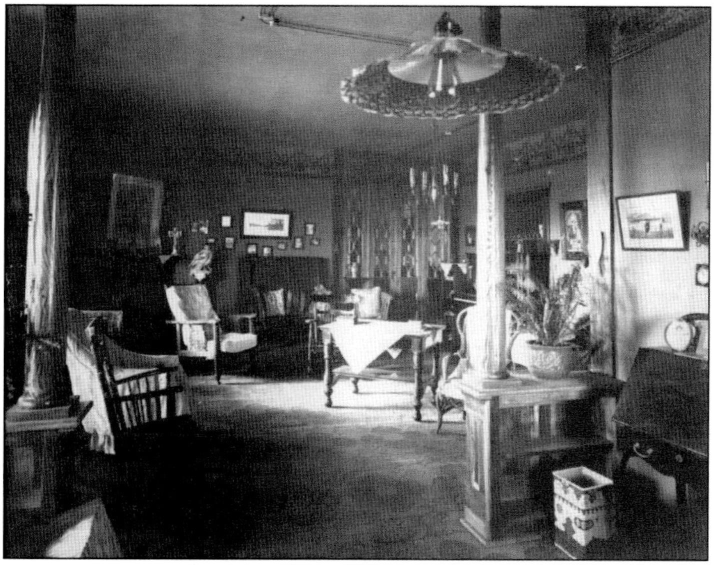

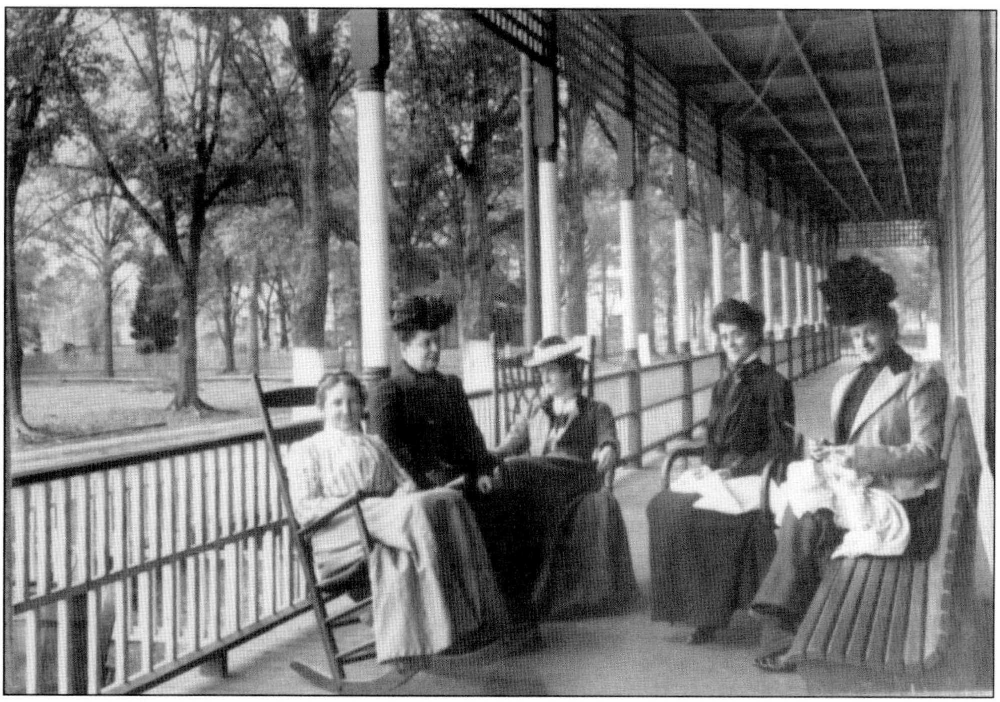

Henrietta Robinson, owner of the Oaks Hotel and known as Madam Robinson, is the lady sitting in the rocker on the far left. Hotel guests and owner frequently relaxed on the porch on the south side of the Oaks Hotel, spending their time reading, doing needlework, or socializing. Some took advantage of daily passenger trains to travel to New Orleans for a day of shopping.

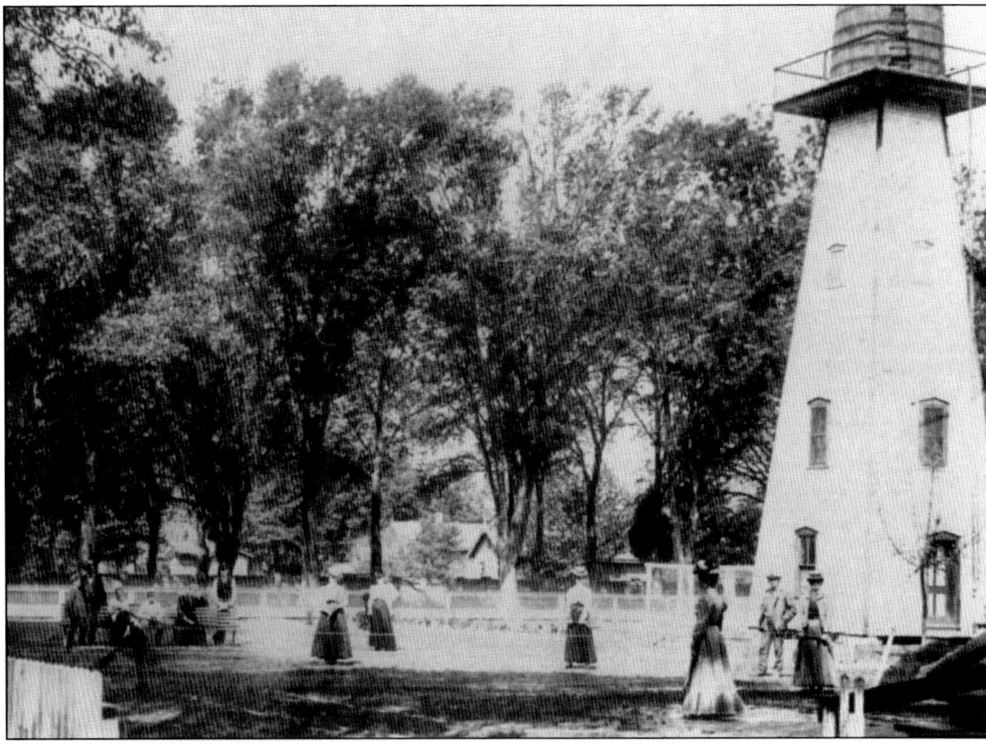

Visitors at the Oaks Hotel enjoyed the fresh country air and socializing on the shady hotel grounds. Several guests gather around a bench while four others enjoy a game of lawn tennis in the west gardens. The large structure to the right is the water tower for the hotel. Cate Square, Charles Emery Cate's home and gardens at the time, is visible in the background.

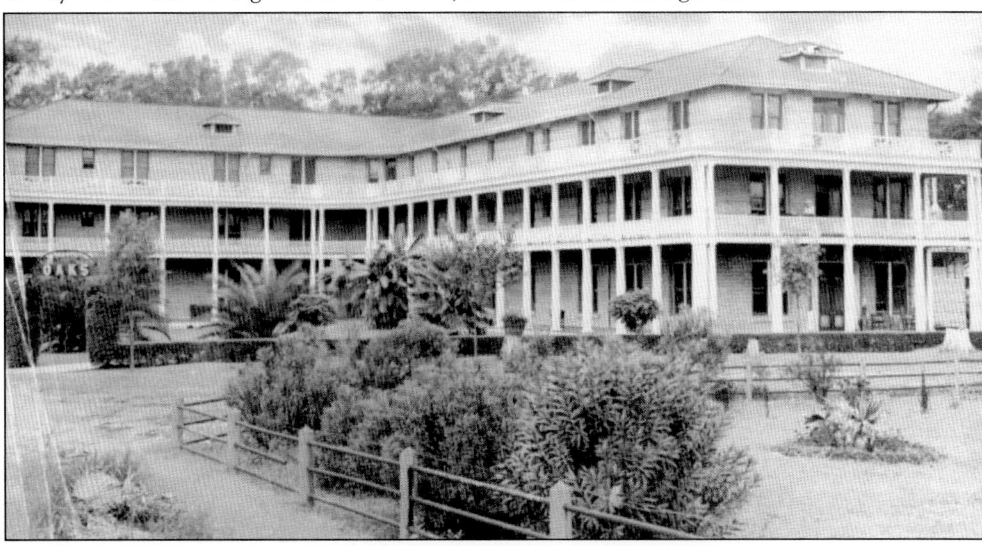

The Robinsons' second Oaks Hotel, built on the site of the original, was completed a year after the 1905 fire, opening on January 1, 1907. The hotel was a three-story, *L*-shaped building constructed of masonry and brick and fronted by beautiful gardens with a statue of Mercury. The lobby contained chairs, magazines, a card table, and two oak telephone booths. The hotel closed after a fire on October 7, 1929.

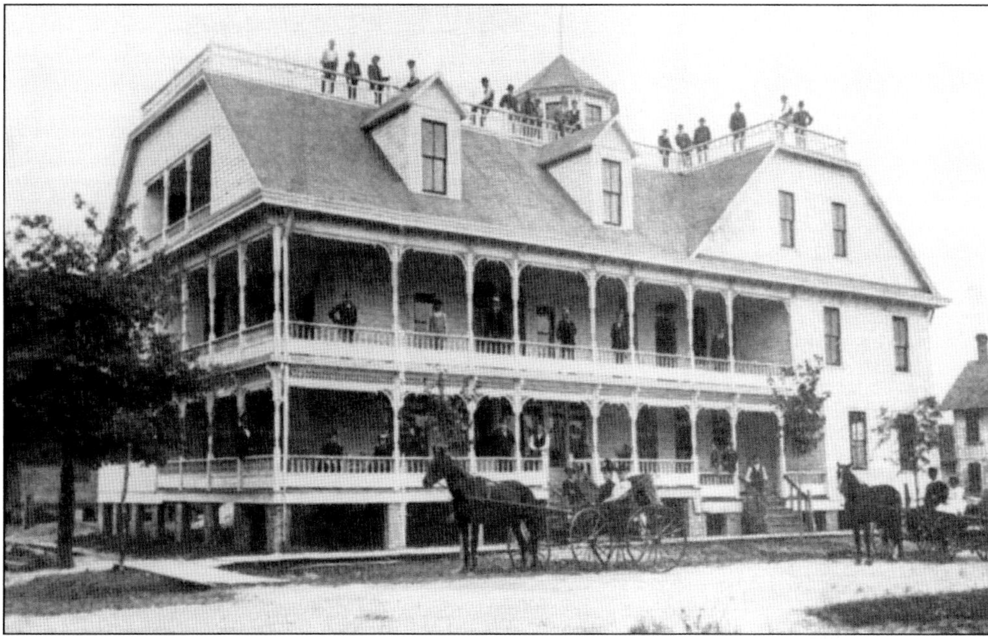

The Newport Hotel, above, was located on the corner of East Thomas and Cherry Streets. Originally built as the Southern Hotel in 1895, the Newport opened in 1907. Pictured below is the Newport after it was renamed the Hotel St. James just a year later in 1908. The main building is shown with wide galleries full of guests in wooden rockers. The hotel frequently hosted dignitaries and politicians, who used the galleries to address constituents and win supporters. William Jennings Bryan once addressed a crowd from the gallery. The three-story hotel, with a widow's walk on top, operated for 35 years before it burned on January 31, 1930.

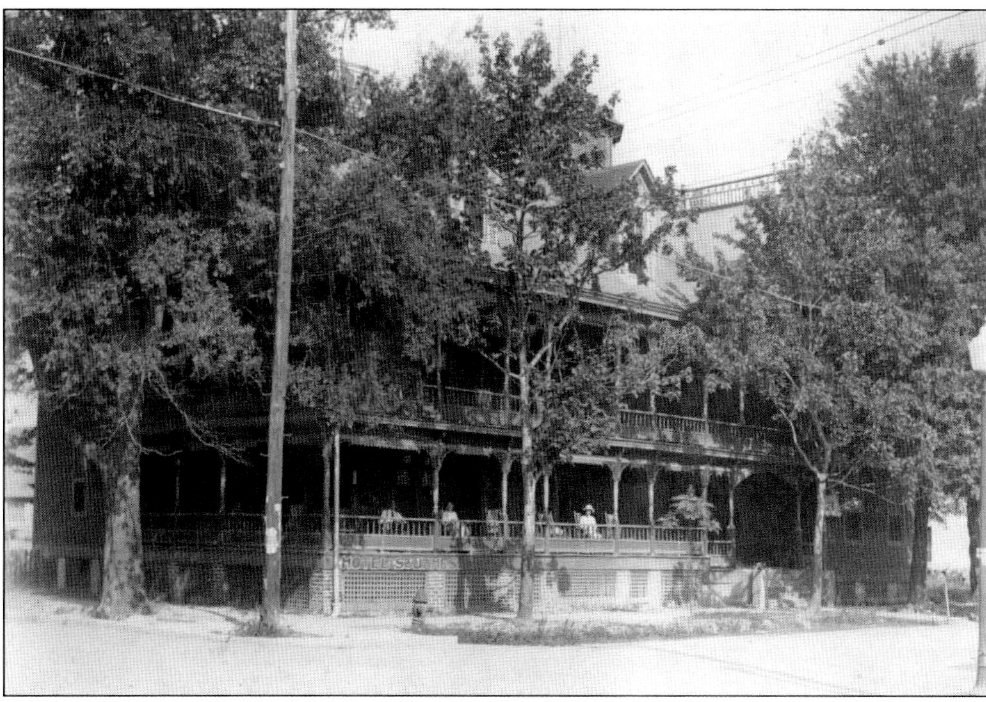

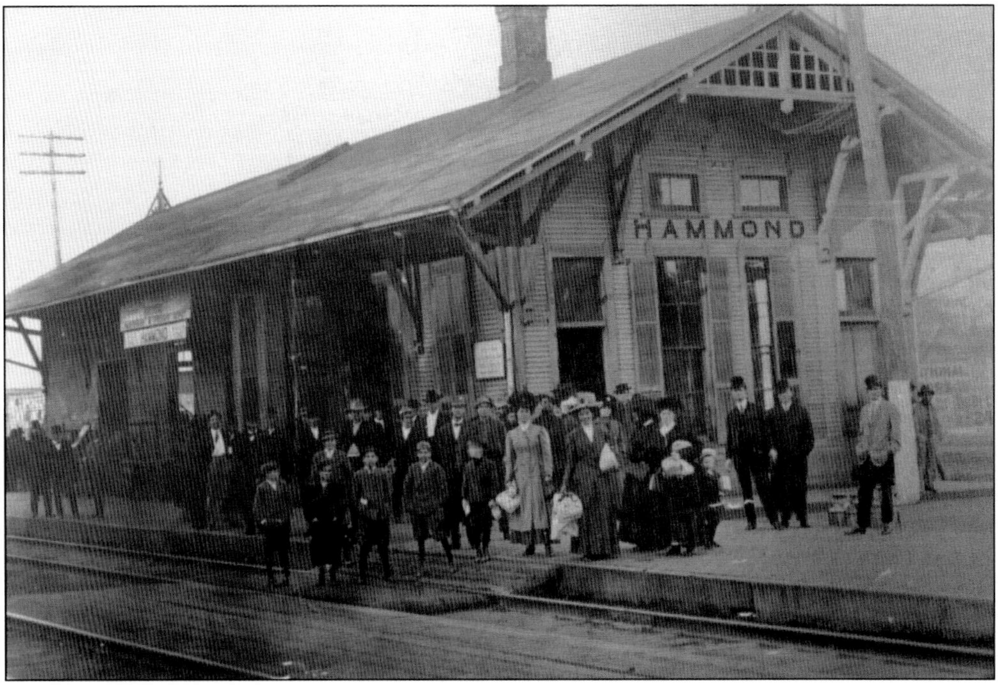

Travelers wait outside the old Hammond Depot. This passenger depot was located on the east side of the railroad tracks. The existing brick depot on the west side replaced it in 1912. The original building became a freight depot and was moved a few blocks south in 1923 and enlarged. It closed in 1962, later housed retail businesses, and is currently a restaurant and bar.

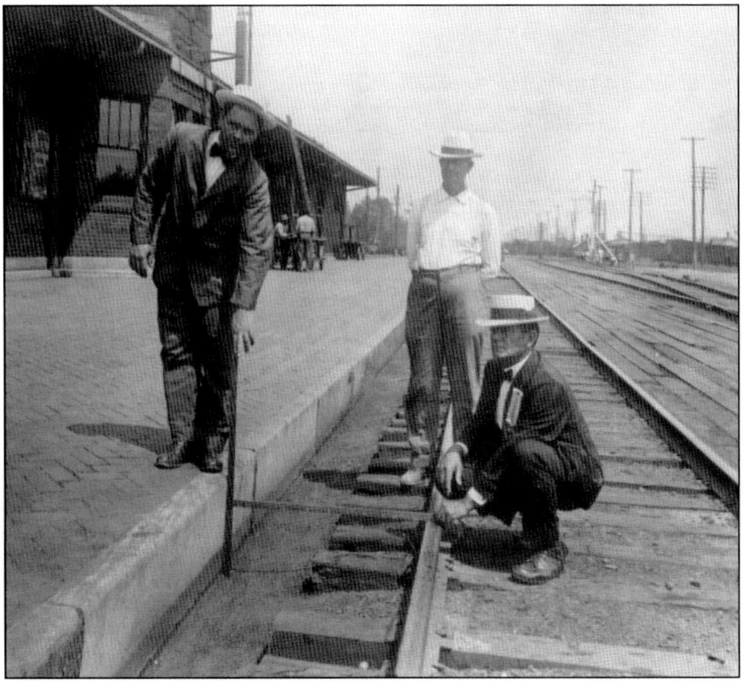

Men measure the height of the platform and the distance from the platform to the tracks at the Hammond Depot in response to a lawsuit. Problems remain today with non-standardization of platform heights depending on type of railcar (commuter or freight), the area of the country, changes in manufacturing of cars, and disability issues. As a result of the lawsuit, the tracks were raised to lessen the disparity in height.

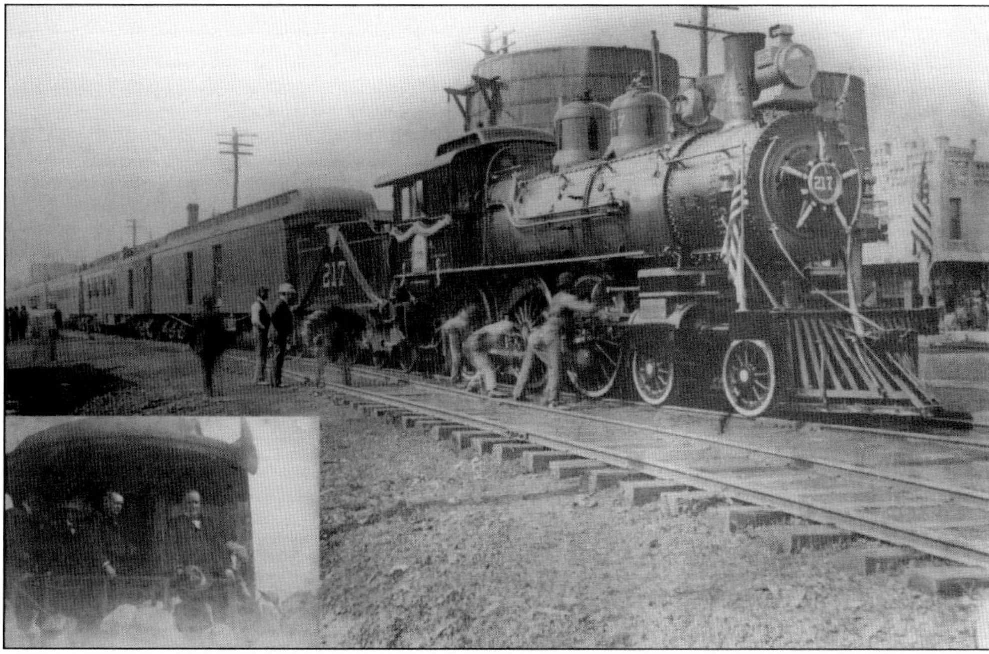

In celebration of his reelection and victory over William Jennings Bryan in the presidential election of 1900, Pres. William McKinley embarked on a six-week rail tour with his wife, Ida, soon after the inauguration of March 4, 1901. The train was nicknamed the *McKinley Special* and made a stop in Hammond. McKinley is pictured on the right in the inset.

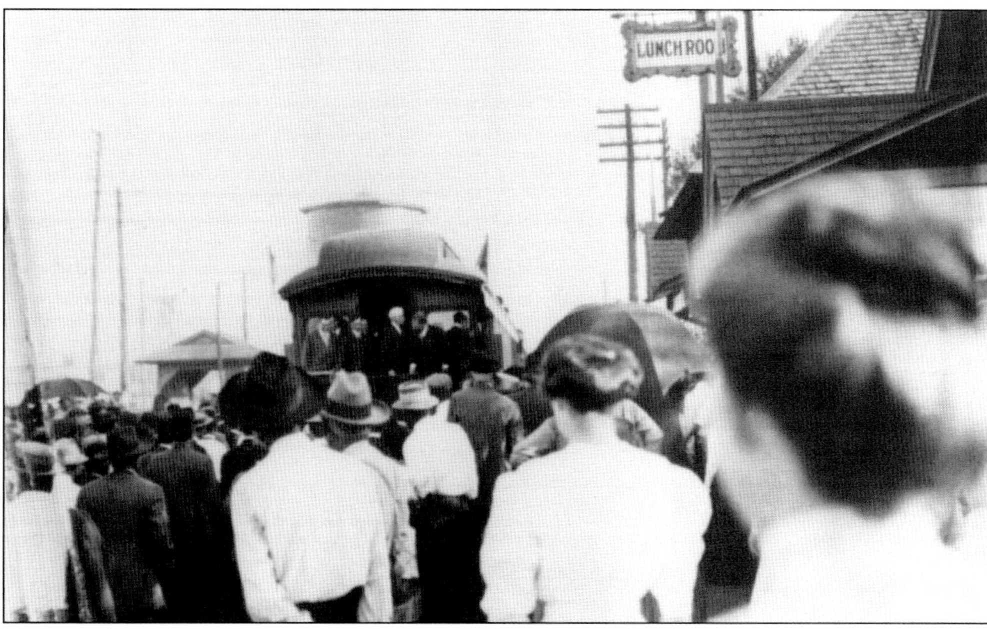

Hammond residents turn out to see Pres. Theodore Roosevelt as his campaign train makes a stop in Hammond in 1912. Having failed to secure the Republican candidacy, Roosevelt formed the Progressive Party and ran against two opponents: incumbent and Republican Pres. Howard Taft and Democrat Woodrow Wilson. Wilson won the presidential election of 1912 with 41 percent of the vote.

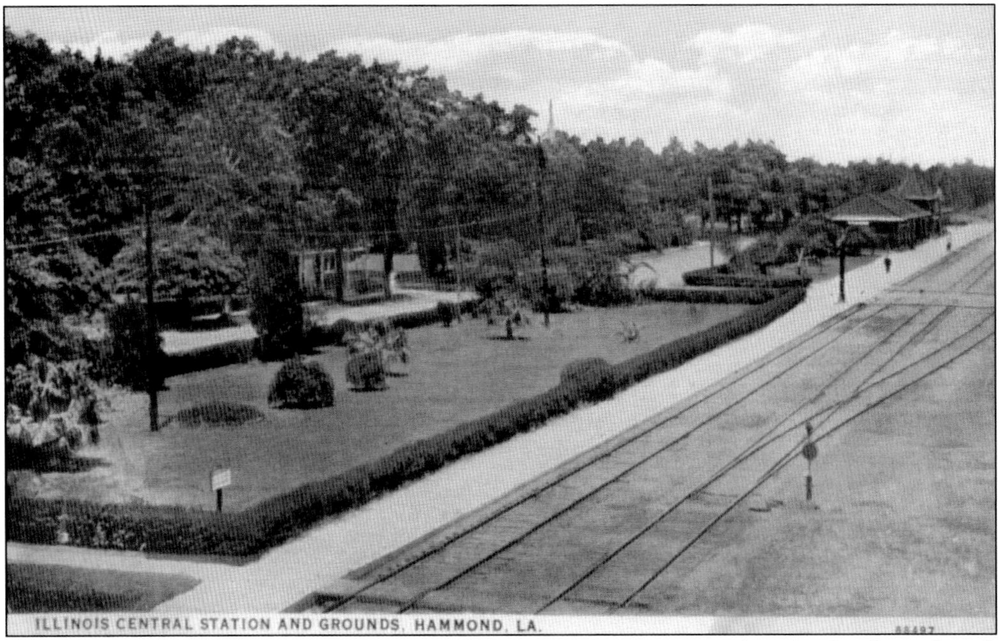

The Illinois Central Railroad (ICRR) provided not only transportation but also freight and mail. Hammond became its most famous stop in Louisiana between Jackson, Mississippi, and New Orleans, and the city's history is intertwined with the ICRR. The beautiful grounds south of the railroad station added to the charm of the area.

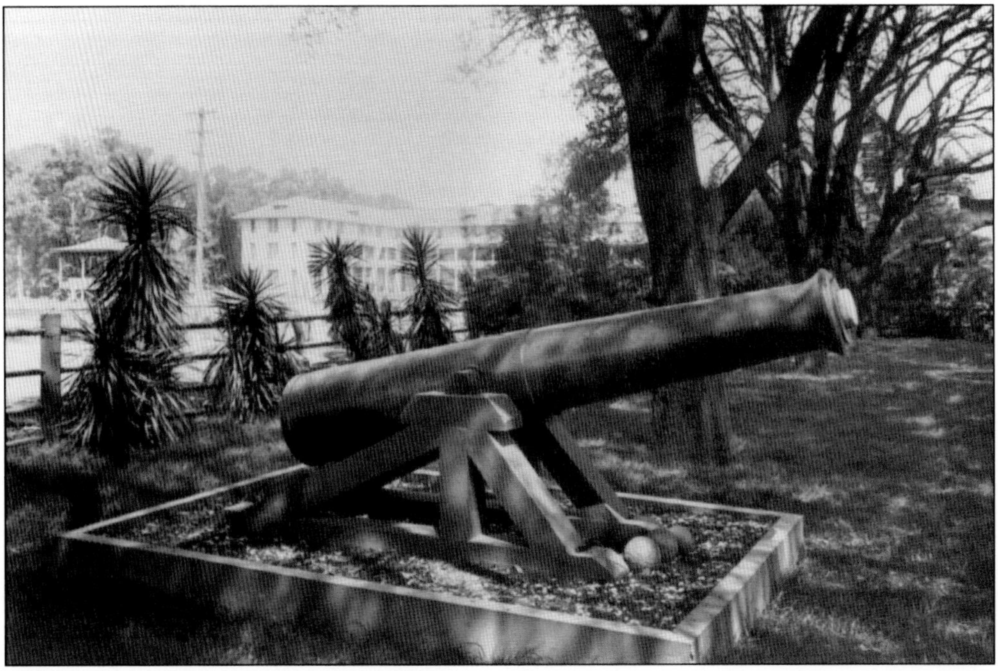

The cannon displayed in the railroad park near Thomas Street was later moved to a spot near Robert Street. Illinois Central Railroad crews had pulled it from Lake Pontchartrain near Frenier, south of Hammond. In the summer of 1942, it was removed and given to the World War II scrap drive. The Oaks Hotel can be seen in the background.

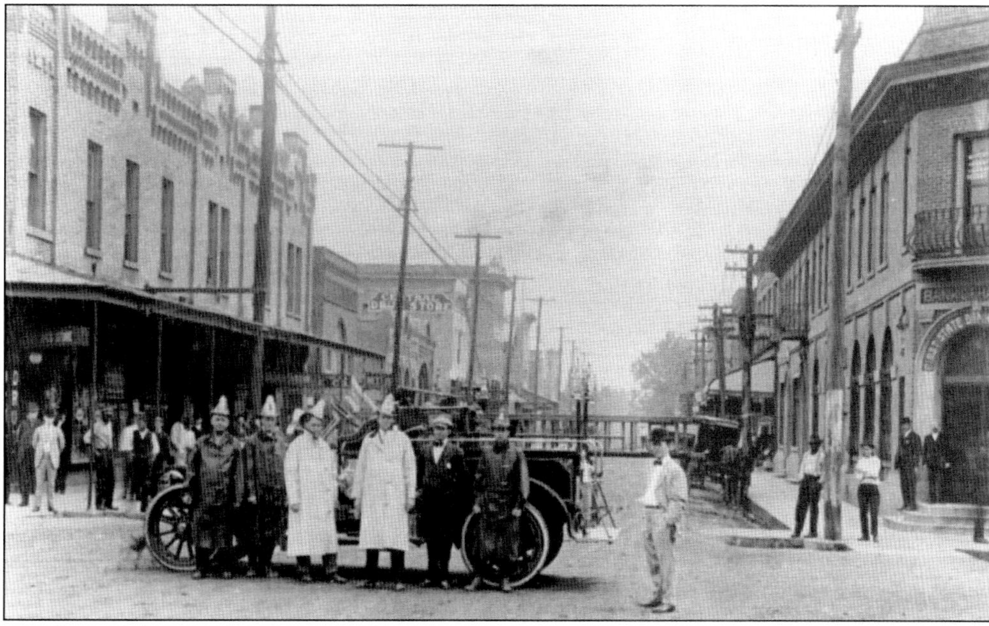

Members of the 1915 Hammond Volunteer Fire Department pose in front of their new chemical and hose car christened *Captain Tom* in honor of Capt. Thomas W. Cate, commander of the Hammond Light Guards in the Spanish-American War. The new car was a welcome addition to the resources of the fire department given the repeated fires that destroyed hotels, businesses, and residences throughout Hammond in its early history.

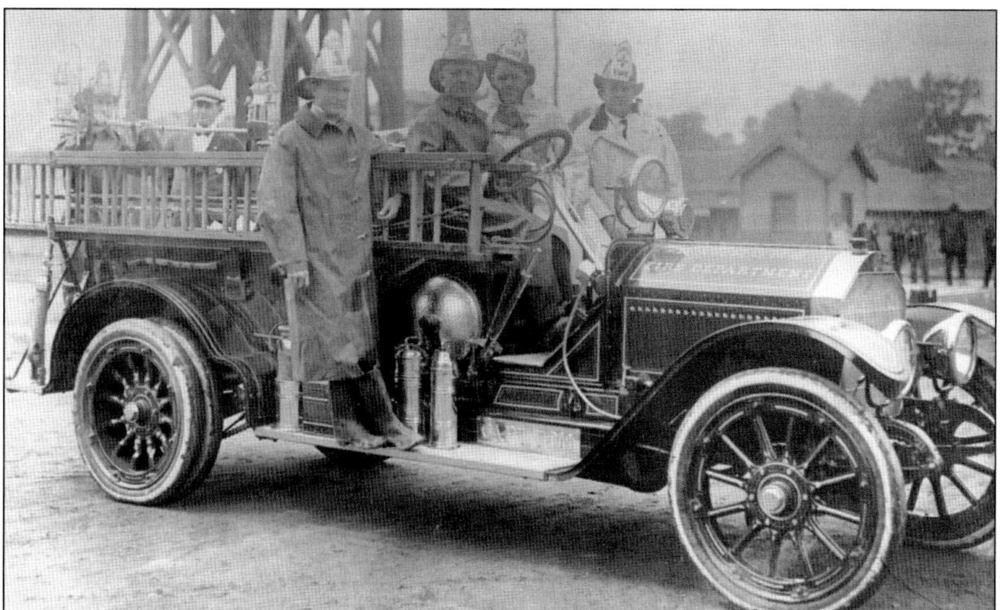

Gathering around the chemical and hose car are, from left to right in the foreground, fireman Will Carter, an unidentified man, fireman Charles Congreve Carter (known as "Bull" Carter), and fireman Norman Bowers. Besides being a fireman, C.C. Carter was elected mayor in 1917, holding office for 16 years. During his tenure, Hammond's main streets were graveled and paved, water works and fire protection were improved, and a city hall was erected in 1922.

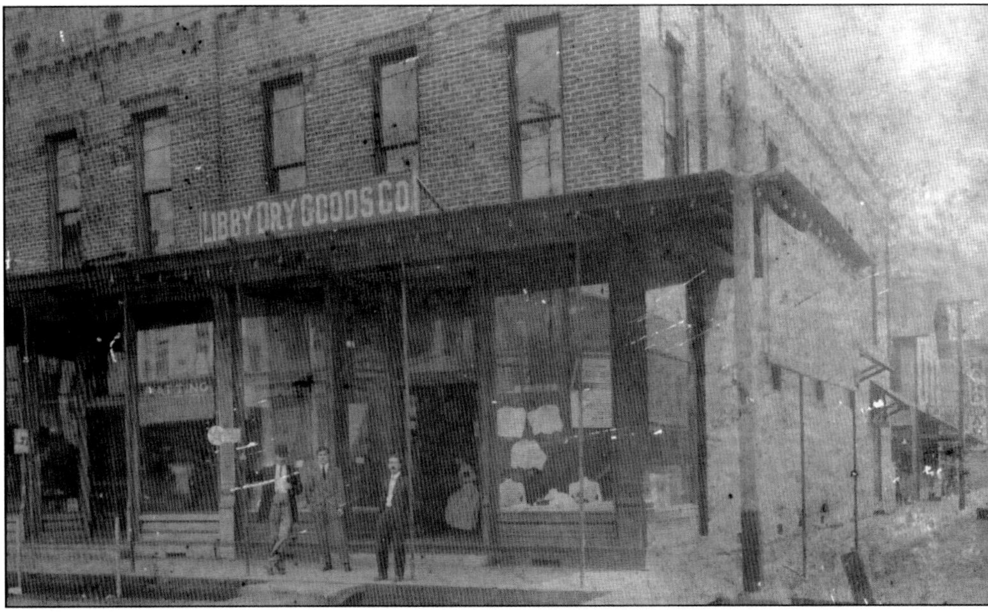

Watson and Libby Dry Goods and Clothing was founded in 1891 by W.R. Watson and notary public W.E. Libby to sell dry goods, clothing, and gents' furnishings. Surviving the 1896 fire, it became the W.E. Libby Dry Goods Company in 1904 and occupied two different sites in the 200 block of East Thomas Street—one on the corner of Cypress Street—in the ensuing years.

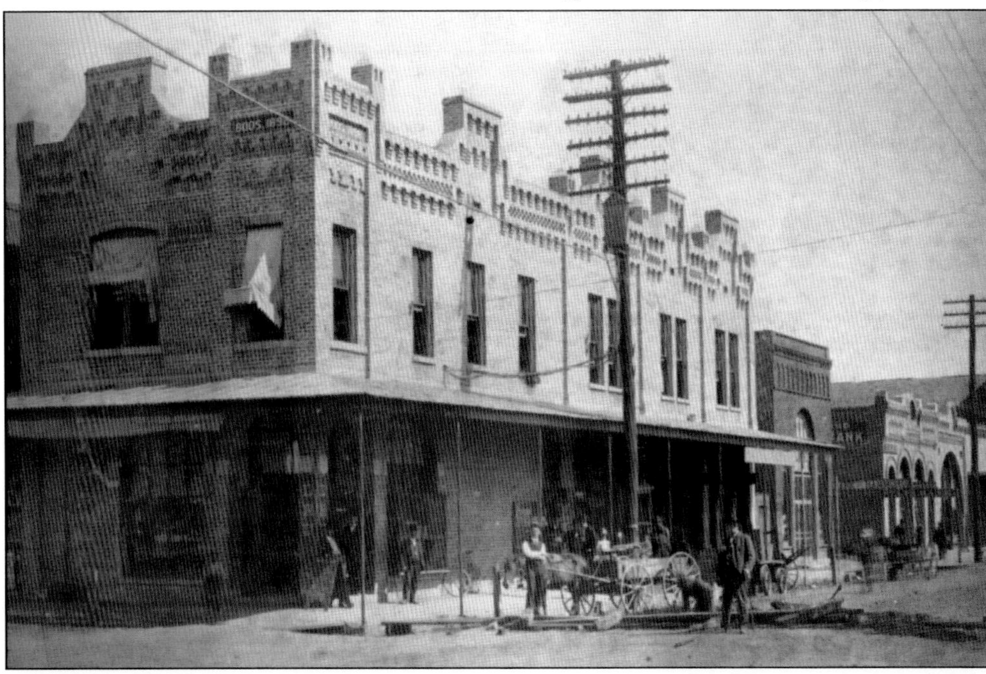

Mayor John W. Skinner (right foreground) supervises early street improvements. Said to be Hammond's oldest building, the Boos Building, on the corner of East Thomas and North Cate Streets, was built in 1898 by a barber. It features corbeled brickwork and a distinctive parapet courtesy of a German architect. In addition to the barbershop, the building housed other businesses, including drugstores.

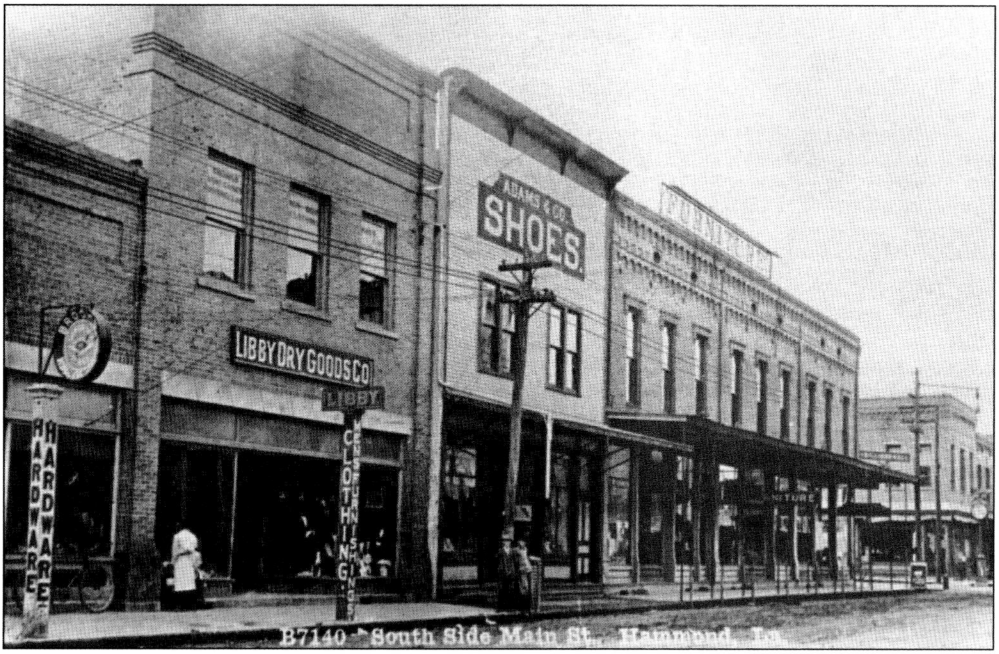

Looking west, the above image depicts businesses that lined the south side of the 200 block of East Thomas Street. The merchants include Brooks Hardware, Libby Dry Goods, Adams and Company Shoes, and Thomas Furniture and Undertaking Parlor. Also looking west, the photograph below shows some of the businesses on the north side. The first discernable buildings are Central Drugs and the first three-story building constructed in Hammond, the Morrison building. Next is the columned Hammond State Bank, followed by the post office, a hardware store, and Hansen and Brooks Groceries and Vegetables. The presence of the Morrison building dates this photograph after 1904, when it was erected.

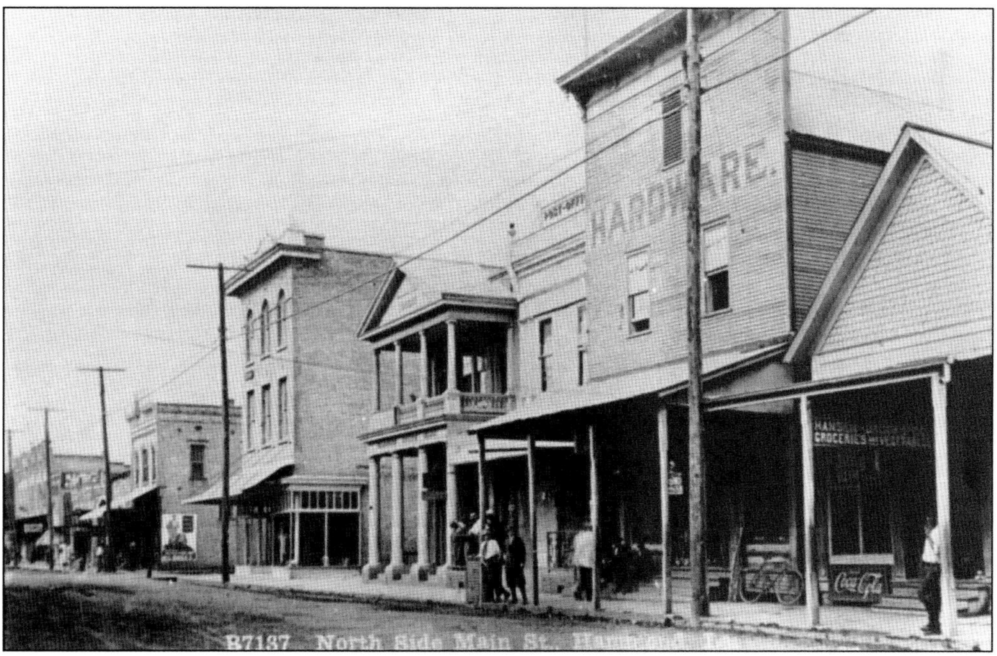

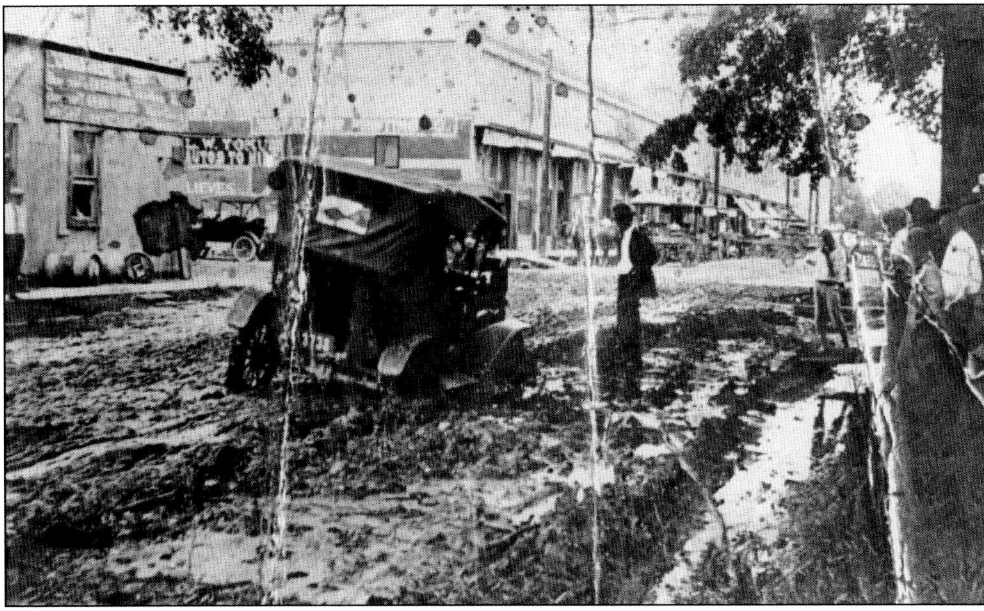

The first Model T left the Ford Motor Company factory in September 1908, and the automobile quickly became popular for the mass market. At one point, half of the automobiles in the world were Model Ts. One Hammond resident recalled in the 1970s that there were few cars in town in 1912, so an automobile in the early teens would have been a novelty of great interest to everyone. Cars moved slowly, competing with horse-drawn wagons, and drivers had to be careful navigating muddy, unpaved streets, as in the photograph above taken on South Cypress Street looking north. By the 1920s, streets were paved and cars of different makes and models were in abundance.

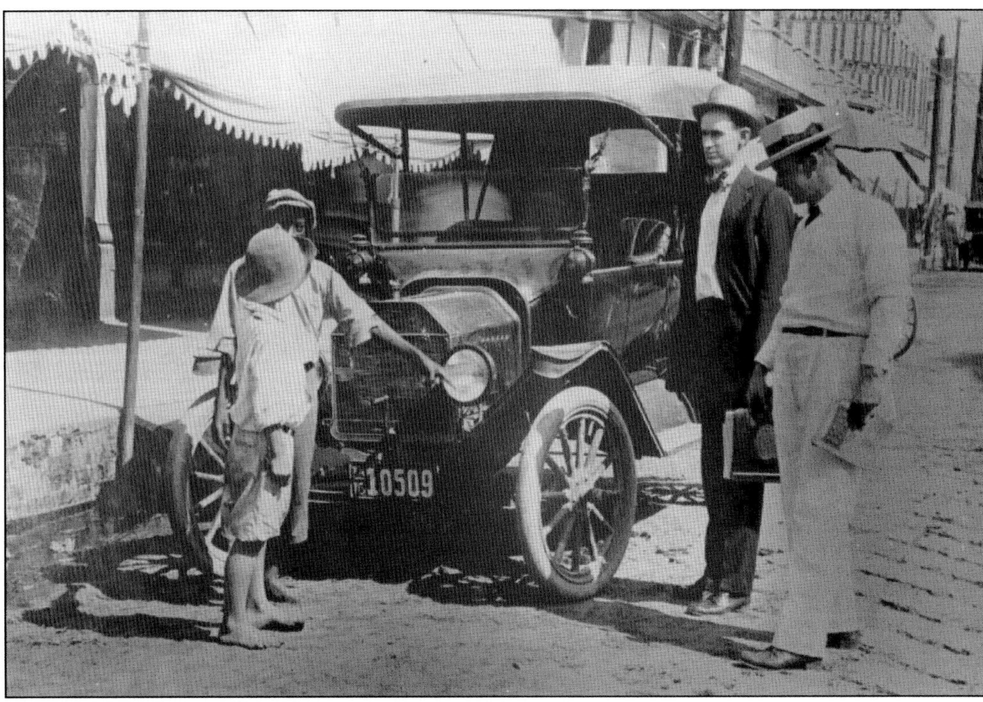

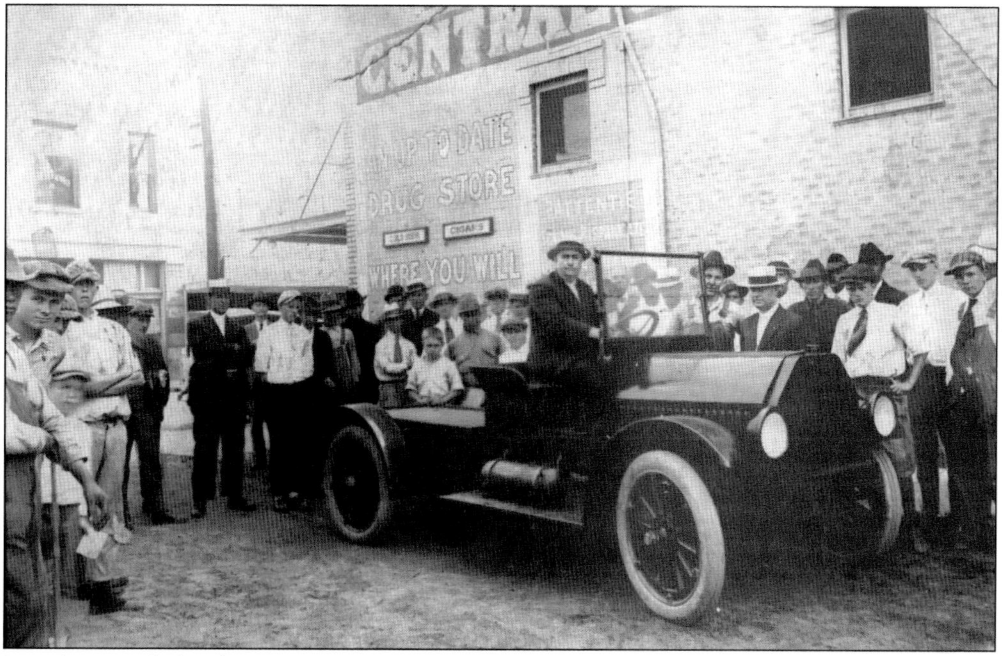

In a photograph dated May 14, 1919, Arthur Richard Carter proudly shows his car, *A.R.C. Steamer*, to a crowd next to Central Drugs on North Cypress Street. Carter, a local luminary of the time, invented several improvements to the steam-propelled engine, receiving numerous US patents, such as one for a water-carrying hood in 1919. He went on to establish a car-manufacturing plant in Gulfport, Mississippi, in 1920.

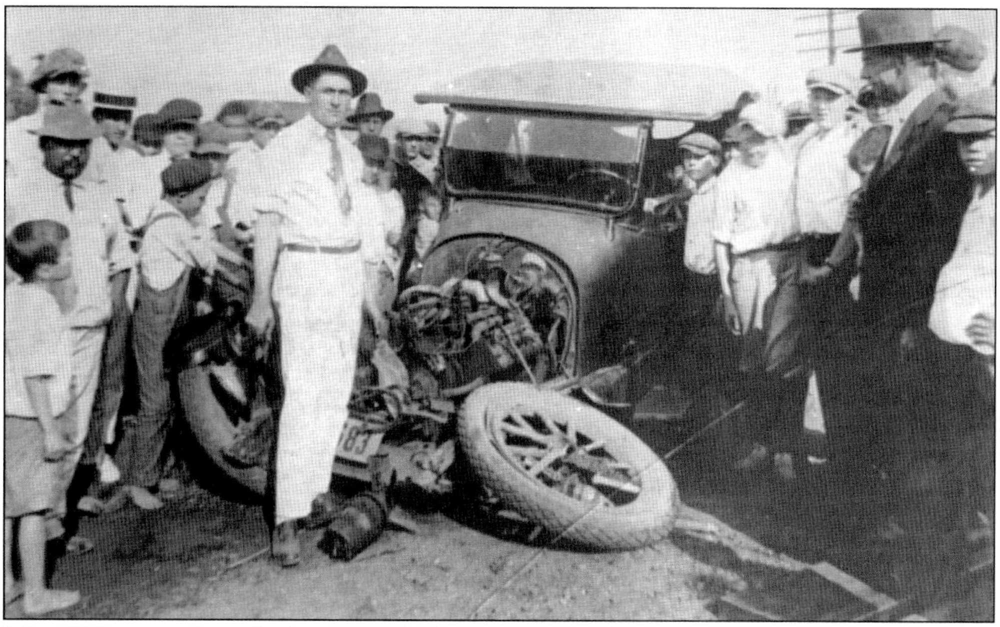

John W. Patenotte's crushed automobile draws a crowd at the site of his accident with a train at the Charles Street crossing before the days of crossing gates or flashing signals. Patenotte was a member of the 20th Engineers Forestry Regiment in World War I and the son of the owner of the Graves and Patenotte lumber mill, located east of Hammond in Robert.

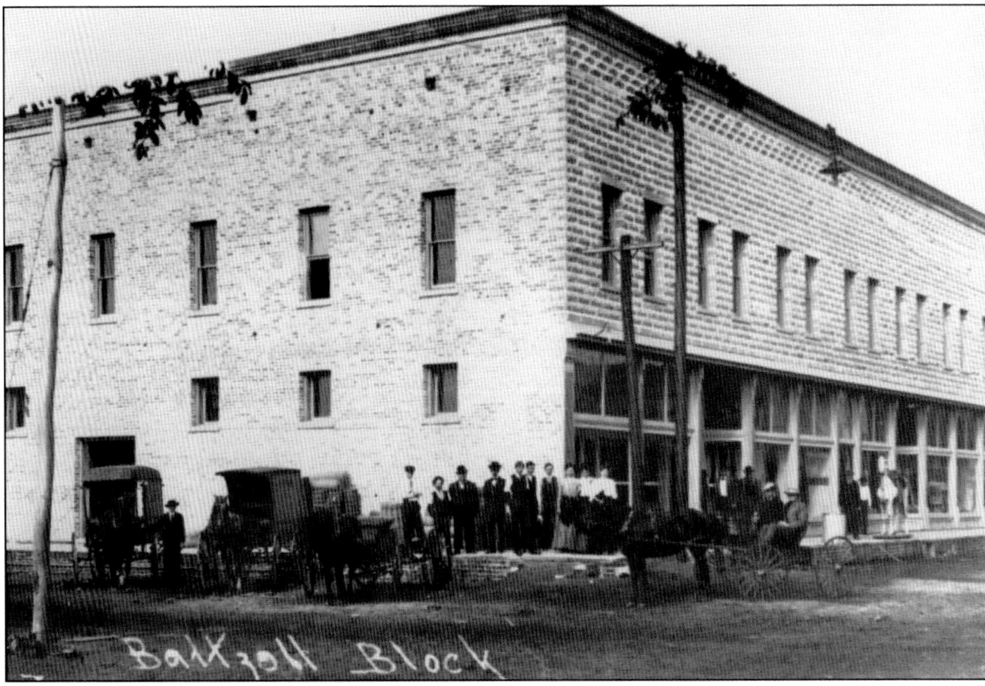

The Baltzell building, which occupies the corner of East Morris and South Cypress Streets, was built in 1905. It was originally part of a full block, which at various times housed the Baltzell, Donaldson, and Black Department Store; the Baltzell Opera House, later the Ritz Theater; a skating rink; the Hammond Hardware and Supply Company, owned by Charles R. "Chum" Anderson; and the Himel Auto Parts Company. The top story was removed after a fire in 1911. The building features a cast-iron storefront manufactured by the Southern Foundry Company of Owensboro, Kentucky. The view below is of South Cypress Street looking north. Grocery stores were located north and south of the Baltzell building.

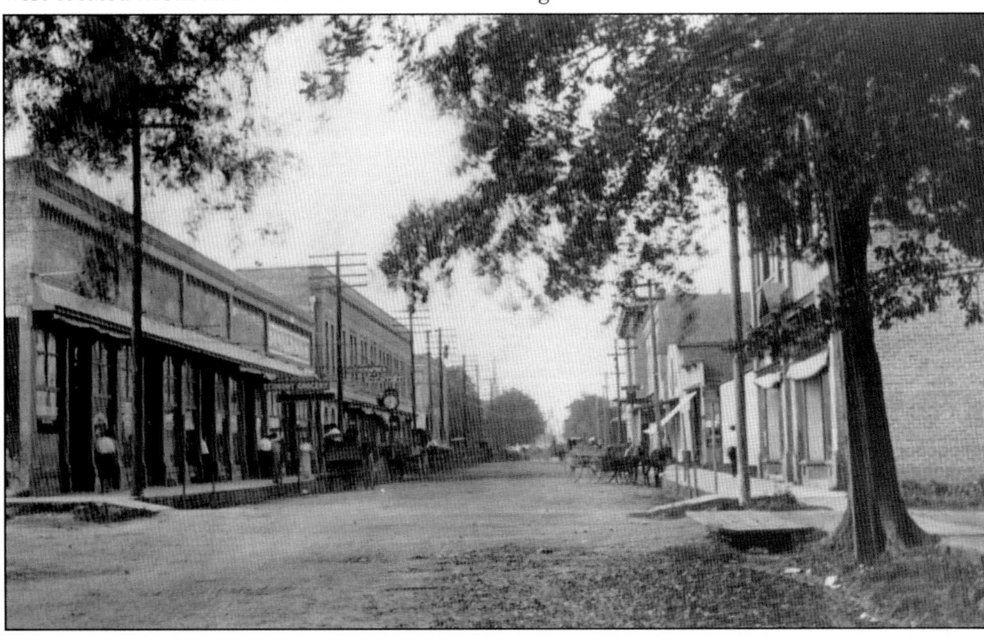

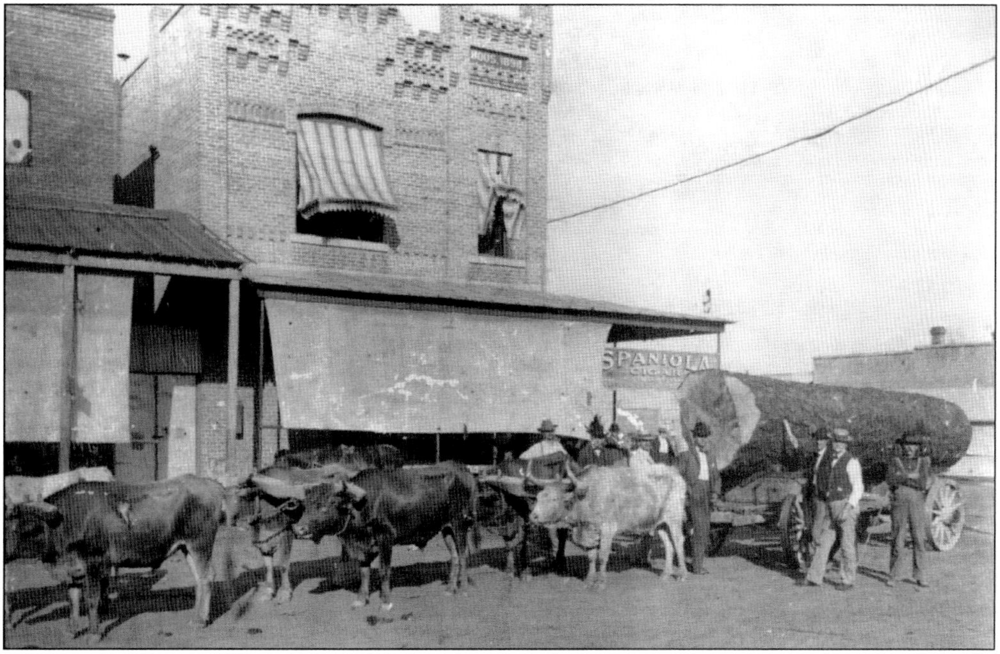

Oxen pull a cart carrying a large pine log, presumably headed towards the Hammond Lumber Company mill that was located on the east side of the railroad tracks near the end of present-day West Dakota Street. Logging was the first industry in Hammond, and several mills were located in the Hammond area by the late 1800s and early 1900s.

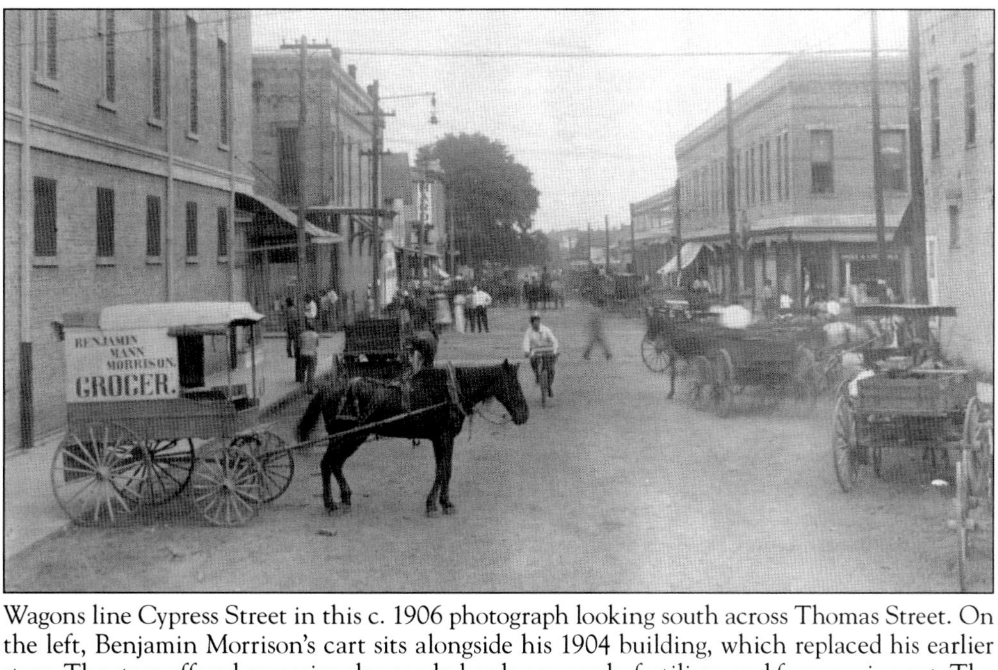

Wagons line Cypress Street in this c. 1906 photograph looking south across Thomas Street. On the left, Benjamin Morrison's cart sits alongside his 1904 building, which replaced his earlier store. The store offered groceries, dry goods, hardware, seeds, fertilizer, and farm equipment. The Morrison building, which now houses a restaurant, featured walls with 18-inch bricks instead of the typical 13-inch ones used at the time.

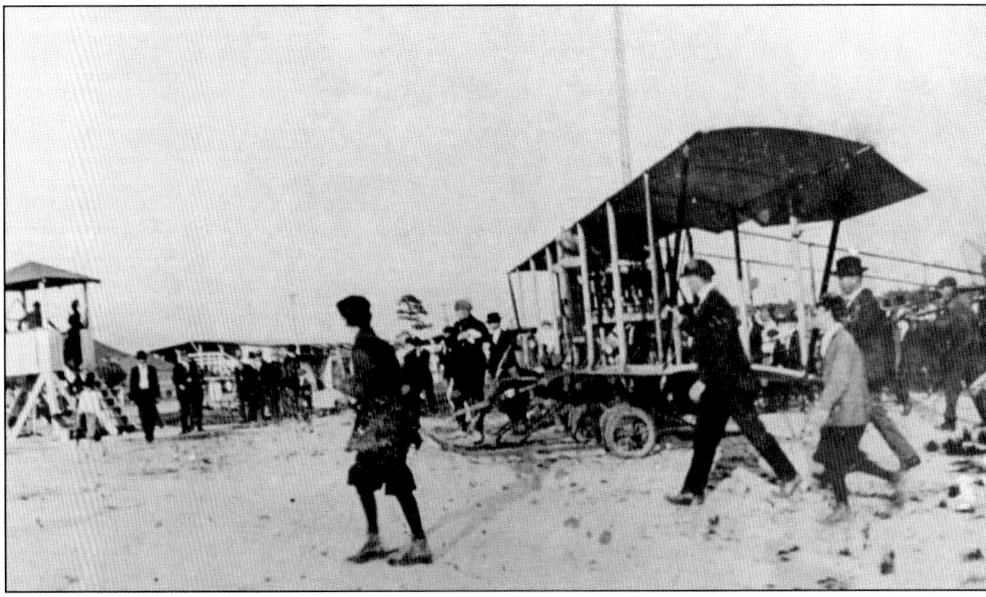

The first airplane flight in Hammond took place on October 26, 1916, during the Tangipahoa Parish Fair at the "Old Fairgrounds." A Thomas biplane arrived by train, and aviator William S. "Billy" Brock thrilled fairgoers with a half-hour flying show at an altitude of 3,400 feet, landing in front of the grandstand. He repeated the maneuvers daily between the afternoon horse races.

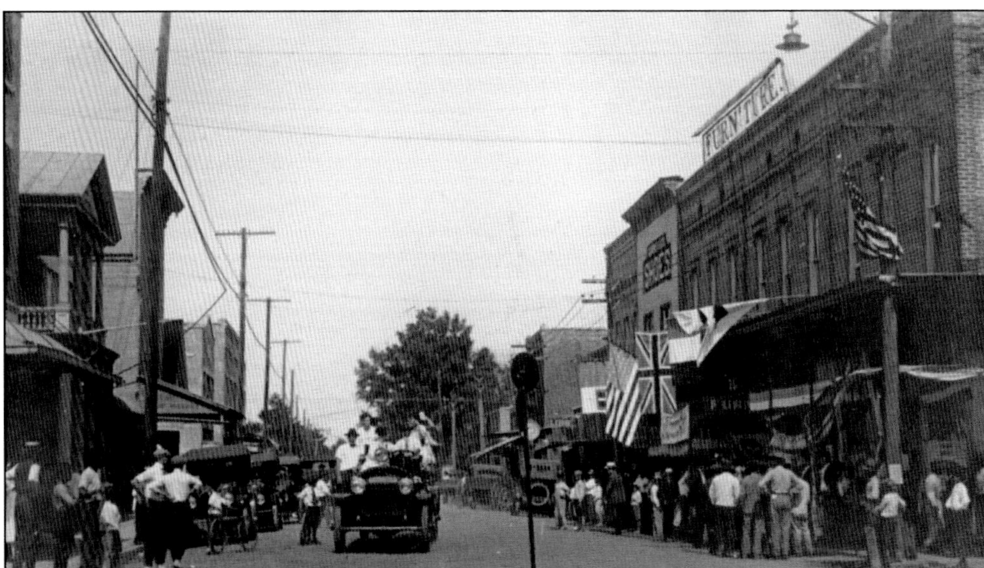

Parades were a regular form of entertainment, and the town was decked out for this World War I parade on the 200 block of East Thomas Street in the late 1910s. On the left, the building with pillars is the Hammond State Bank, and across the street are Adams and Company Shoes and the Thomas Furniture Store and Undertaking Parlor.

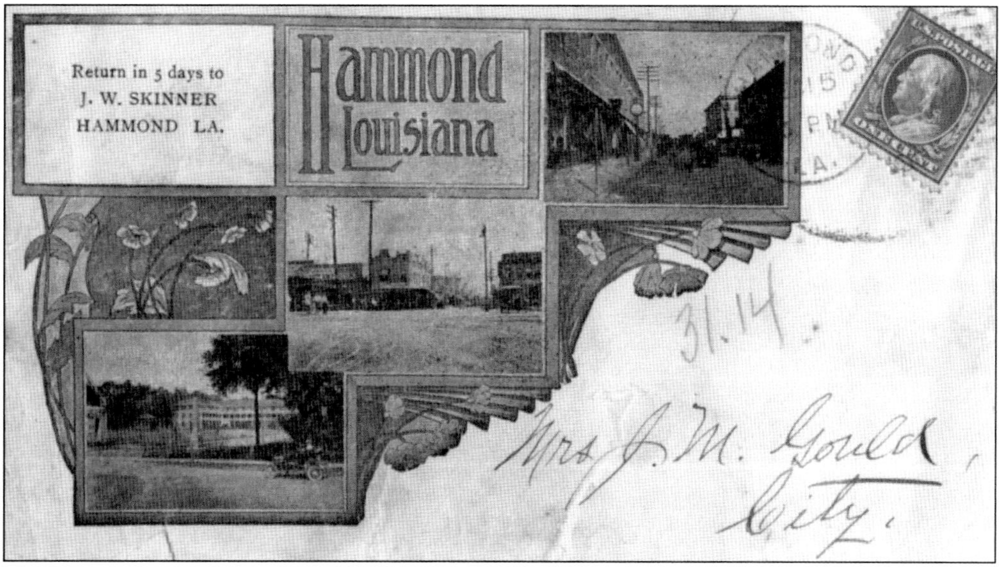

The image above is a custom-printed envelope by Hammond Progressive Union, touting Hammond as the "Queen City of the Ozone Belt." The front cover features the streets of downtown Hammond, including a car passing by the second Oaks Hotel. The return address shows that the envelope was used by J.W. Skinner. The back of the envelope, shown below, lists enticements for the prospective settler, such as "graded and high schools, churches of all denominations" and "the greatest milk producing town and the most famous truck growing section in the Southern States." If that were not enough, the envelope also notes that a person is "only ninety minutes from Canal Street, New Orleans" via Illinois Central Railroad, which boasts "fourteen passenger trains daily."

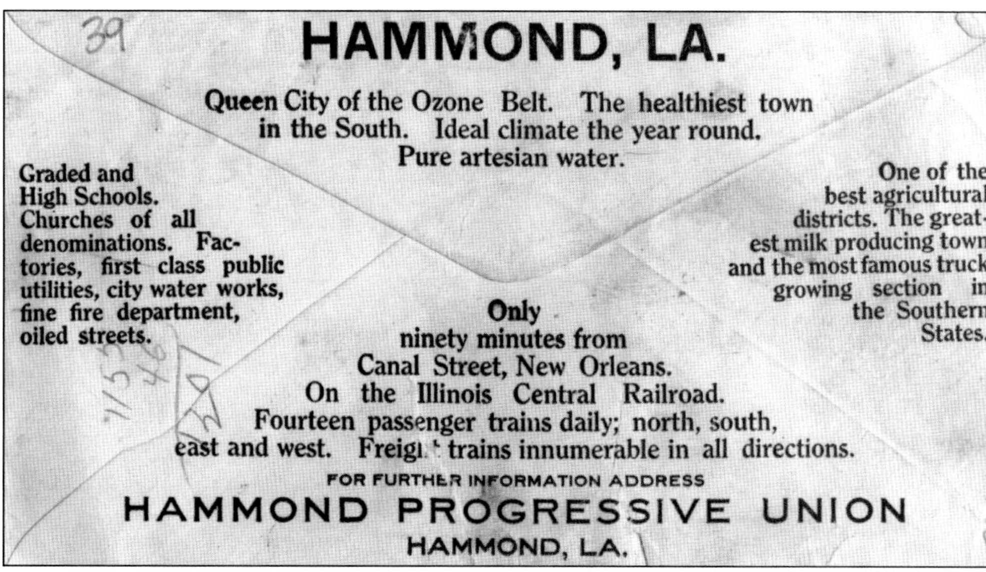

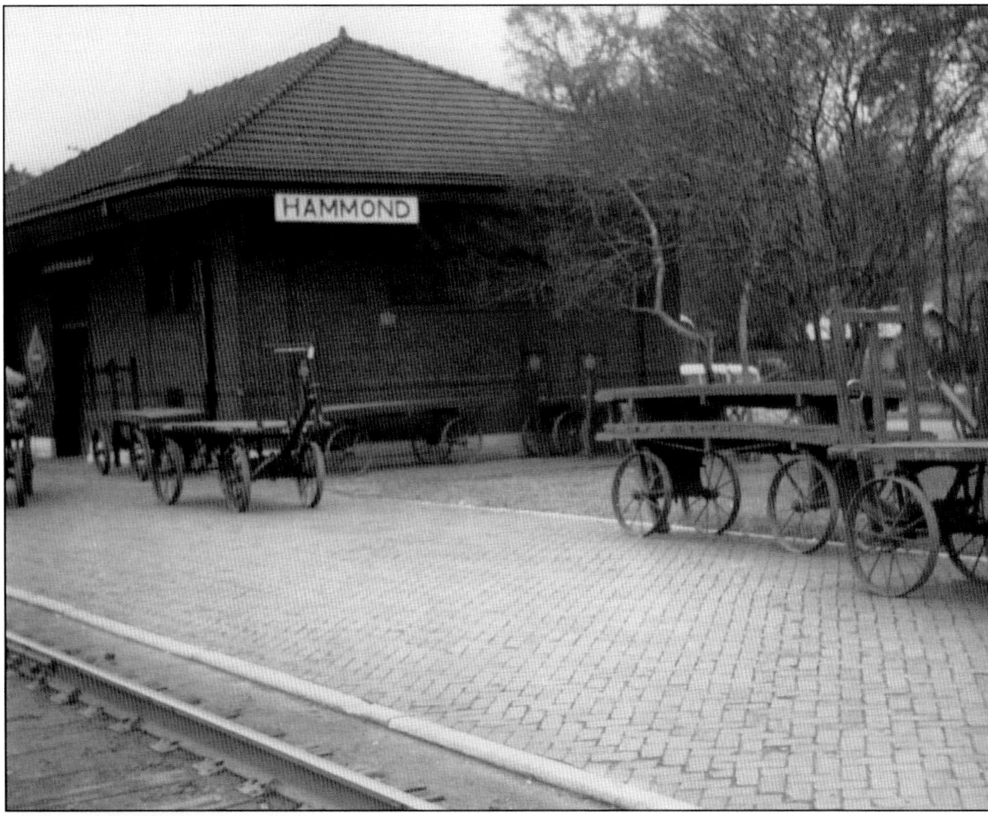

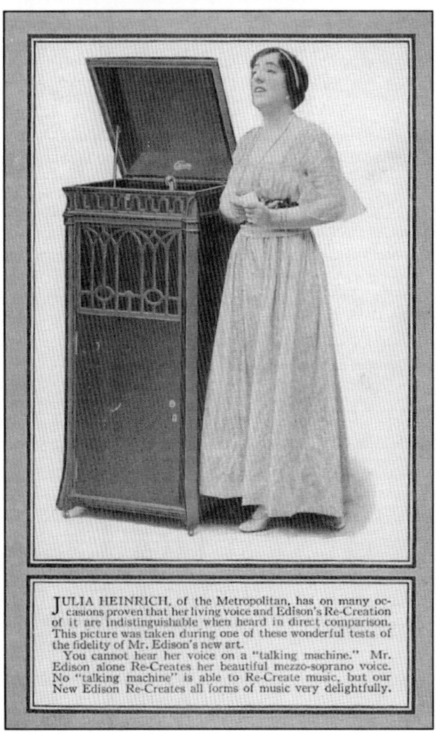

Carts used for loading baggage and cargo sit in front of the Hammond Train Depot. On September 18, 1919, soprano Julia Heinrich was waiting for a train to New Orleans while on a concert tour of the South. A locomotive hit a baggage cart that had been left on the tracks, and Heinrich was struck in the head by the cart's handle and killed. Heinrich, the daughter of German baritone Max Heinrich, sang for two seasons with the Metropolitan Opera, was also a voice teacher, and made comparison tests of her voice against Edison cylinders. Her accompanist, Lucille Colette, was uninjured in the accident. (Above, courtesy of LF/TD.)

Sports celebrity Sidney Bowman competed in the triple jump in the 1928 Olympics in Amsterdam and the 1932 Olympics in Los Angeles. Bowman set a national interscholastic record and was a 1932 national Amateur Athletic Union champion. He participated in track and football at Louisiana State University and was inducted into the Louisiana Sports Hall of Fame in 1976 for track and field. (Courtesy of LF/TD.)

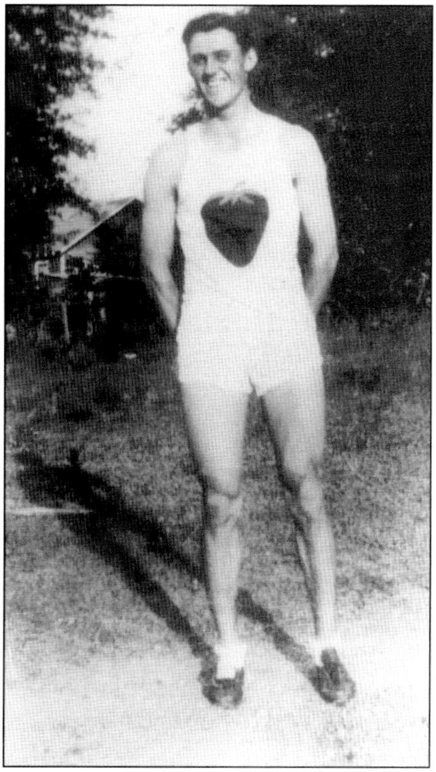

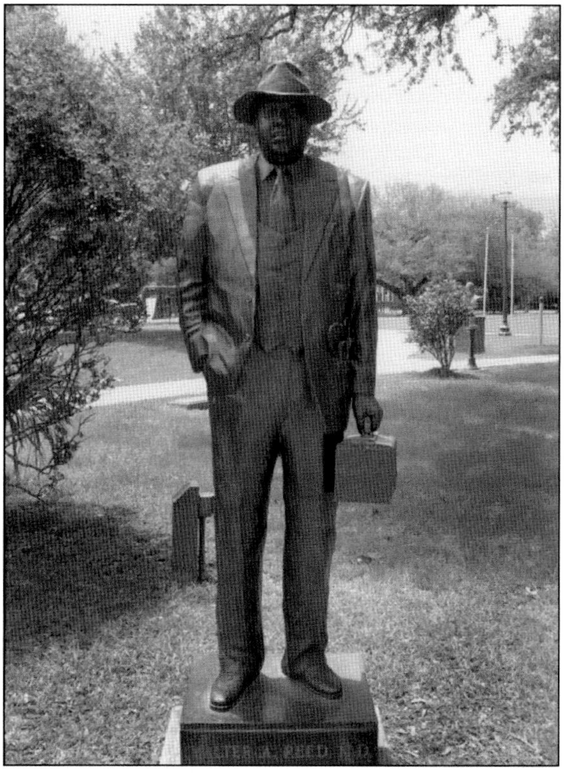

A bronze statue in Cate Square honors the first African American doctor in Hammond, Walter A. Reed. Reed received his medical degree in New Orleans and resided in Hammond from the early 1900s until his death in 1945. He frequently made house calls in either his horse and buggy or his Ford Model T. His Dr. Reed's Cough Syrup was available for many years at Central Drug Store. (Photograph by RT.)

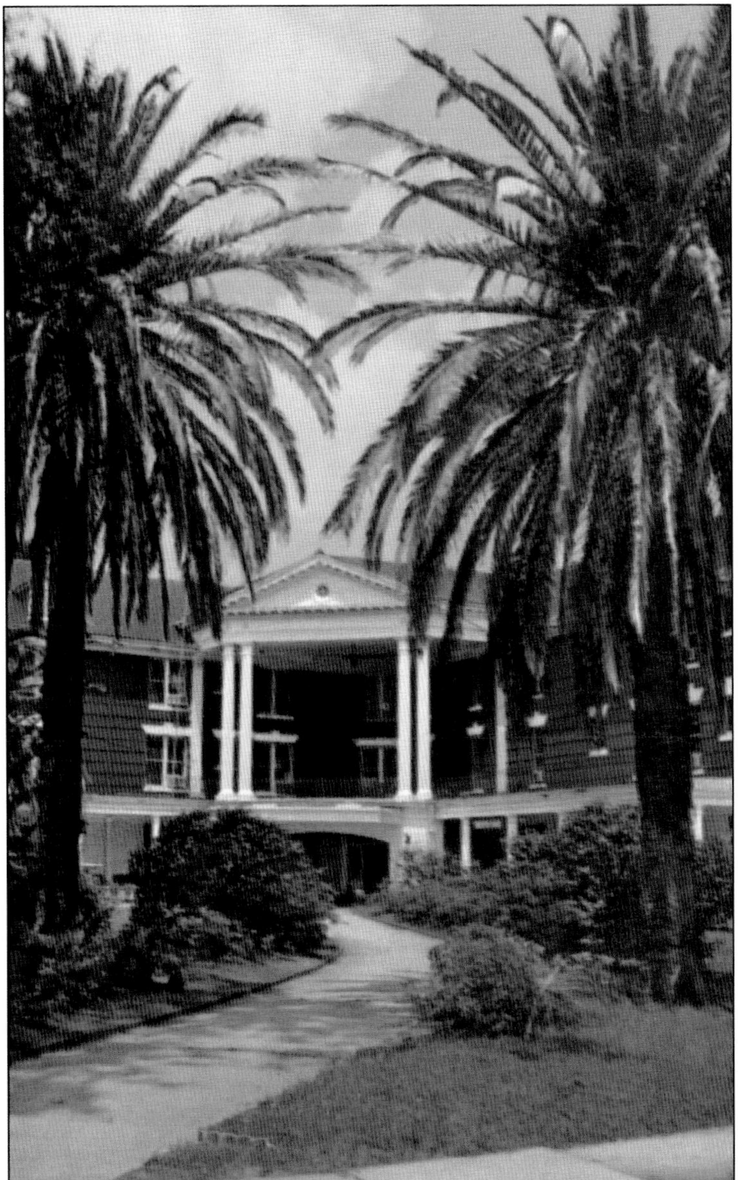

After the 1929 Oaks Hotel fire, a new hotel was built using the same masonry and brick walls. The Alvis Hotel opened in February 1932, but ownership was relinquished to the Strawberry and Vegetable Auction, Inc., which renamed the hotel Casa de Fresa (House of Berries). Guests included strawberry buyers and their families, traveling salesmen (known as "drummers"), politicians, visitors to the relatively new Southeastern Louisiana College, and such notables as Bing Crosby, Robert Merrill, Leopold Stokowski, and Gloria Vanderbilt. The hotel featured 60 rooms, 40 baths, five efficiency apartments, a telegraph office, and a popular coffee shop and dining room. The decline of the berry industry and the rise of motel chains led to the closing of the hotel in August 1966. Later, it briefly housed Valley Forge Academy (later Southwood Academy) in several rooms on the first floor. Despite concerted efforts to save the deteriorating building and its placement in the National Register of Historic Places, the former hotel was destroyed by fire in April 1979. Regions Bank (formerly Citizens National Bank) now occupies the site.

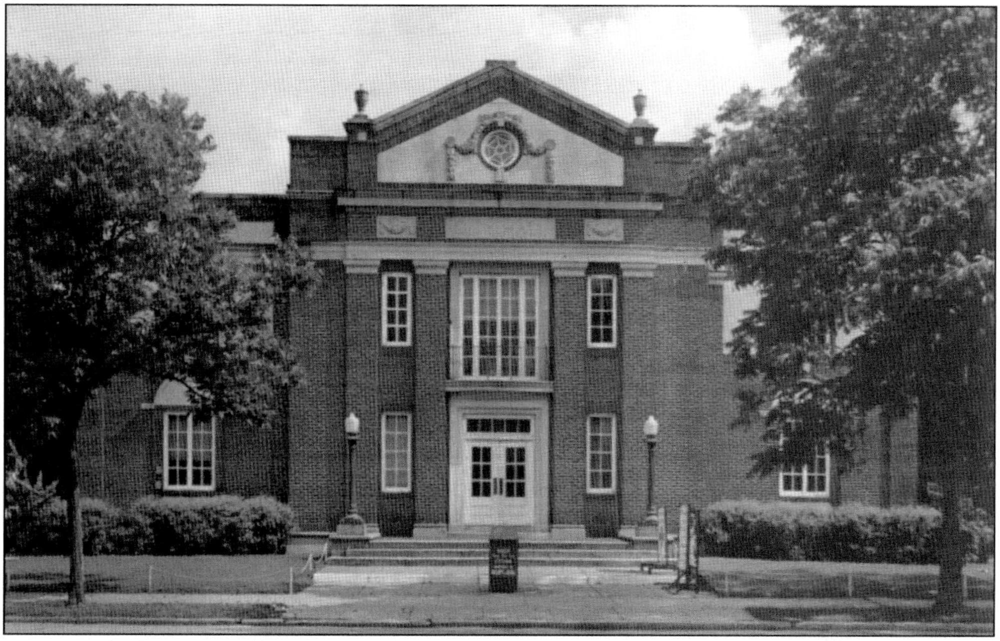

Hammond's first city hall was built in 1926 under the administration of Mayor Charles C. Carter, who served as mayor from 1917 until 1922. Other mayors serving in this building included William B. Jordan, James A. Stire, John C. Morrison, and Sam A. Saik. The building was demolished in the late 1960s to make room for the current city hall, which was built in 1969.

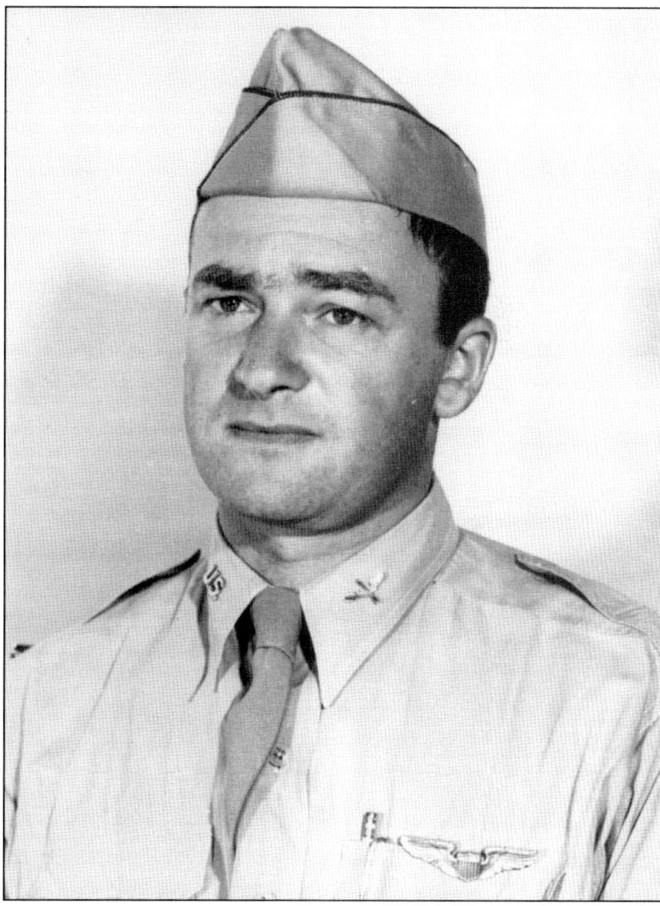

Maj. Samuel Zemurray Jr., son of a famous United Fruit Company president, was killed with three others over Morocco in 1943, piloting a plane while seeking an aircraft missing from their squadron. His father later purchased land and donated it to the city as a memorial park to his son. Zemurray Park has a pond, trees, and sports fields and courts and hosts holiday lights and fireworks.

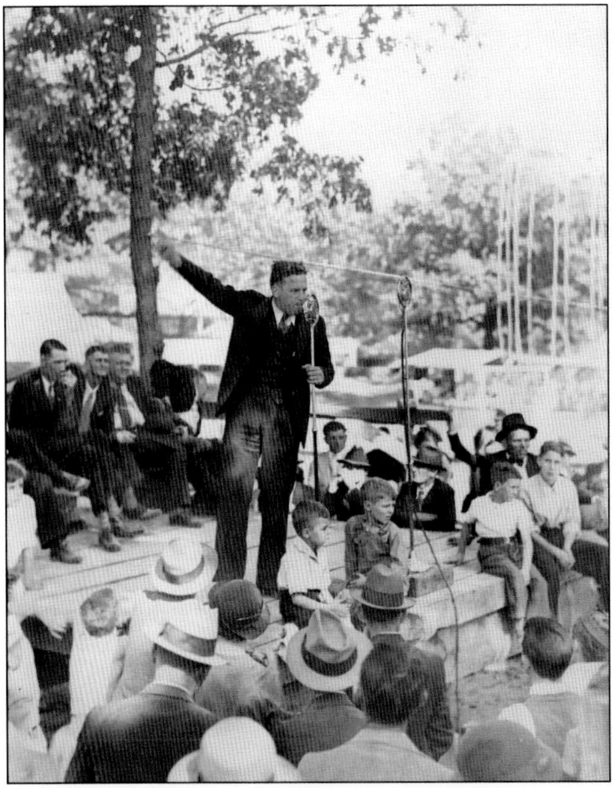

At left, James H. "Jimmy" Morrison speaks at a political rally in the mid-1930s. Morrison, the son of pioneer merchant and banker Benjamin M. Morrison, was an attorney before unsuccessfully running for state senator in 1936. In 1942, he was elected to the US House of Representatives, serving Louisiana's District 6 for 12 terms from 1943 to 1967. Among other accomplishments, he is remembered for his liberal politics, support for federal social programs, and his support of the Voting Rights Act of 1965. Below, Morrison sits outside with strawberry farmers and their wives. Morrison had the support of the strawberry growers in the entire area because of his passionate activism for their rights.

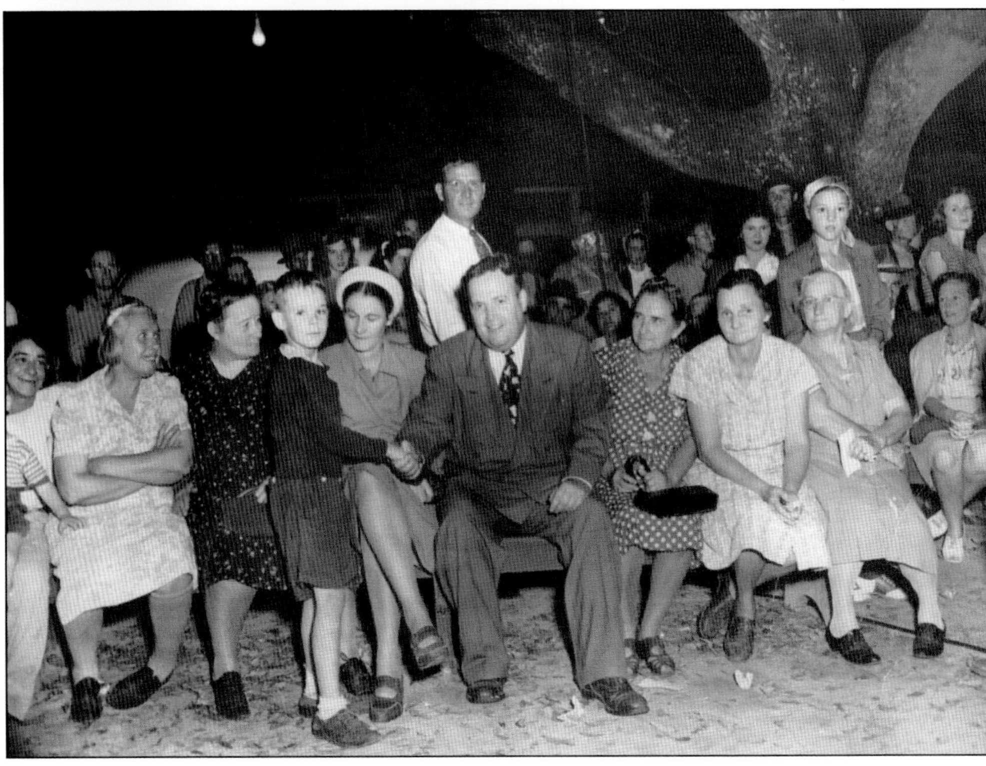

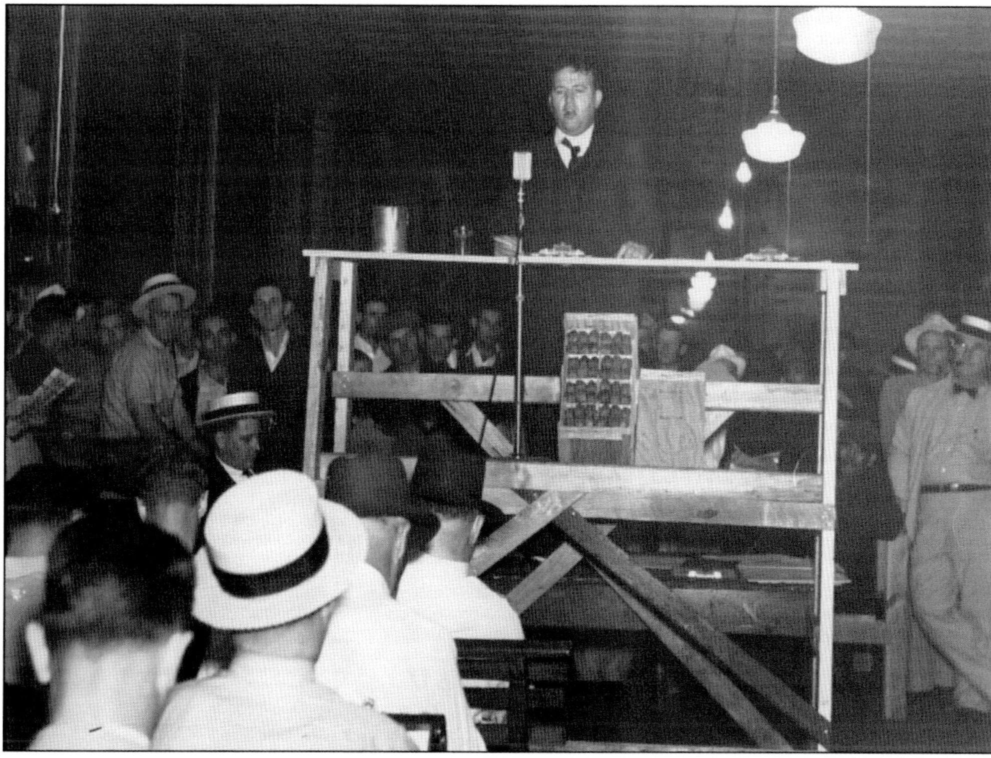

Attorney James H. Morrison auctions off the first express railcar of Louisiana strawberries for the 1939 season. In 1937, Morrison wrote the charter of the newly formed Louisiana Farmers Protective Union and launched a public-relations campaign to ensure that auctions were carried out fairly and only quality strawberries were shipped from the state. Morrison's support for the farmers left a lasting mark on the Louisiana strawberry industry.

This iconic image of US congressman James H. Morrison shows him sharing Louisiana-grown strawberries with Pres. Harry S. Truman. The prize-winning strawberries were presented to Morrison, who offered them to President Truman at the White House. Morrison served under five presidents: Franklin Roosevelt, Truman, Eisenhower, Kennedy, and Lyndon B. Johnson.

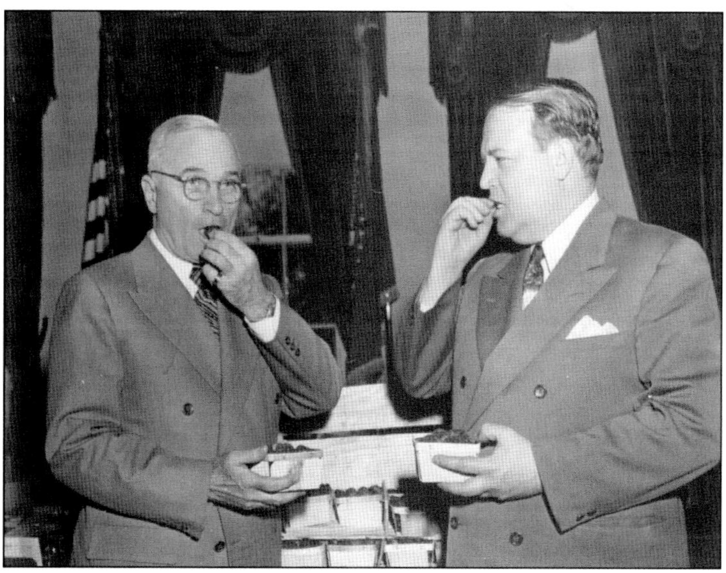

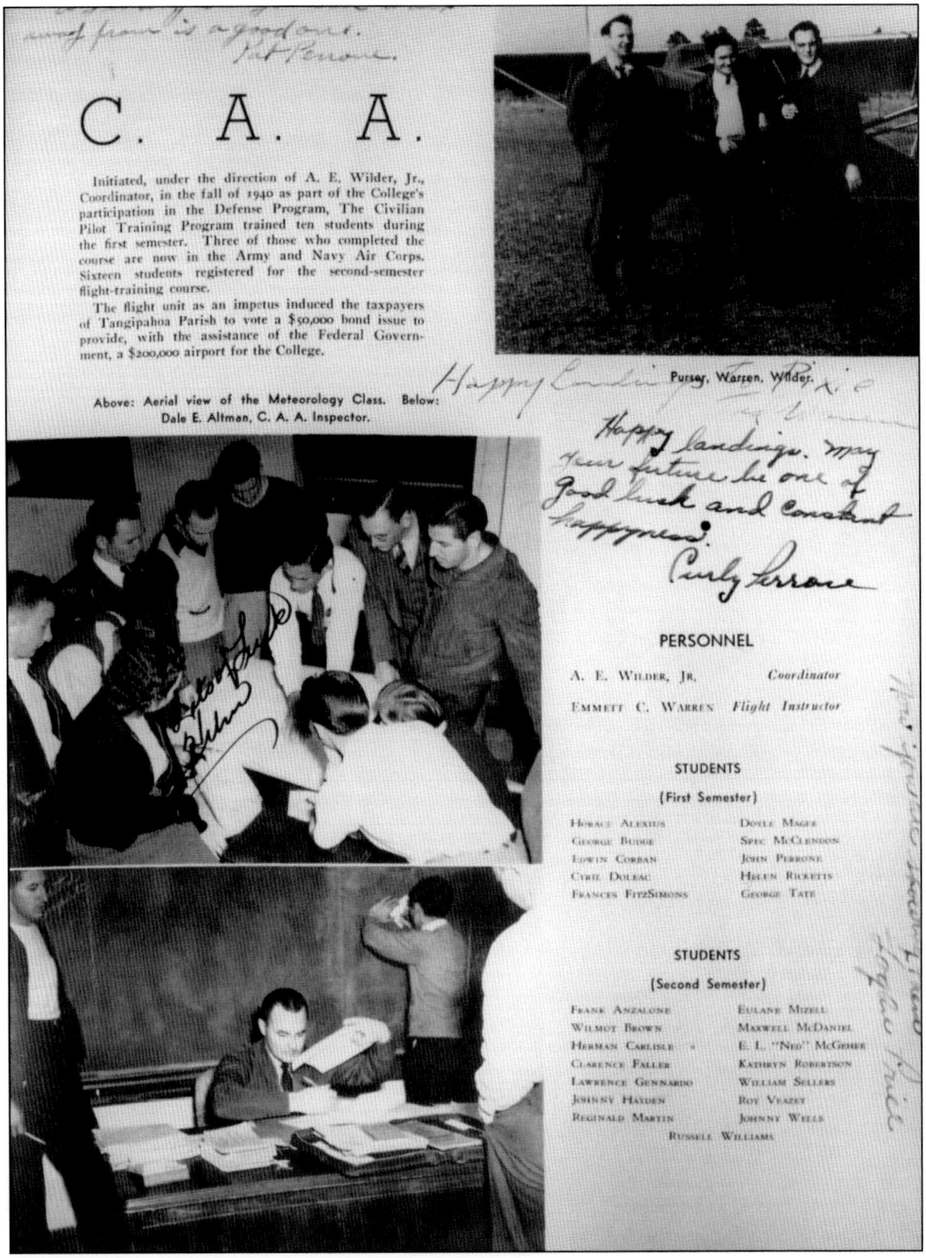

C. A. A.

Initiated, under the direction of A. E. Wilder, Jr., Coordinator, in the fall of 1940 as part of the College's participation in the Defense Program, The Civilian Pilot Training Program trained ten students during the first semester. Three of those who completed the course are now in the Army and Navy Air Corps. Sixteen students registered for the second-semester flight-training course.

The flight unit as an impetus induced the taxpayers of Tangipahoa Parish to vote a $50,000 bond issue to provide, with the assistance of the Federal Government, a $200,000 airport for the College.

Above: Aerial view of the Meteorology Class. Below: Dale E. Altman, C. A. A. Inspector.

Pursey, Warren, Wilder.

Happy landings. May your future be one of good luck and constant happiness. Curly Perrone

PERSONNEL

A. E. Wilder, Jr. — *Coordinator*

Emmett C. Warren — *Flight Instructor*

STUDENTS

(First Semester)

Horace Alexius	Doyle Magee
George Budde	Spec McClendon
Edwin Corban	John Perrone
Cyril Doleac	Helen Ricketts
Frances FitzSimons	George Tate

STUDENTS

(Second Semester)

Frank Anzalone	Eulane Mizell
Wilmot Brown	Maxwell McDaniel
Herman Carlisle	E. L. "Ned" McGehee
Clarence Faller	Kathryn Robertson
Lawrence Gennardo	William Sellers
Johnny Hayden	Roy Veazey
Reginald Martin	Johnny Wells

Russell Williams

In the fall of 1940, with the United States close to war, Southeastern Louisiana College established a Civil Pilot Training Program, coordinated by A.E. Wilder Jr. Ten out of more than 75 students were selected for the program, with flight instruction by Emmett C. "Ted" Warren from the Farley Vincent Aeronautics School of New Orleans. Two were from Hammond: John A. Perrone and, because of a national quota of only one female to every nine male students, the only female, Helen L. Ricketts. The existing airport was abandoned after commercial mail flights had been discontinued and the lights removed, but the training program resulted in the approval of a tax to fund the construction of a new parish airport, with additional funding from a government grant. Spin training was required before a student was allowed to solo, and precision spins were required before a private license was issued. Some of the students went on to careers in the military.

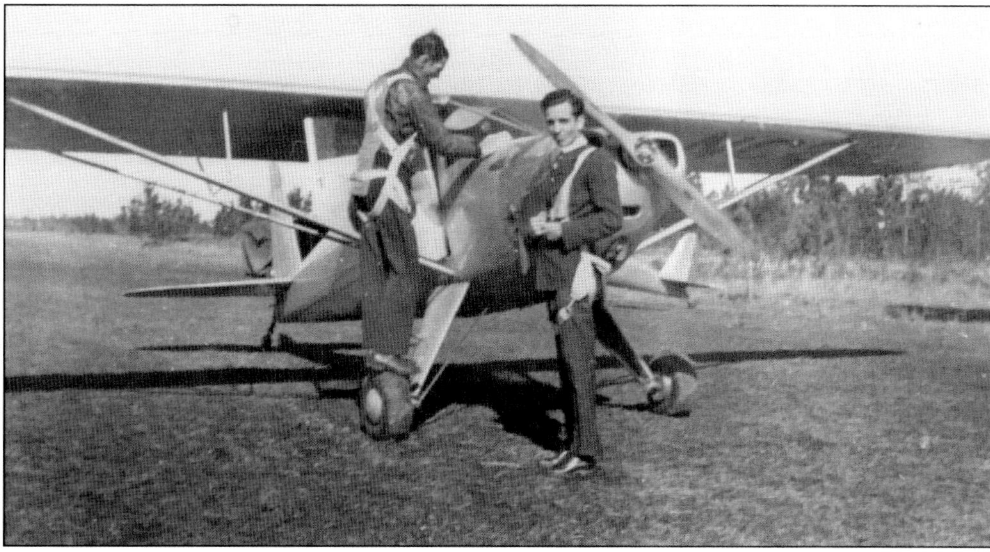

John A. Perrone watches while flight instructor Ted Warren checks the fuel before spin training. After serving in World War II, Perrone returned to Hammond in 1946 and, with his brother Pat, founded Perrone Flying Service. The flying service was short-lived since a hurricane destroyed their hangar in 1947. He returned to military service in 1948 and retired as a colonel.

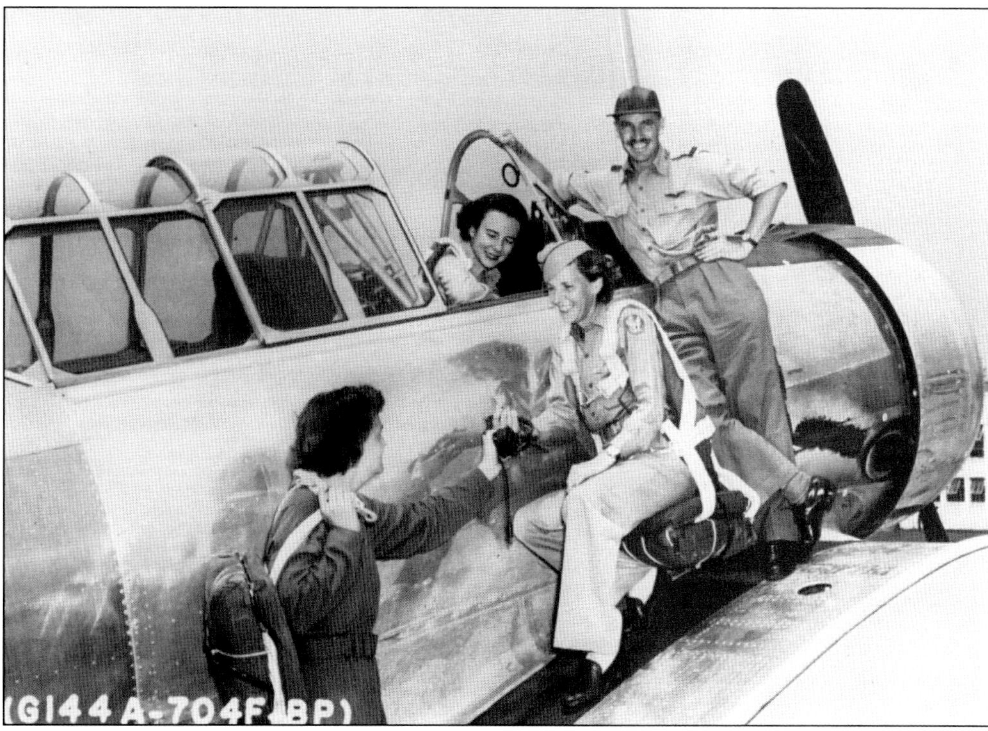

Helen Ricketts Hooks Rownd poses in the cockpit of an AT-6 while training to be a WASP (Women's Air Force Service Pilots). Soon after training, her initial assignment was flying different planes to various destinations throughout the country. Her next and most harrowing task was to tow targets for aerial gunners' practice. She later became a mathematics teacher at Hammond High School.

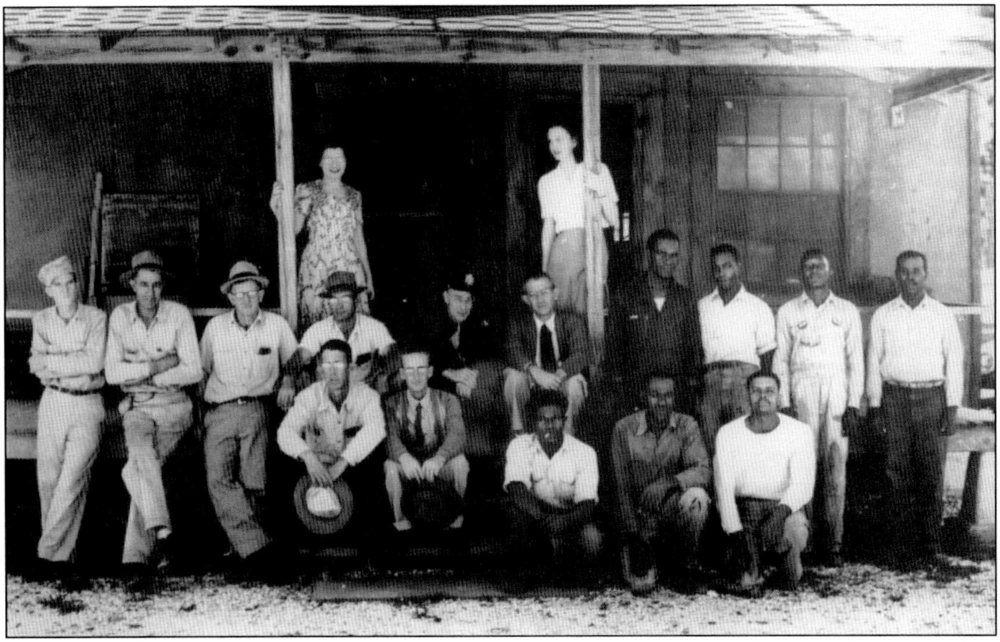

The new airport planned for Hammond was designated as a national defense project, and in August 1942 the US Army Air Forces took over construction of the airport. Additional property was expropriated, the airport became a military air base, and barracks and support facilities for military personnel were built. In this photograph, post engineers pose in front of one of the airport buildings.

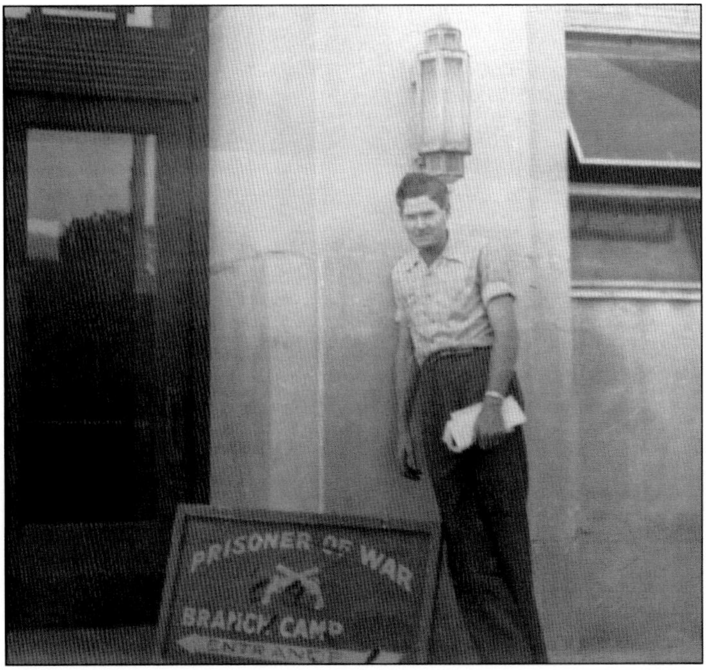

From 1944 to 1946, over 20,000 German soldiers were sent to prisoner-of-war camps near Alexandria and Harahan, Louisiana. Smaller branch camps around the state provided labor for companies that would supply camp construction and security. Bogalusa's Gaylord Container Corporation constructed a camp in Hammond for pulp wood cutting and loading. The camp sign ended up at the door of Southeastern High School the morning after Halloween in 1946.

Two

Business and Industry

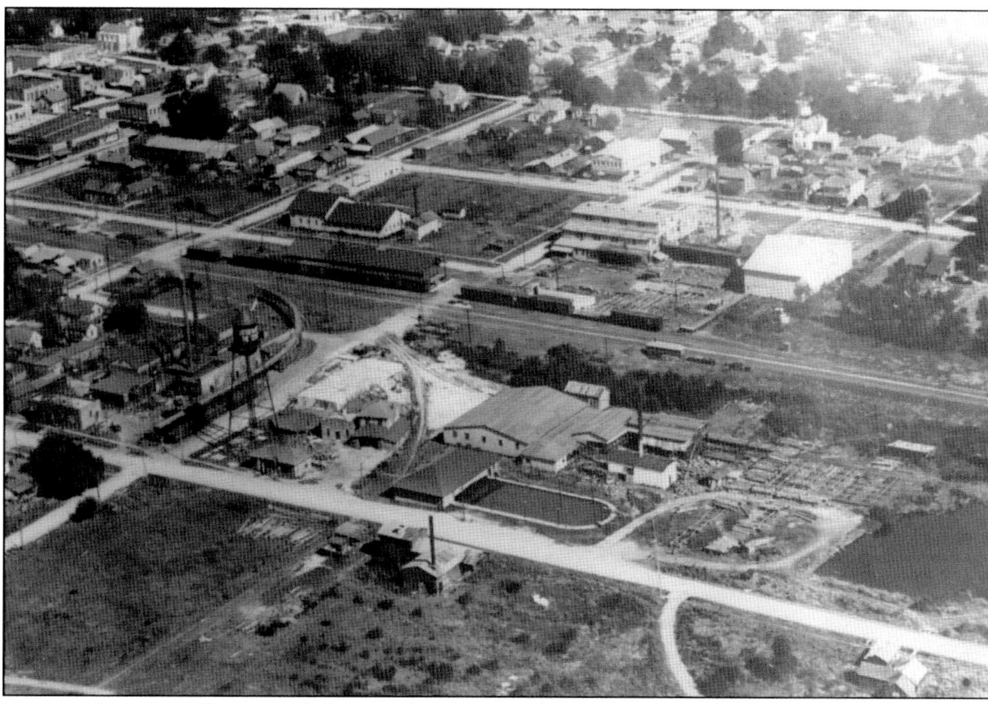

An aerial view of Hammond depicts the area south of Thomas Street around 1923. Running below the railroad, Railroad Avenue stops at Coleman Avenue near the water tower. At this intersection sits the city's source of electricity, Hammond Ice, Light, and Bottling Company. On the other side of Coleman Avenue is Hammond's waterworks and fire station. Moving south, on Oak, is the natatorium, next to the Barney Arnold Sawmill. (Courtesy of DF.)

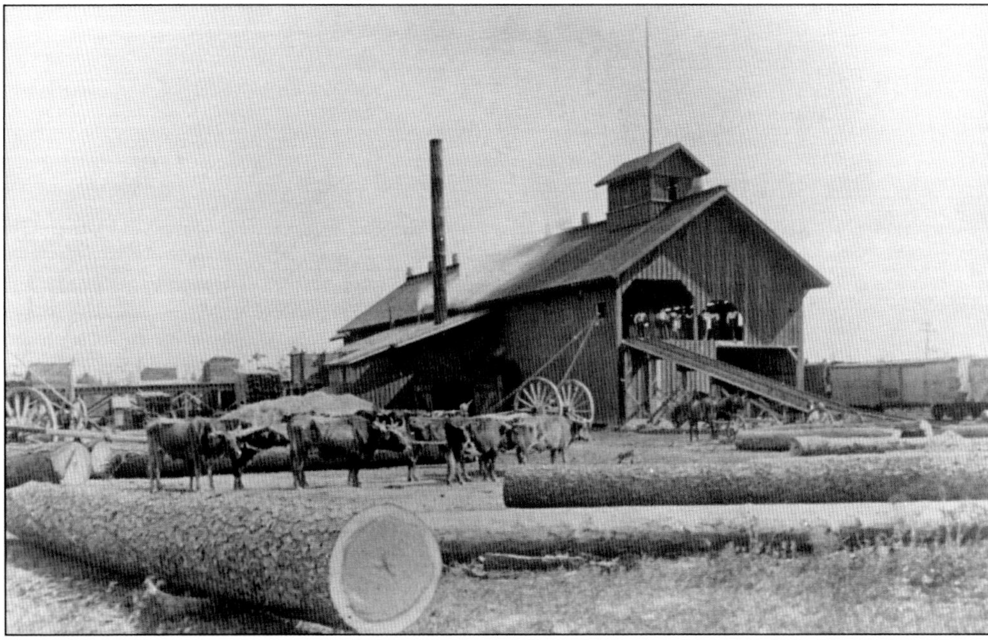

The Charles E. Cate Lumber Company was located between the current Hanson and Coleman Avenues near the railroad tracks. In 1861, Cate built a lumber factory and a boardinghouse for employees of his shoe factory. The complex consisted of a sawmill, gristmill, and tannery. Water barrels on the roof provided fire protection. A brickyard stood in what is now Zemurray Park.

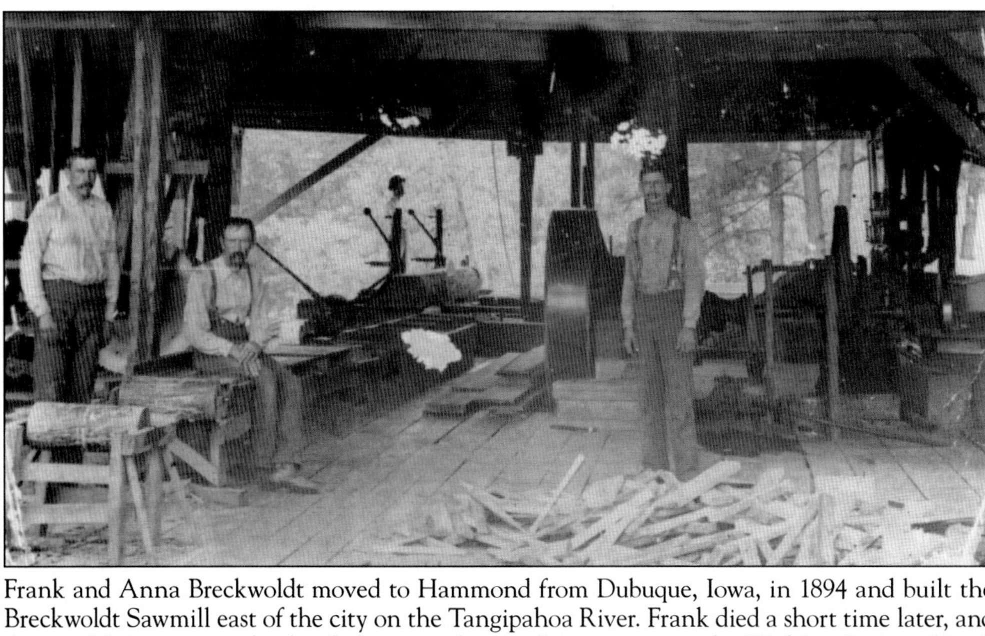

Frank and Anna Breckwoldt moved to Hammond from Dubuque, Iowa, in 1894 and built the Breckwoldt Sawmill east of the city on the Tangipahoa River. Frank died a short time later, and Anna added rooms to the family home and opened it as a resort, the Wishing Springs Hotel, taking in boarders who could enjoy fishing, boating, and swimming. The gravel industry destroyed her business around 1918.

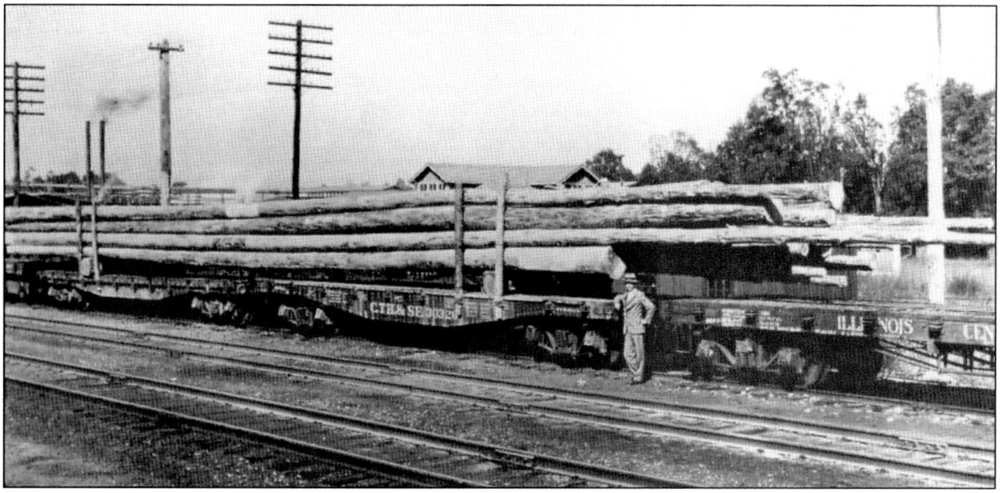

The Hammond Lumber Company supplied wood pilings for construction in the early 1900s, including the building of the Panama Canal, which opened for ship passage on August 15, 1914. Operations manager Will Nalty stands beside a flatbed railcar loaded with 120-foot wood pilings destined for Panama. Pine trees used for pilings were harvested all along the Gulf Coast for the enormous task of building the canal. (Courtesy of LF/TD.)

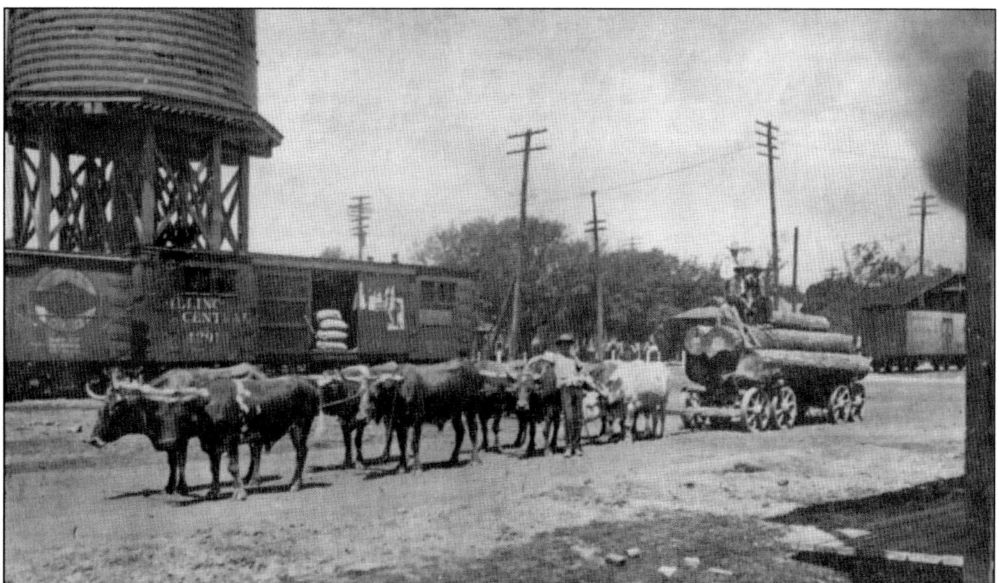

Oxen pull an eight-wheel log wagon next to the water tower and railroad tracks. Most of the log wagons of the day were built in Laurel, Mississippi, by the Lindsey Wagon Company. The wagons, which were patented in 1899 by John Lindsey, were shipped all over the United States and Central and South America. During World War I, the company shipped wagons to France. (Courtesy of LF/TD.)

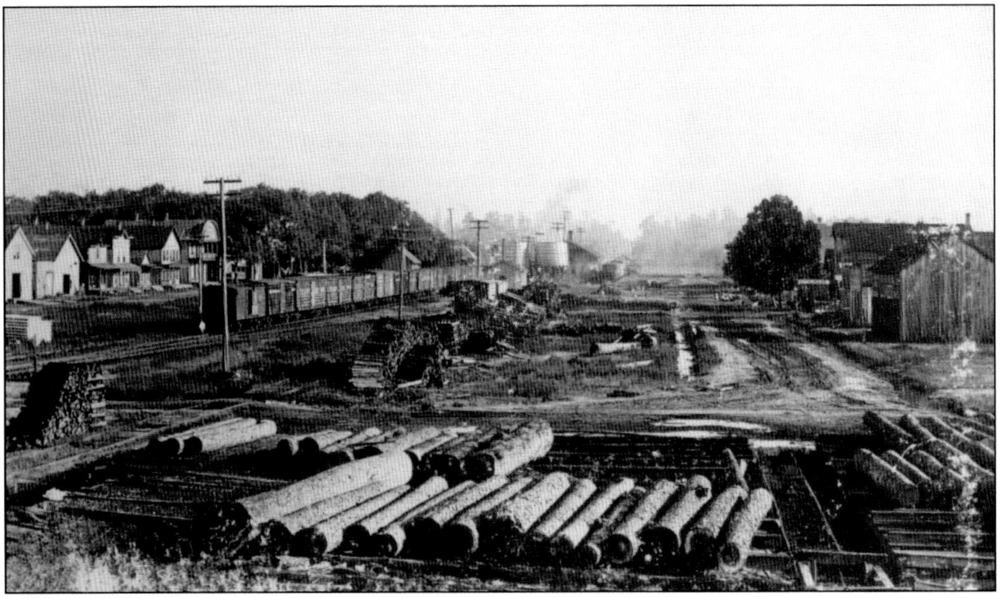

In 1895, a train stops in Hammond, viewed from Charles E. Cate's sawmill, part of the C.E. Cate Lumber and Brick Company located on Southwest Railroad Avenue. By 1892, there were nine sawmills that shipped lumber products from Hammond. Most of the lumber was shipped to St. Louis and other points north.

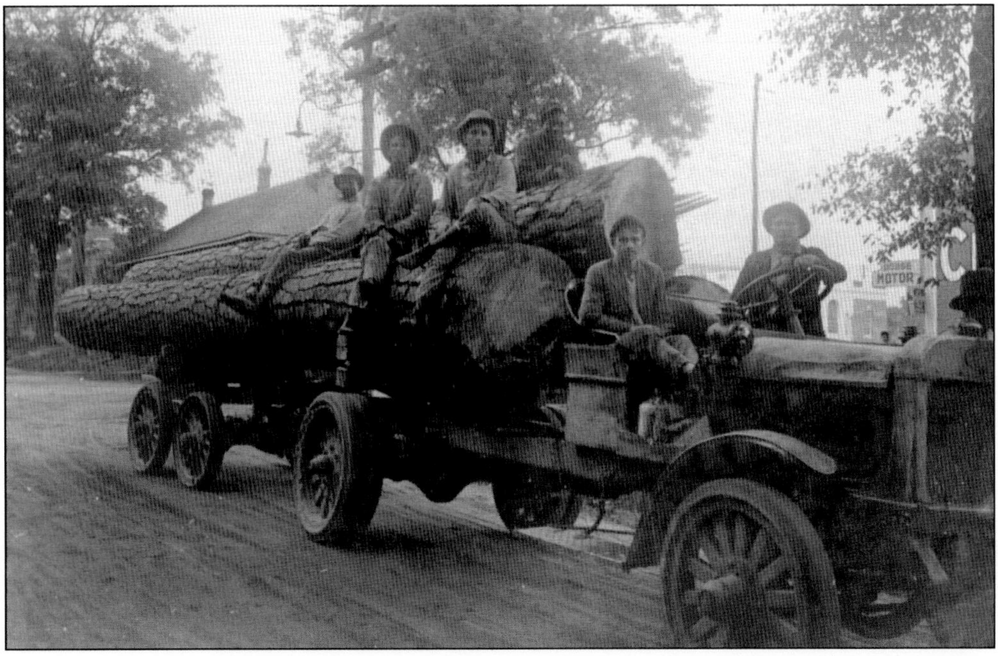

A logger with a truckload of pine logs and lumberjacks pauses for a photograph on the corner of Oak and Thomas Streets sometime in the early 1900s. Lumber and wood products had long been an important industry in Hammond. By the 1920s, the logging industry was in decline, the result of depletion of timber and changes in building materials.

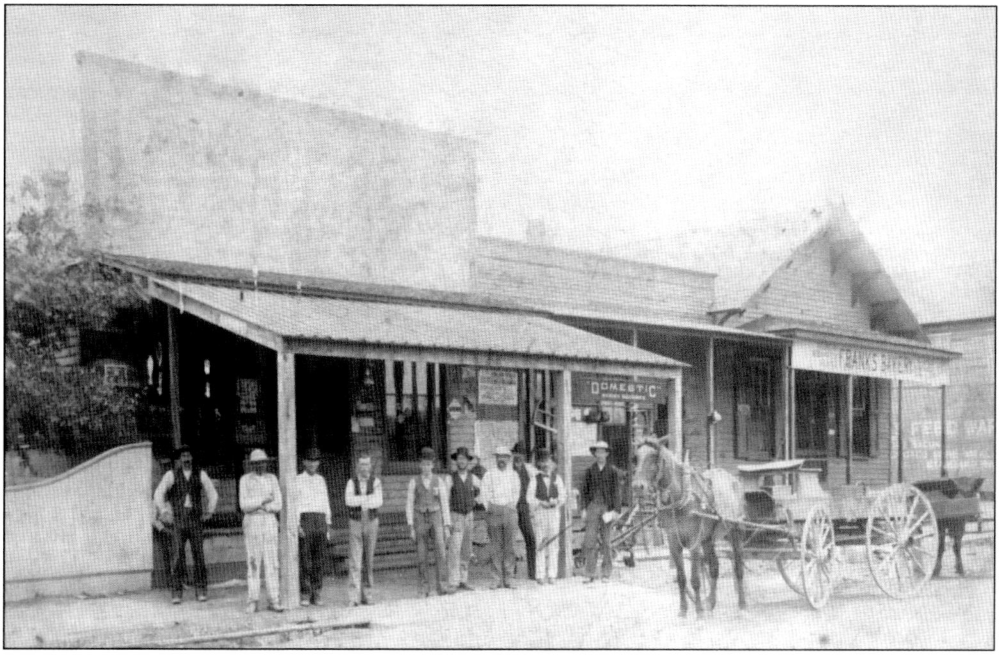

A group of men gathers around the original Neelis General Store on Northeast Railroad Avenue near Thomas Street. Frank E. Neelis became a Hammond merchant when he joined with W.E. Lawson to form Lawson & Neelis in 1889. In 1892, Frank's brothers, John G. and George C. Neelis, bought out Lawson, renaming the entity Frank E. Neelis and Company. The fire of July 1896 destroyed the store.

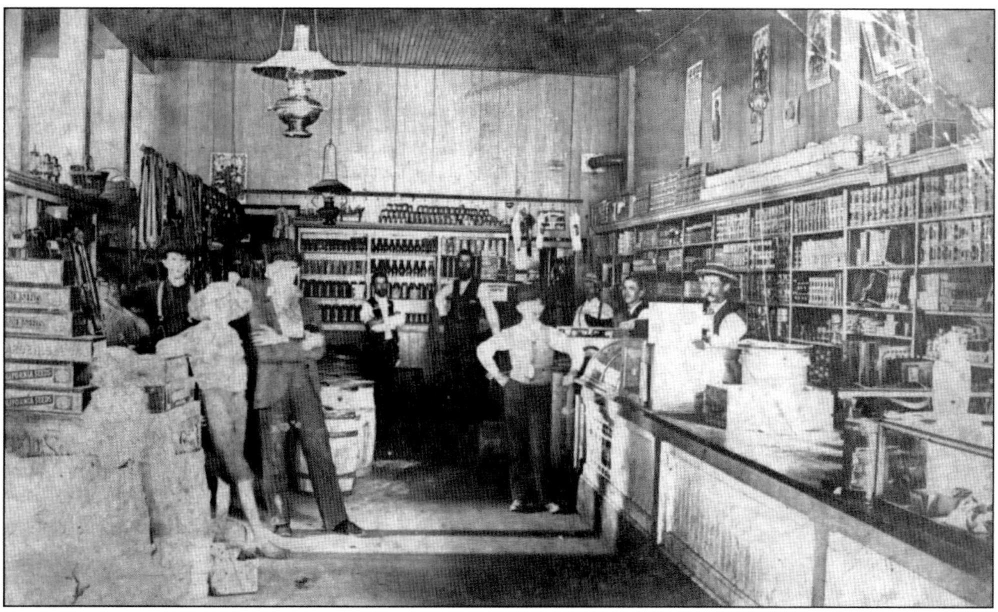

Workers proudly display the interior of the first Neelis store during its heyday at the turn of the century. The store is typical of a general store for that time, with oil lamps hanging from the ceiling, canned and bottled goods lining the shelves, barrels of pickles, hams hanging on racks, various garden seeds, woven baskets, and bridle and tack equipment ready for purchase.

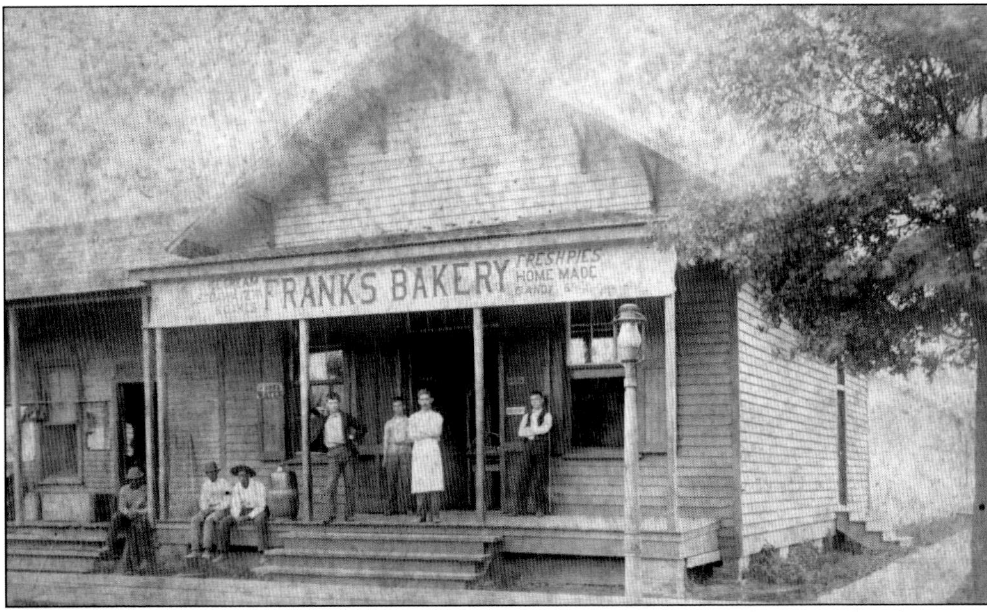

Frank Norman's Bakery stood at the corner of Thomas Street and Northeast Railroad Avenue, next to Frank Neelis's store. In addition to pies and baked goods, the store featured candy, ice cream, and soda water. The site was later occupied by the Boos Building, constructed in 1898, which included G.W. Crook Ice Cream, Candy, Cigars and Tobacco as one of its tenants.

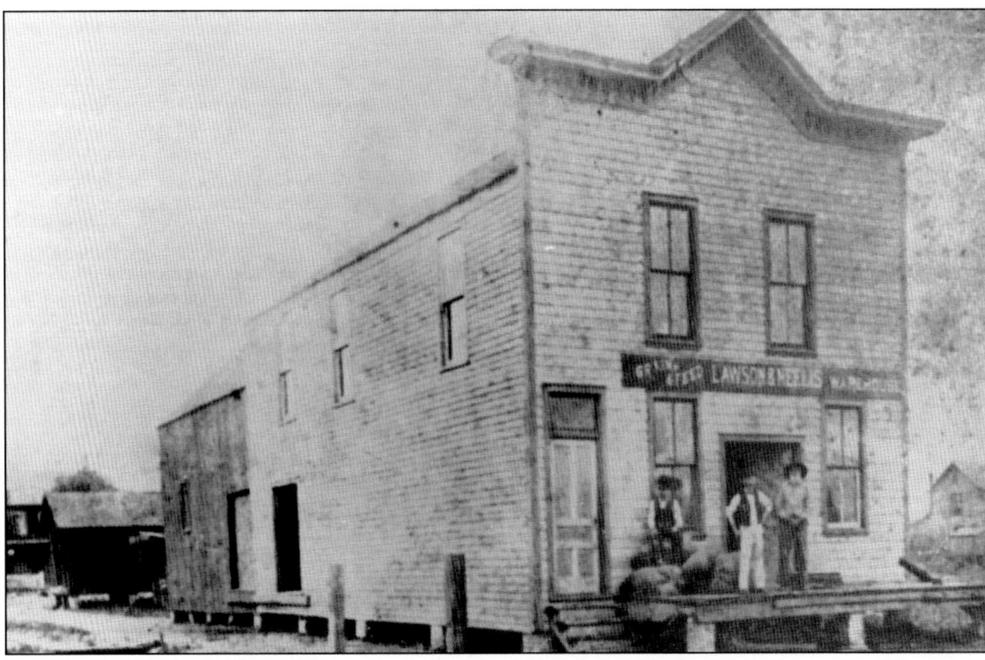

The Lawson & Neelis Warehouse was situated on Southeast Railroad Avenue. Its second floor was the site of the first Catholic Mass in Hammond, offered in 1890 by Fr. Leander Roth, who served as pastor of Catholic churches in Amite and Ponchatoula. Catholics continued to worship there for about 12 years until Holy Ghost Church was built.

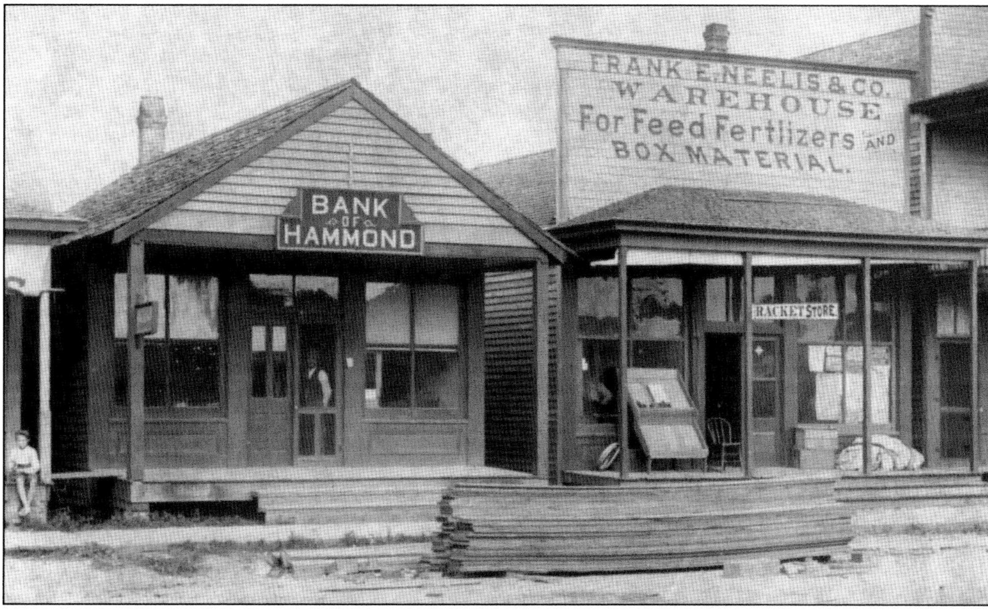

One of Hammond's first financial institutions, the Bank of Hammond, was incorporated in 1894. Its first officials included Frank E. Neelis, president; John E. Wilcombe; Charles E. Cate; and L.I. Way and D.M. Durkee, directors. The bank was located on the 100 block of Southeast Railroad Avenue and was next to the Neelis brothers' warehouse. The two buildings perished in the fire of 1896.

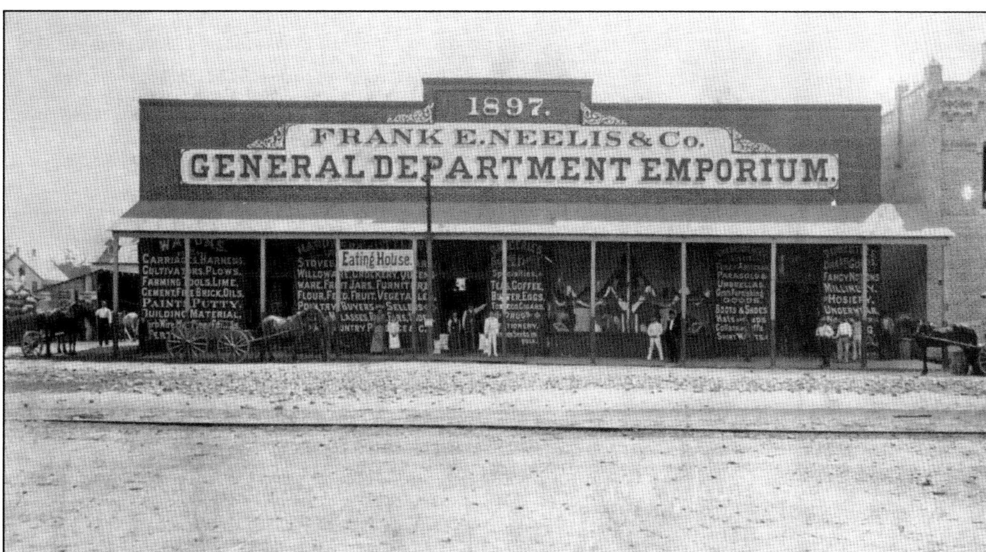

The Frank E. Neelis and Company General Department Emporium opened its doors in a new brick building in 1897. According to the *Souvenir Album of Hammond, Louisiana*, published in 1897, the spacious emporium may have been "the largest mercantile house outside of New Orleans." The new emporium sold carriages, building materials, dry goods, and clothing, among many other useful items. The building burned in 1984.

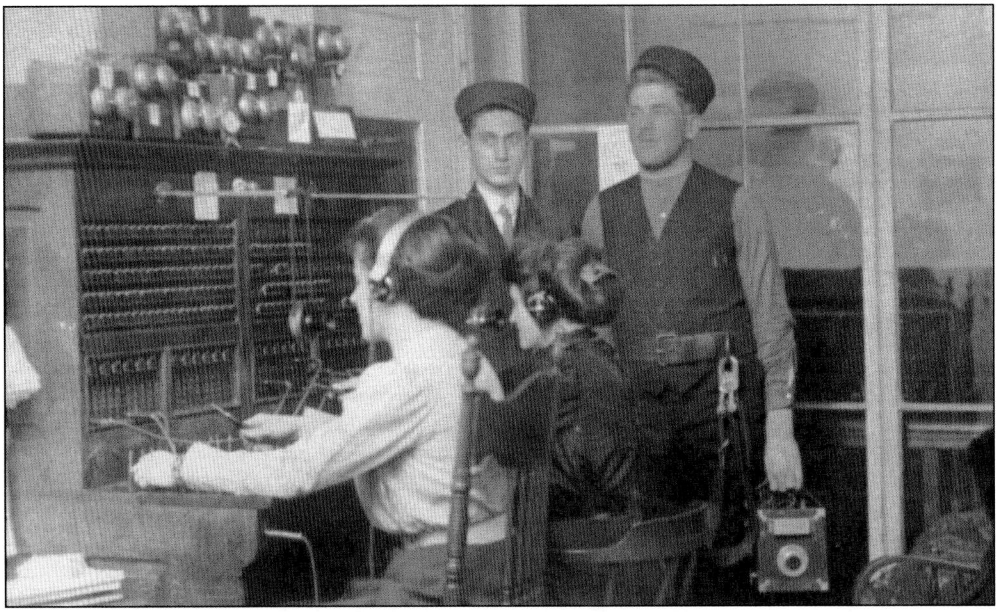

This photograph shows the exchange of the Cumberland Telephone and Telegraph Company. Located on the second floor in the Boos Building on East Thomas Street, the office, which opened in 1898, was the first telephone company in Hammond. By the end of 1900, there were 94 subscribers. In 1913, two years after Cumberland merged with the Bell System, there were 378 phone users; by 1950, there were 2,999 subscribers.

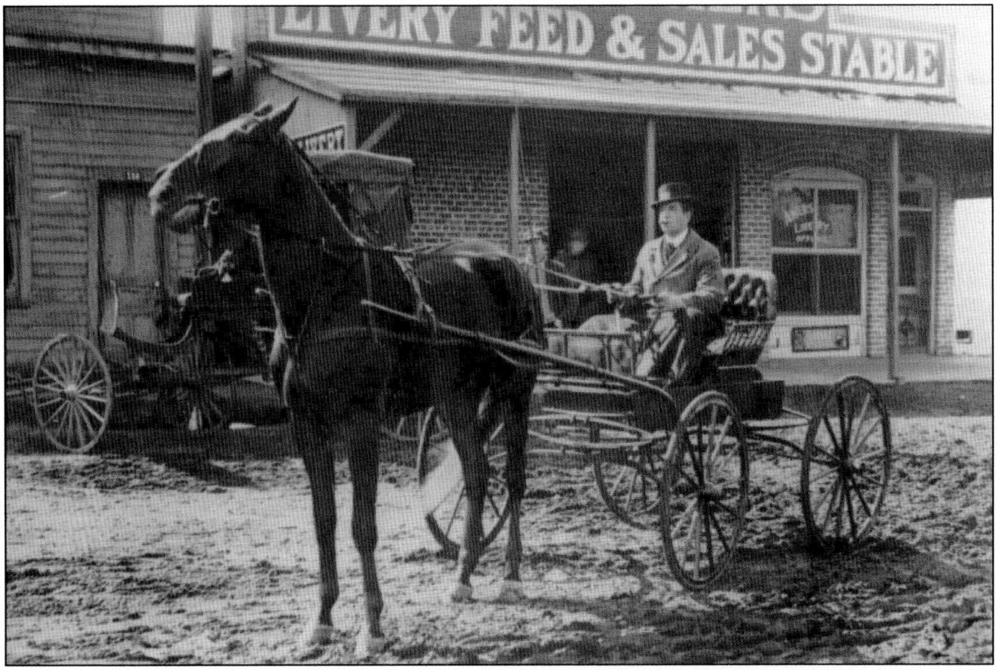

Akers Livery Stable was located on Southwest Railroad Avenue. Other stables of the period included Louisiana Livery, J.C. Farley's, and the Willis Livery Stable. Charles G. Baltzell later operated a livery stable in the building, which eventually became the site of a bus station, first for Hammond Stage Lines and then for Greyhound.

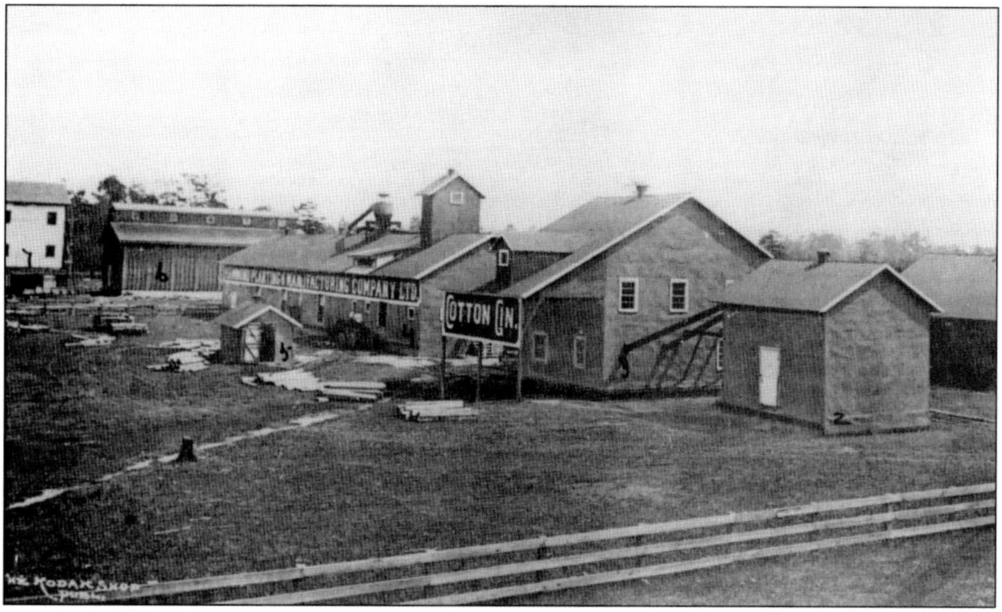

Hammond Planting and Manufacturing Company Limited and Cotton Gin structures were located on Northeast Railroad Avenue across the railroad tracks from the current depot. The *Louisiana Farmers' Institutes Bulletin, No.10–11* notes that the manufacturing company won a prize of a "sack of cracked corn" for producing the richest milk at the November 7, 1906, Hammond Exhibition. The photograph was taken sometime between 1910 and 1920.

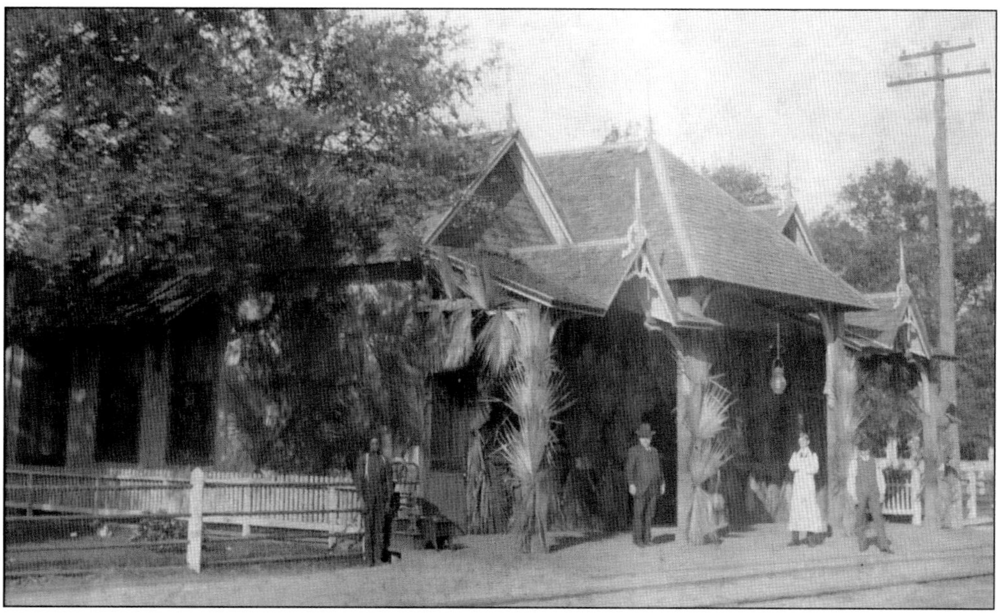

Festooned with palm fronds, the Railroad Lunch Stand offered meals and drinks to rail travelers. Hotel owner Thomas Kidder, standing in the center, operated the stand. The building was connected by a covered walkway to the hotel in back before the hotel burned in 1899. Col. Henry W. Robinson later purchased the lunch stand.

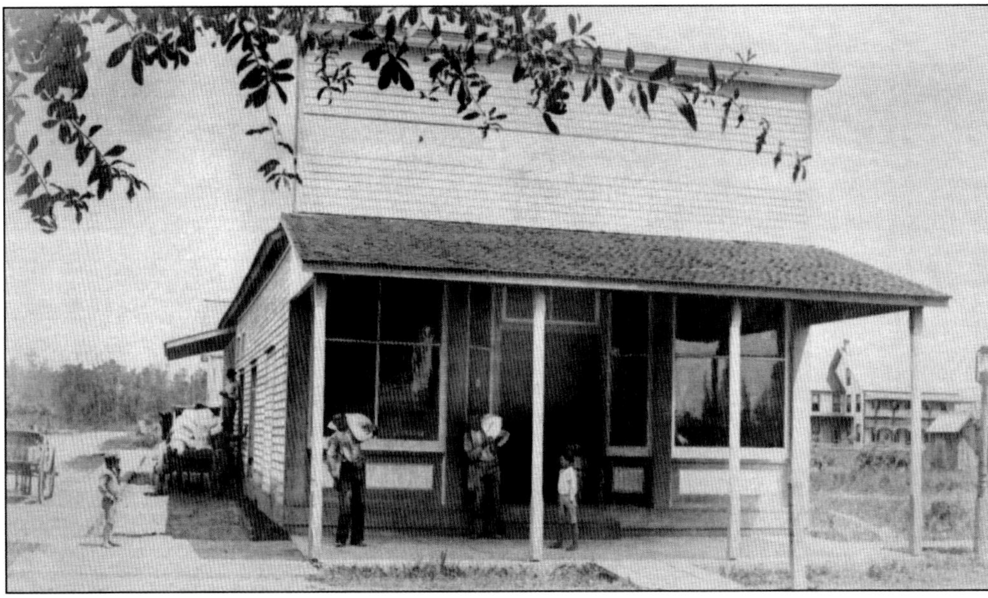

Merchant and banker Benjamin M. Morrison opened his first store around 1894 on East Thomas and North Cypress Streets. In the right background of the photograph above is the Andrews Home, a boardinghouse on Charles and Cherry Streets. After the store burned in a fire in 1903, Morrison replaced it the following year with a brick structure that stands today. Morrison's feed and seed warehouse, below, was situated on North Cherry Street between Charles and Thomas Streets. Its walls were insulated with sawdust, and ice was stored in the building to maintain cooler temperatures in the days before electric refrigeration.

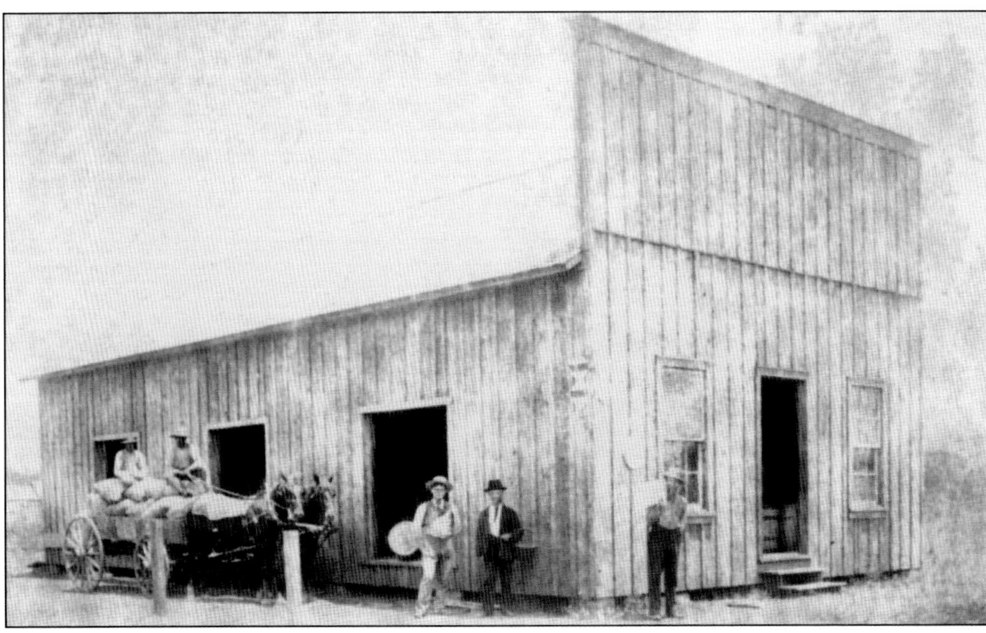

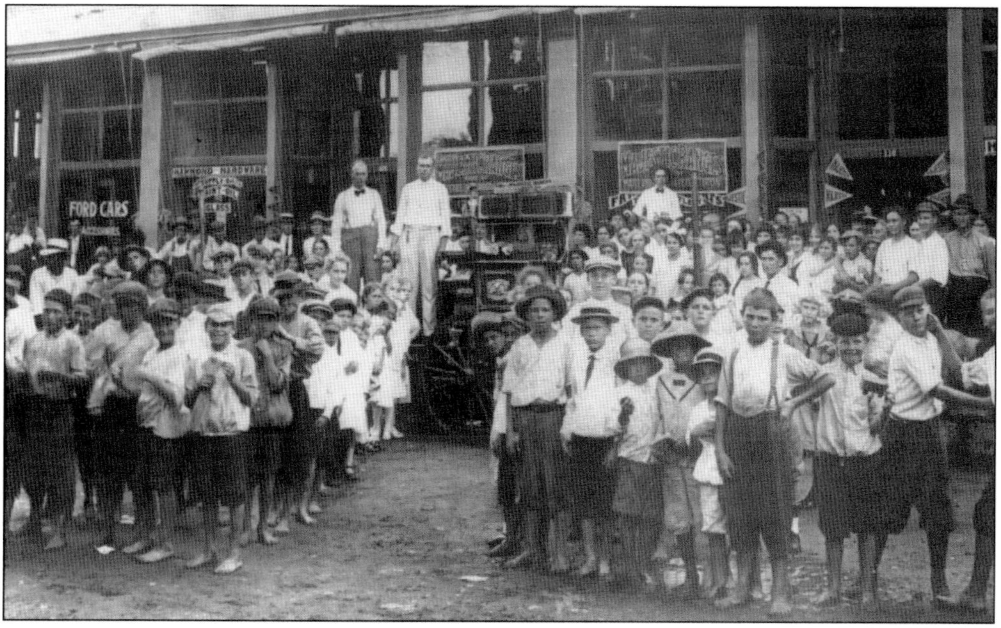

In the above image, a group of school-age children gathers around the entrance to Hammond Hardware, located on the corner of South Cypress Street and East Morris Avenue. The store is advertising its stock of Majestic Ranges, as seen by the oven on the cart. The Majestic Stove Company produced approximately two million stoves from the 1880s until the 1940s. The company was one of the 10 largest stove manufacturers in the United States prior to World War II. The photograph below shows the interior of the Hammond Hardware store. From left to right are Dick Whitaker, store clerk; Charles R. "Chum" Anderson, store owner; and ? Walker, store clerk. Anderson and his wife purchased the store in 1912. Whitaker was Anderson's brother-in-law.

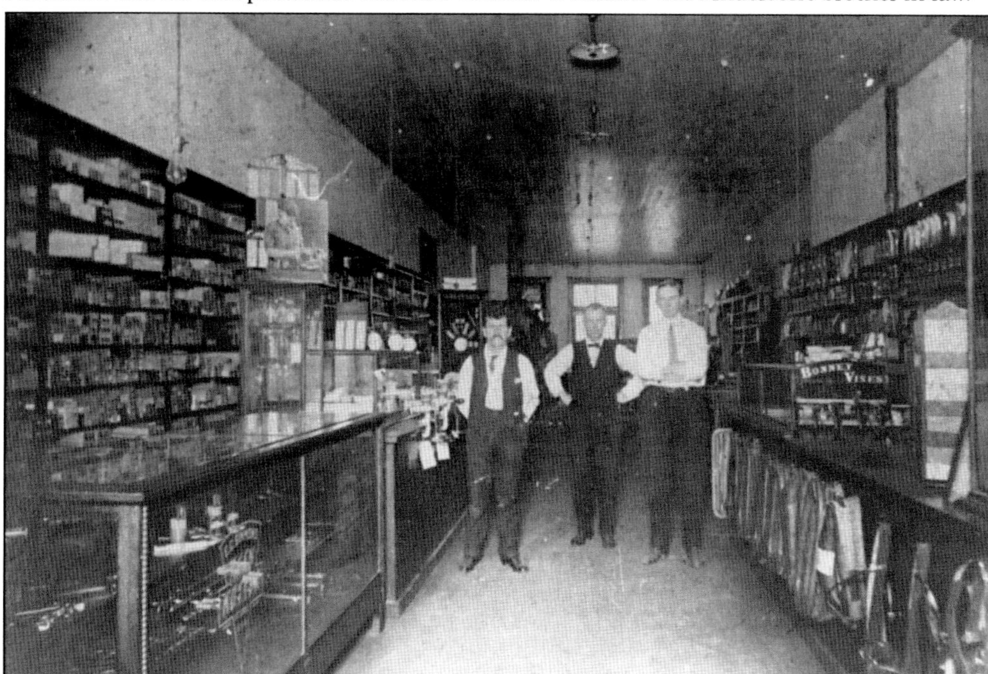

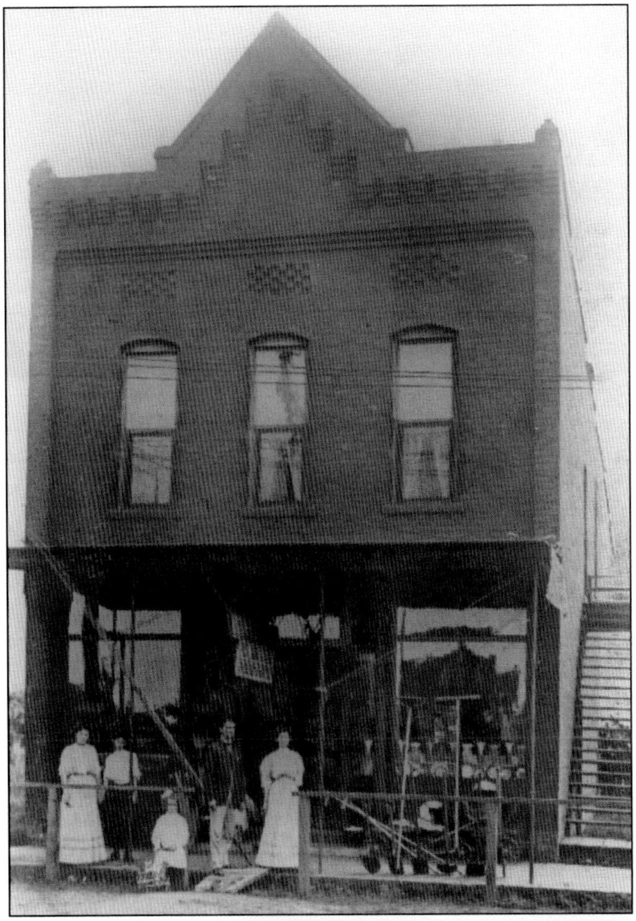

Noah's Ark was a novelty store on the second block of East Thomas Street next to the Columbia Theater. Owned and operated by early pioneer Michael "Mike" Seib, the store sold a variety of goods. Seib also published postcards of Hammond, many of which can still be found online and in antiques shops.

The Dantone family poses in front of their fruit shop on the corner of North Cherry and East Thomas Streets around 1912. Dantone's Grocery was one of the largest fruit sellers in the area. Owner Joseph Dantone is pictured inside, flanked by his wife, Mary Serio Dantone, and her sister Annie Serio, respectively. Outside the grocery are Mitchell Dantone and Joseph's brother-in-law Samuel Serio.

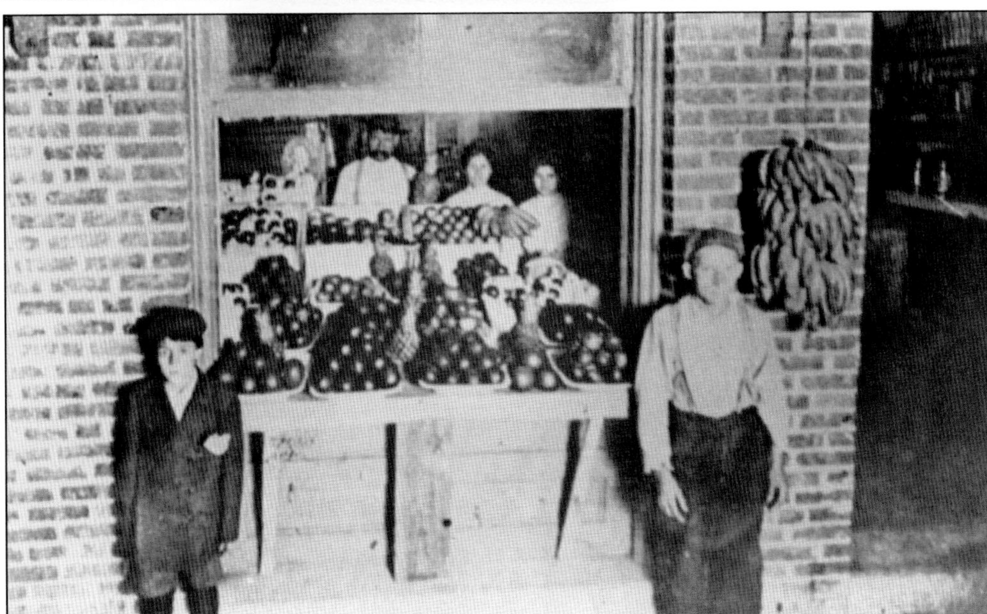

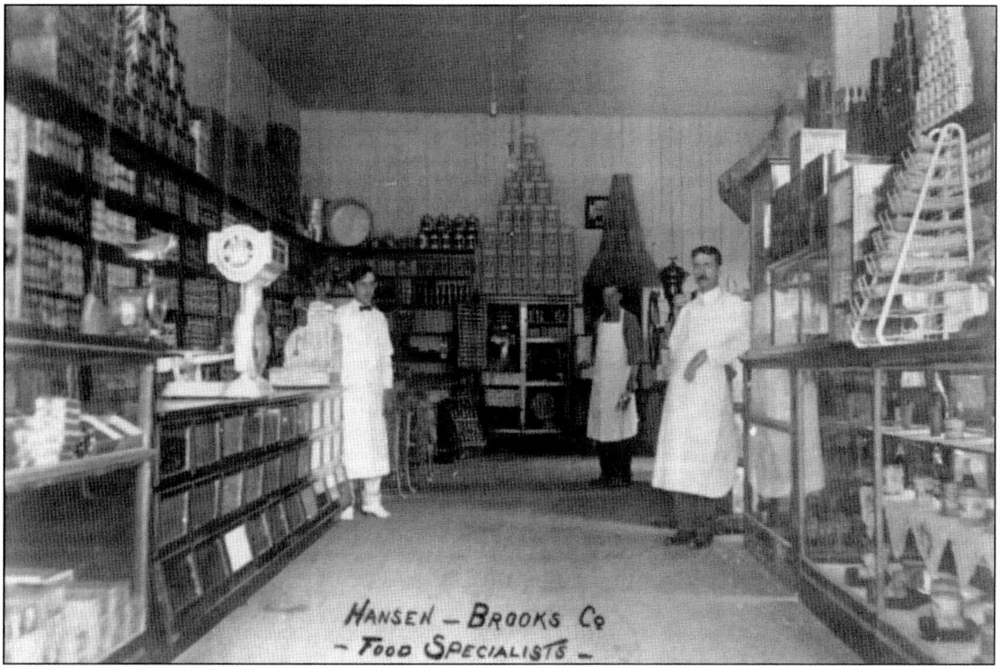

Located in the 200 block of the north side of East Thomas Street, Hansen Brooks Company Groceries and Vegetables billed themselves as the "food specialists." With a population of 2,000 in the early 1900s, the city had a number of grocery stores, with others operated by Willis and Penniman, Bacon and Sisson, and John Bondurant.

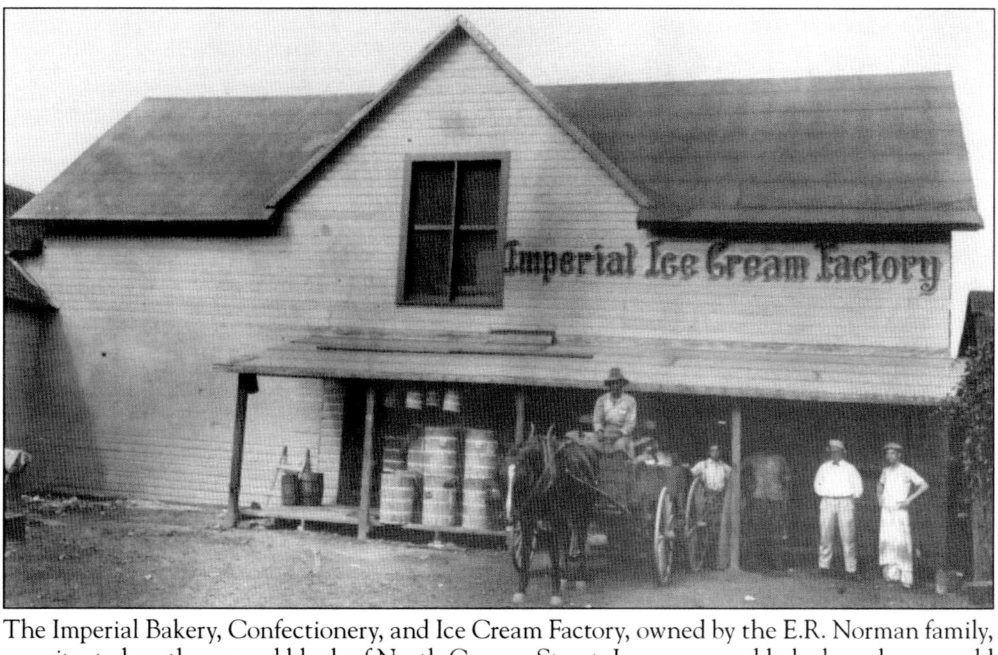

The Imperial Bakery, Confectionery, and Ice Cream Factory, owned by the E.R. Norman family, was situated on the second block of North Cypress Street. Ice cream and baked goods were sold in the building that faced Cypress, while the image shows the factory building in the back. Jessie Smith Bunce, the second man from the right, was the manager of the ice cream factory, while Edwin Norman managed the bakery.

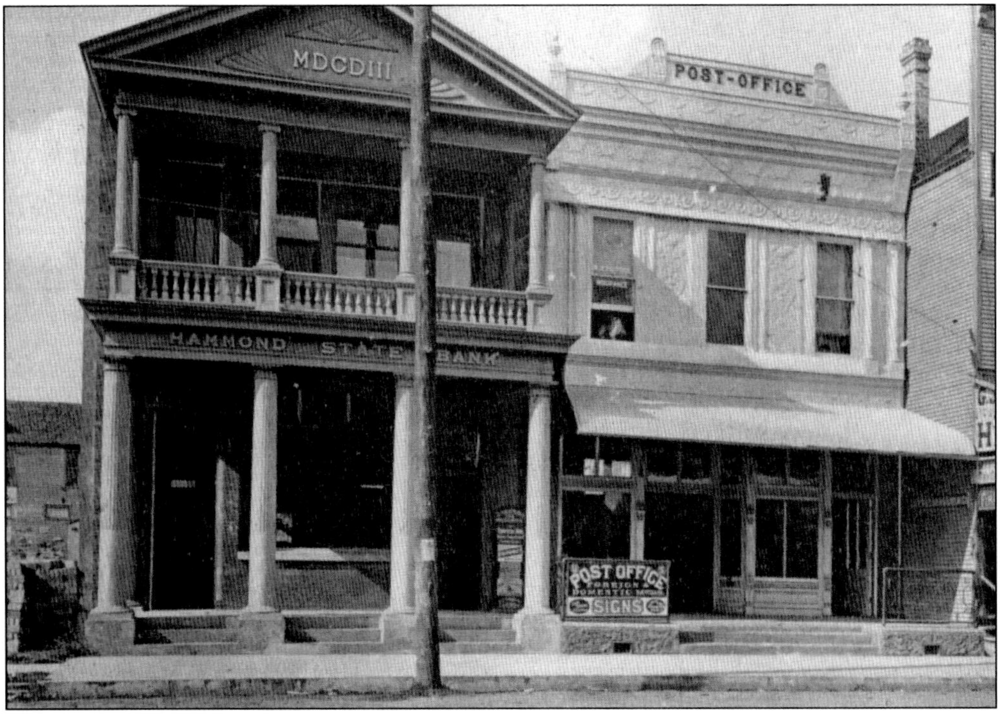

The Hammond State Bank, built in 1903 on the north side of East Thomas Street, was one of many of the structures that housed the post office before the present one was constructed. Unlike most other businesses on the main street, both buildings were set back several feet from the sidewalk. The facade of the post office is still visible.

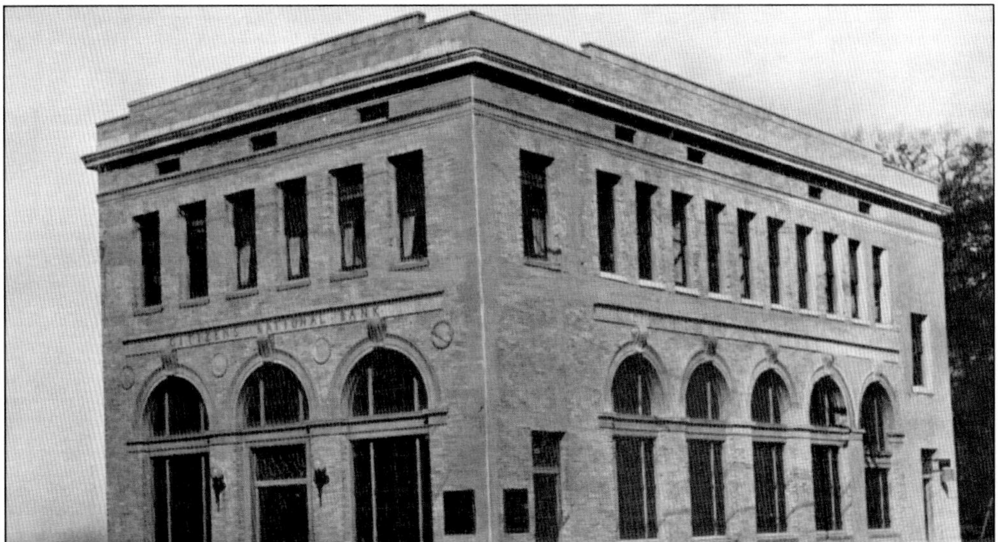

The original Citizens National Bank, formed in 1921 by a group of community members from Hammond, Ponchatoula, and Amite, opened its doors on Thomas Street in 1922. Closed during the Depression, it reopened its doors in 1934 and expanded in the 1960s and 1970s. The current bank headquarters was built on the site of the Oaks Hotels and the Casa de Fresa.

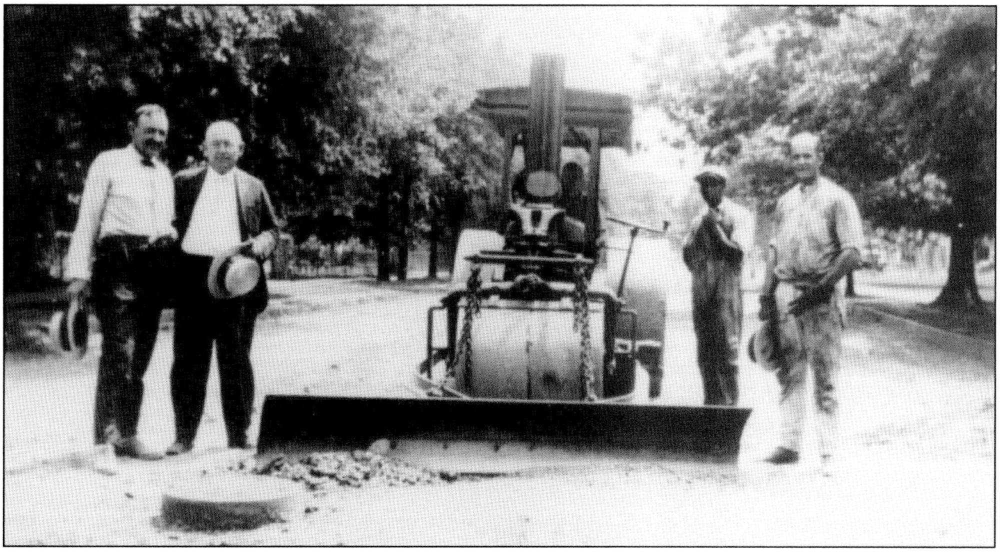

The Hammond Street Department prepares a street for paving in 1921. At the time, Will H. Thomas was the street commissioner and Charles C. Carter was mayor. Although utility lines came first, the city initially paved the main streets in the commercial thoroughfares of downtown, such as Oak, Thomas, Cypress Streets and both Railroad Avenues. Other streets were graveled, a huge improvement for business owners and citizens. (Courtesy of LF/TD.)

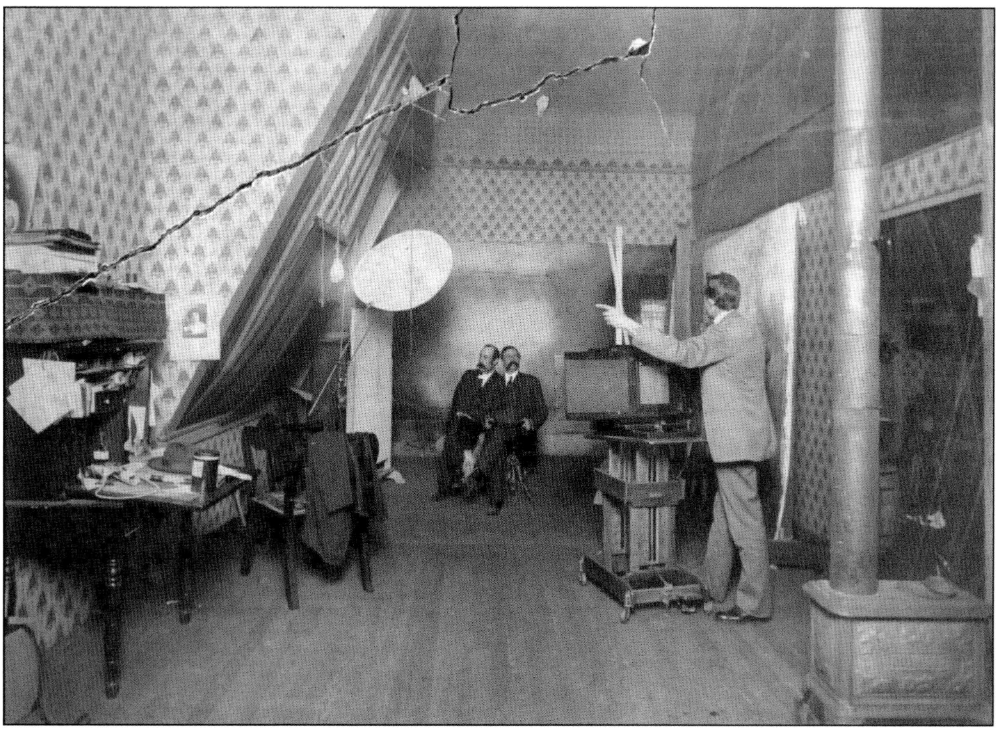

A photographer poses two subjects for a snapshot at the Hammond Studio. Photographs were very popular at the turn of the century, marking important occasions as well as daily activities. They were often printed on postcards for mailing to family and friends. The invention of the Brownie camera by George Eastman in 1900 revolutionized mass-market personal photography.

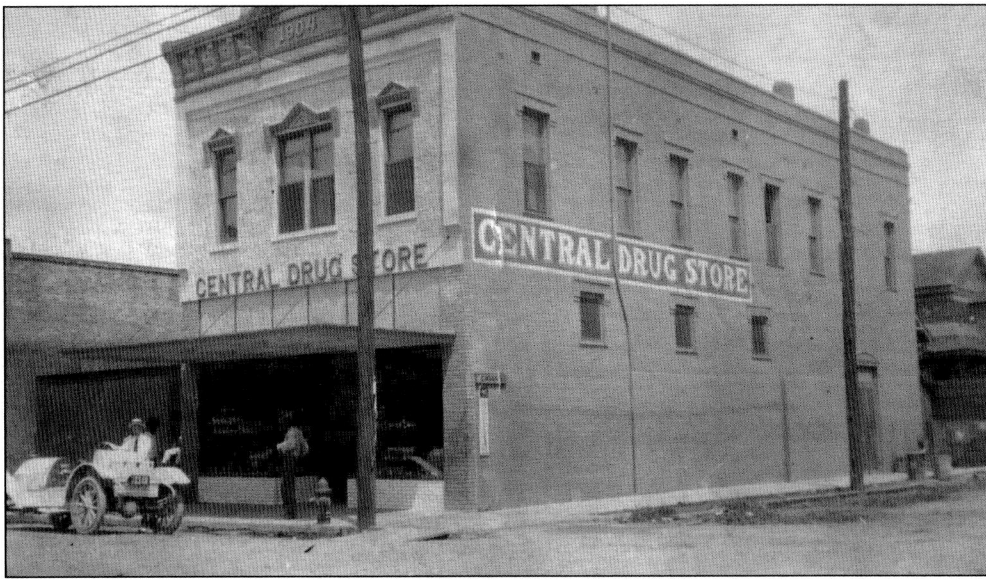

The Central Drug Store began life as Robinson's Central Drugs around 1896, founded by Dr. J.L. Robinson, who had relocated to Hammond from Illinois about seven years earlier. The store was sold in 1910 to Michigan natives Rol D. Fellows and his partner E.S. Wiseman, who moved it across the street from its original location on the south side of East Thomas Street in 1917. Fellows's nephew Donald took over operation of the drugstore in 1948, followed by his son Don Fellows Jr., the current owner and operator. The drugstore is a nationally recognized leader in pharmaceutical compounding. Below, Rol Fellows stands against the counter in the interior of the store.

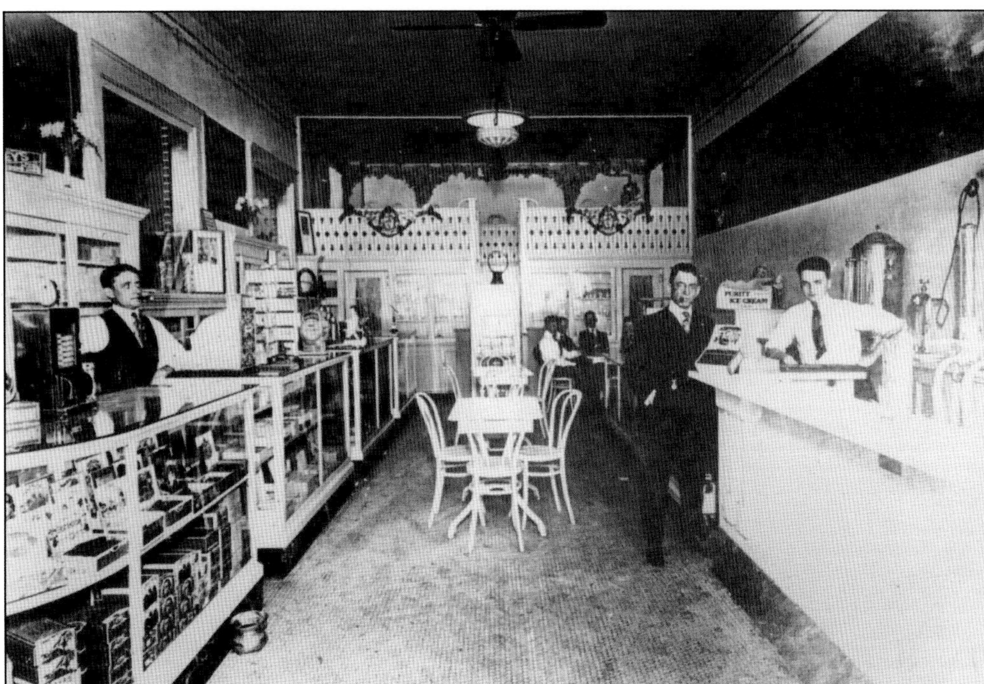

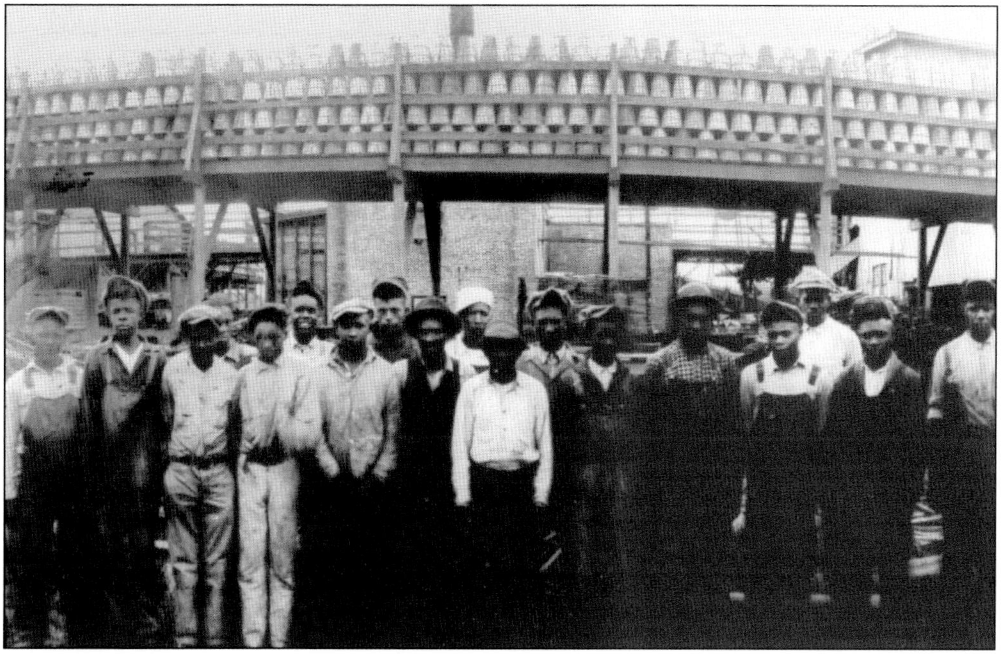

Several workers from the Hammond Box Factory, located in the 100 block of East Coleman Avenue, pose for a photograph. The Hammond Box Factory was one of two box factories in the city; the other was located directly across the railroad tracks, on the west side. The box factories supplied strawberry crates and other containers for packaging to the farming industries.

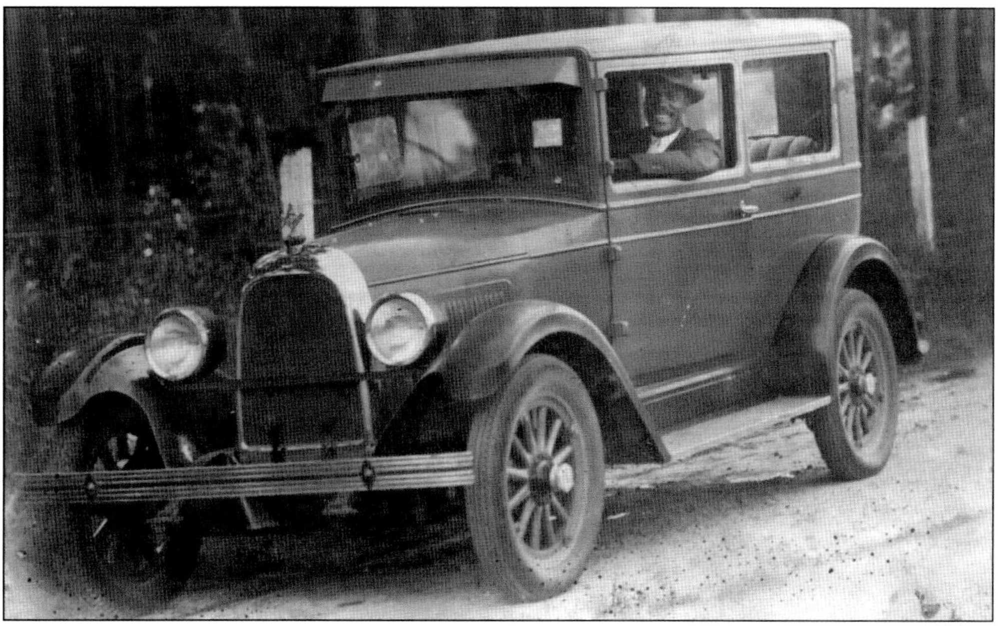

In 1931, Noah A. James Sr. opened the N.A. James Funeral Home, Hammond's second African American–owned funeral business, in his residence on South Cedar Street (later Noah A. James Drive). James was a Mason, as shown by the automobile hood ornament in this 1930s photograph. The business, which moved to its own building across the street, is still operated by the James family. (Courtesy of N.A. James Funeral Home.)

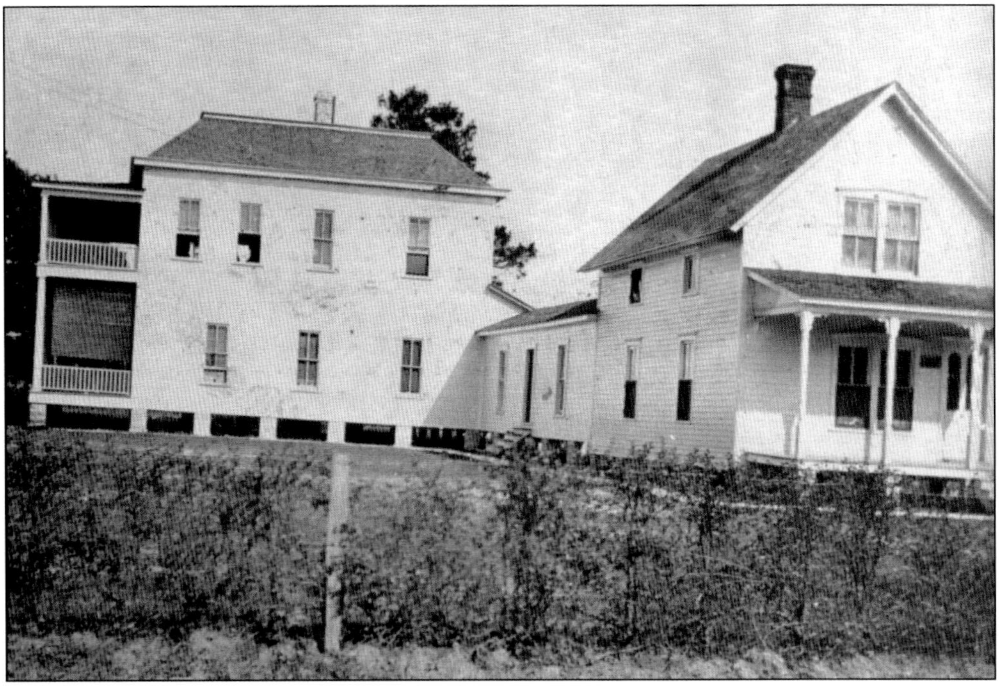

Above, Hammond's first hospital, the Hammond Sanitarium, was located on South Holly Street and Sanders (at that time Saunders) Avenue. The hospital was founded in 1907 by Tulane University graduate Dr. Edward L. McGehee, his sons Lucius D. McGehee and Edward L. McGehee Jr., and A.F. Gates. The sanitarium, which was ahead of its time in treatment and practice, could not compete with free care in New Orleans and lasted until 1912. The McGehees also founded the Cottage Colony Sanitarium in 1909, pictured below. This private sanitarium treated patients with tuberculosis and had space for between 20 and 24 beds. James M. Braxton served as superintendent, and the sanitarium was still in existence in 1921. The disease was not brought under control until the 1940s, although it is still prevalent worldwide.

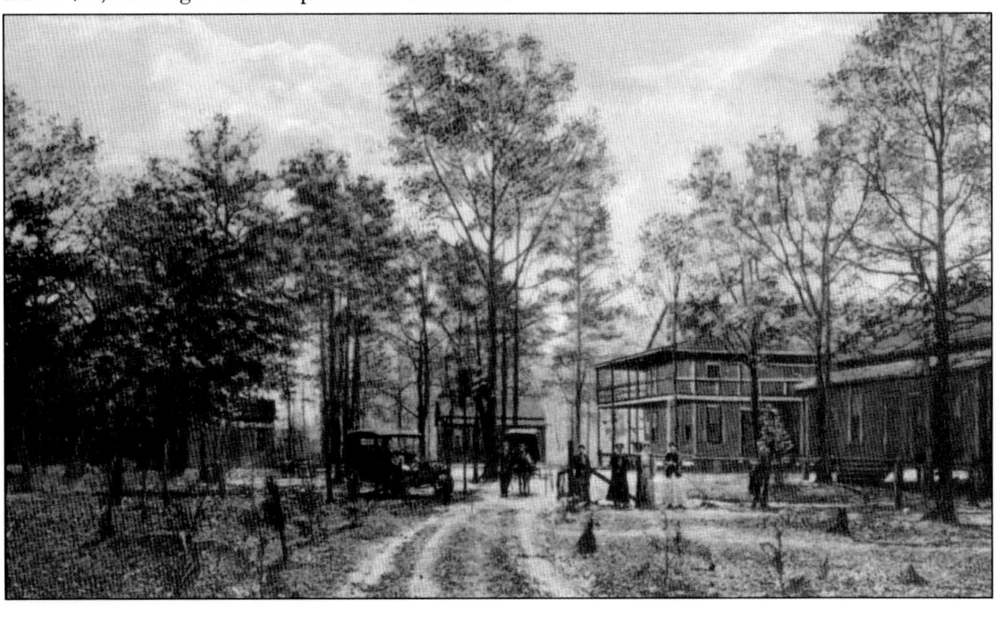

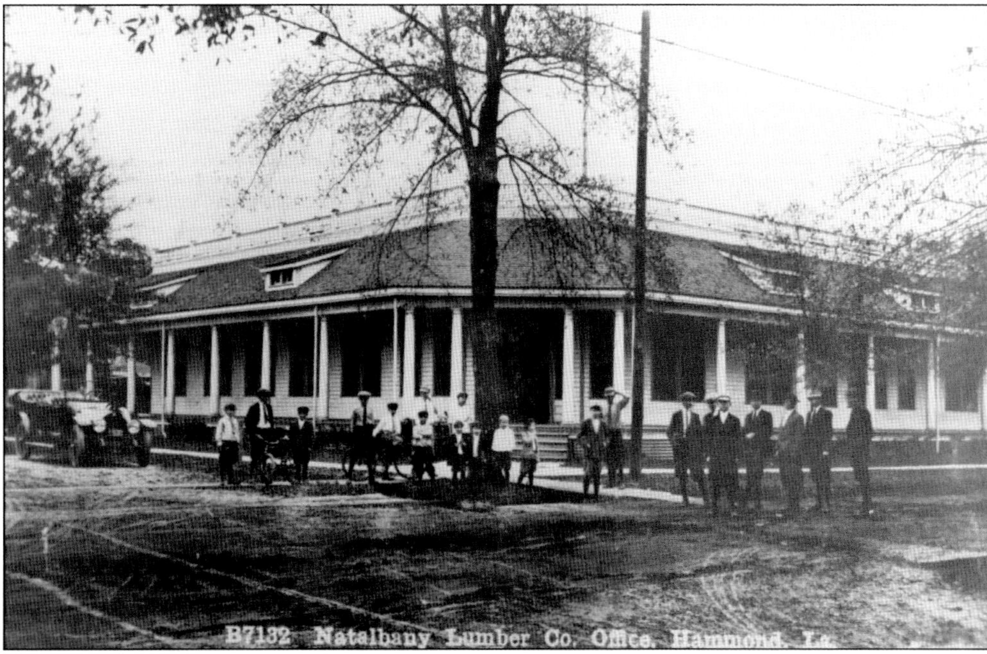

Built in 1906, the Natalbany Lumber Company office building operated at the corner of West Thomas and North Pine Streets. The mill, which was located in Natalbany, north of Hammond, was destroyed by fire and the offices relocated to Canton, Mississippi. Soon after, Dr. Marquis Wiginton converted the building to a hospital and named it the Wiginton Memorial Hospital. The hospital facility operated until the early 1960s.

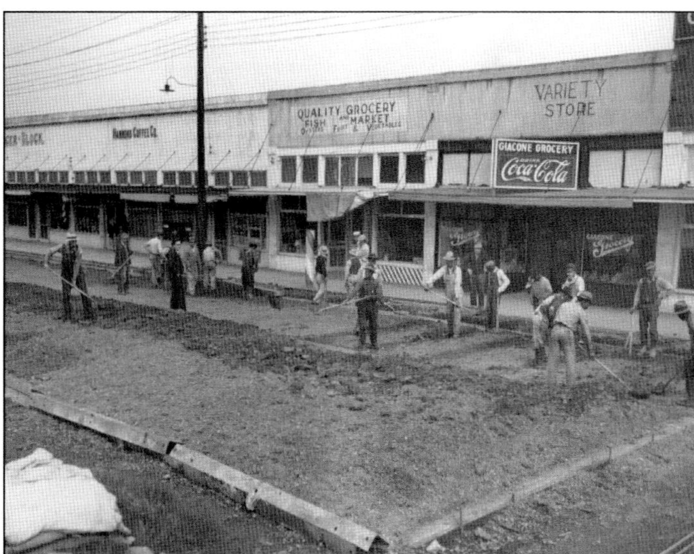

Northeast Railroad Avenue gets repaved in front of the Giacone Grocery and Hammond Coffee Company in 1937 as part of a Louisiana WPA project. A lack of industrial equipment meant that paving work was mostly done by manual labor, as illustrated by the number of workers. Today, the offices of Holly and Smith Architects stand in the location of the Giacone Grocery. (Courtesy of State Library of Louisiana.)

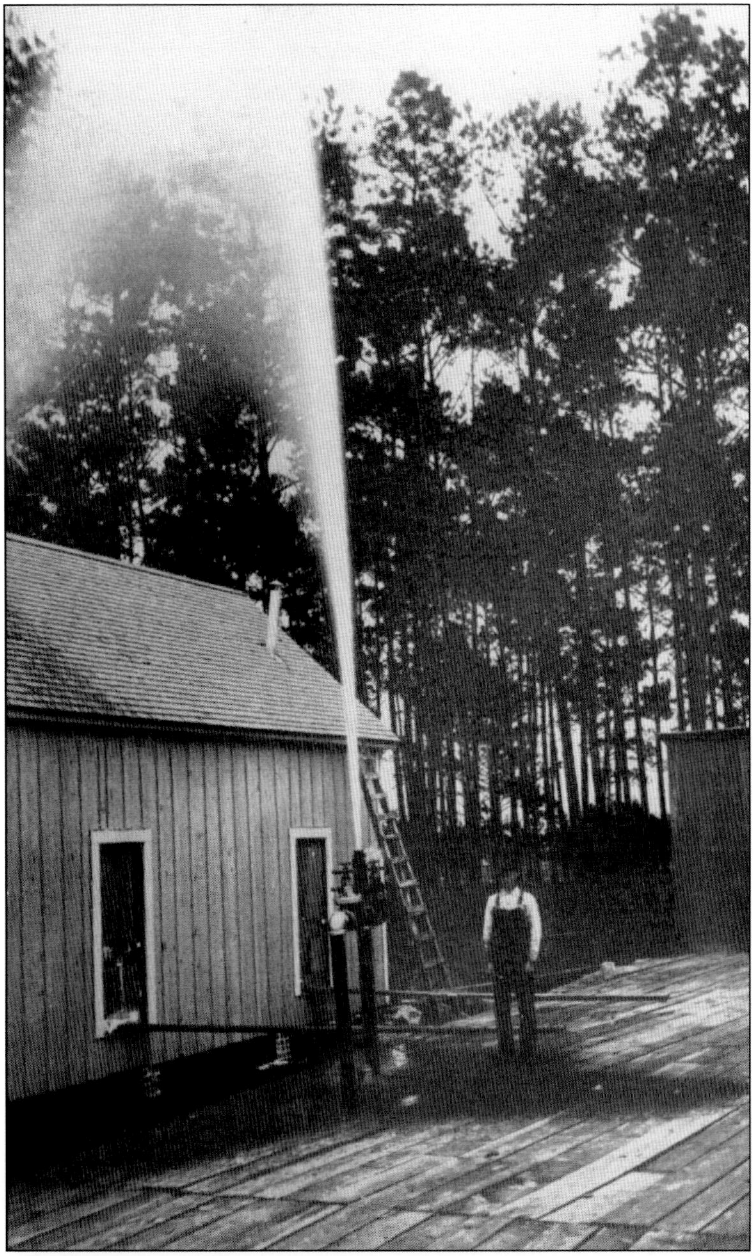

The Hammond Oil and Development Company was organized in 1901 by a group of Hammond area citizens to drill for oil next to the Illinois Central Railroad right-of-way. Water was struck at a depth of 2,200 feet, and the oil venture was abandoned. The resulting geyser had a flow of 576,000 gallons per day at a pressure of 85 pounds per square inch. The Geyser Water Company was organized in 1908 to sell the pure water, and for many years thereafter Hammond Geyser water was used in the ICRR dining cars and in hotel dining rooms; in fact, it was shipped all over the South. A pamphlet issued by the ICRR in 1910 stated, "If there is a point in the South where the supply of artesian water is as abundant as in this parish, we do not know where it is located." The well was located near the northwest corner of the Ross and Wallace Bag Company warehouse on Old Covington Highway.

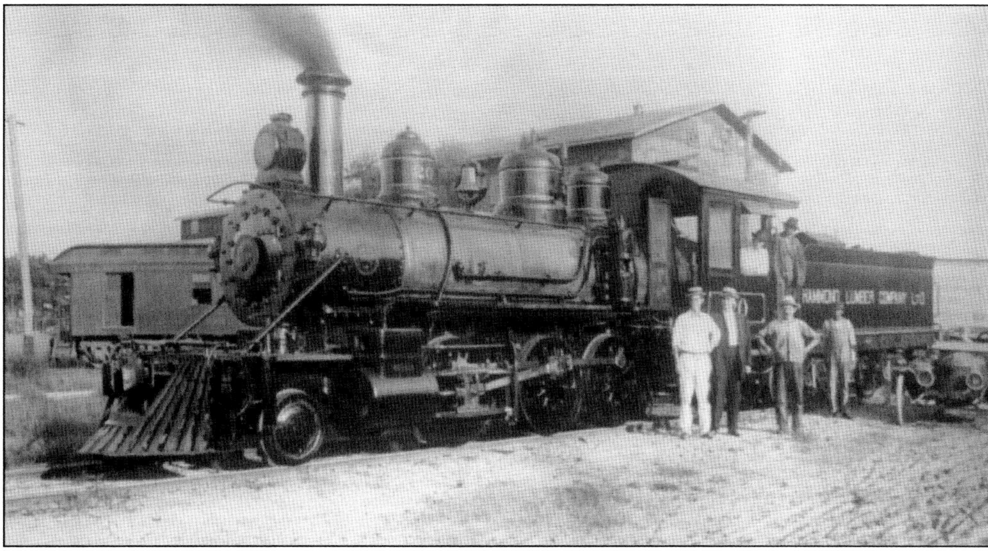

Will Nalty (far left), operations manager of the Hammond Lumber Company; Dr. Richard Carter (second from left), inventor; and several workers stand beside new Hammond Lumber Company Locomotive No. 20 in a 1911 photograph. Dr. Carter was an inventor of steam-powered engines and owned a steam engine manufacturing plant in Gulfport, Mississippi.

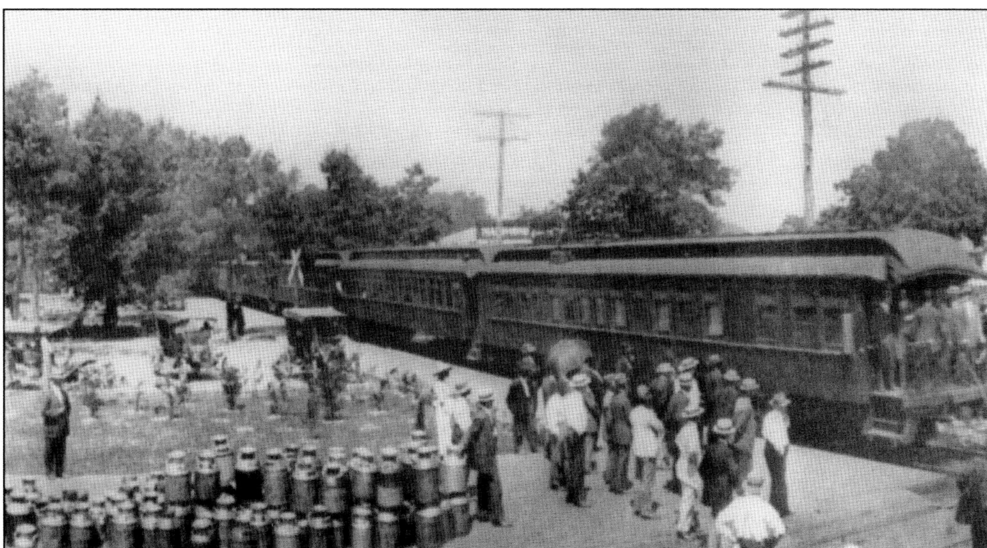

Milk canisters along the tracks are waiting to be shipped or delivered. A 1934 article in the *Hammond Vindicator* states that the "total numbers of gallons of milk shipped in 1900 was five or ten gallons, shipped to a drug store and restaurant . . . while the total number of gallons shipped in 1914 was 3,650 gallons per year at 18c [sic] per gallon."

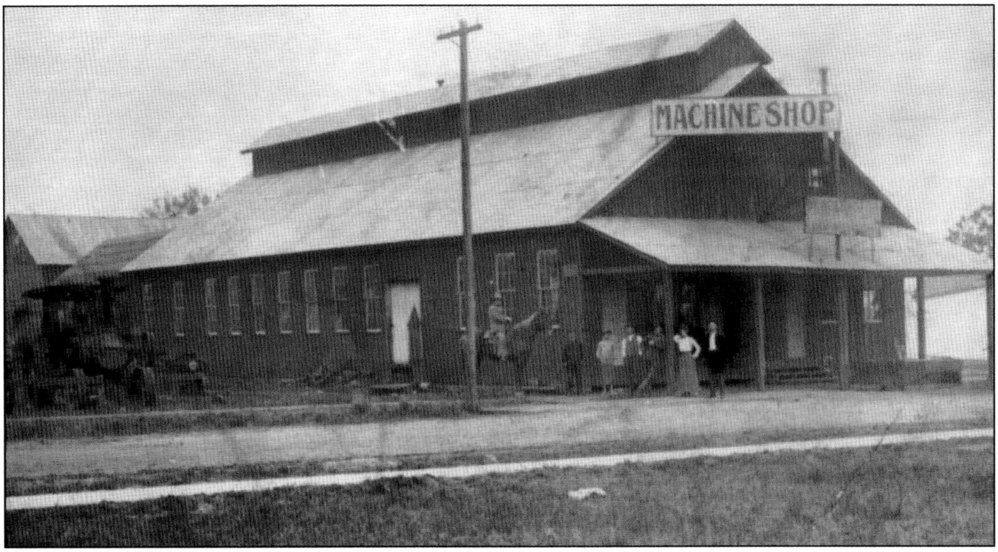

The Hammond Machine Shop became the Diamond Machine Shop in 1909, when it was bought by Diamond Iron Works. A gray iron foundry was added, and the shop was operated by machinists George F. Smith and A.L. Way; the latter was the owner of the original shop. The store was located on the corner of East Coleman Avenue and South Cypress Street, site of the former Hammond Coca-Cola bottling plant.

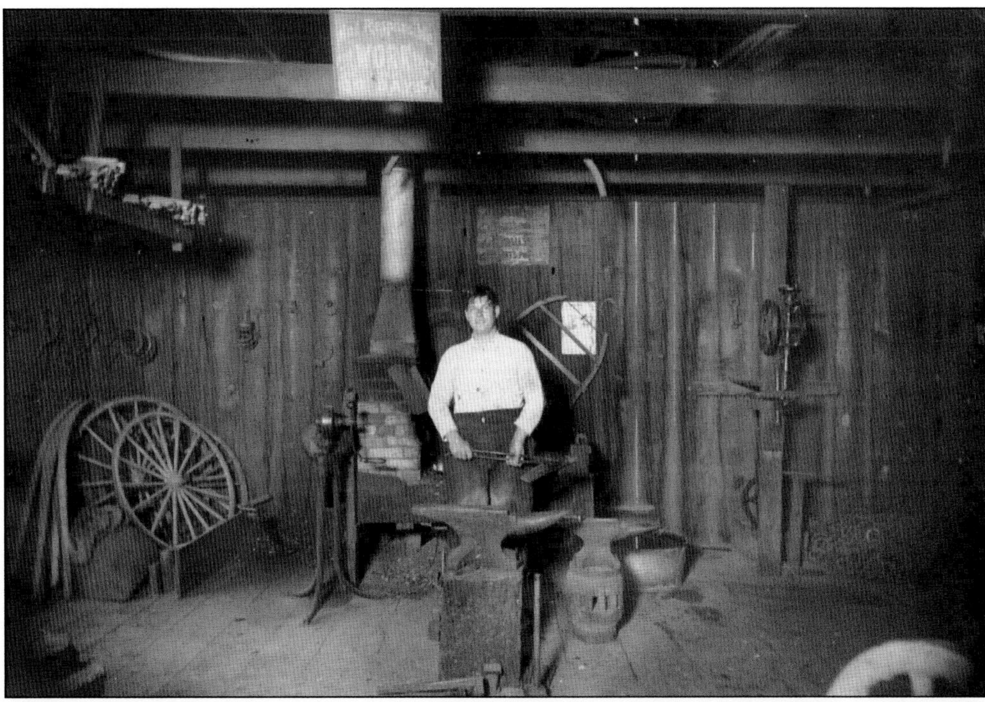

In this photograph, Guy Skinner, son of Mayor John W. Skinner (1913–1917), works in the blacksmith shop located on the corner of East Hanson Avenue and South Cypress Street. Built in 1890, the wood framework shop, with walls of 12-inch-thick lumber, was the first of its kind in the area. The shop eventually became a general repair shop owned by Edward J. Rolling Sr. and was demolished in October 1962.

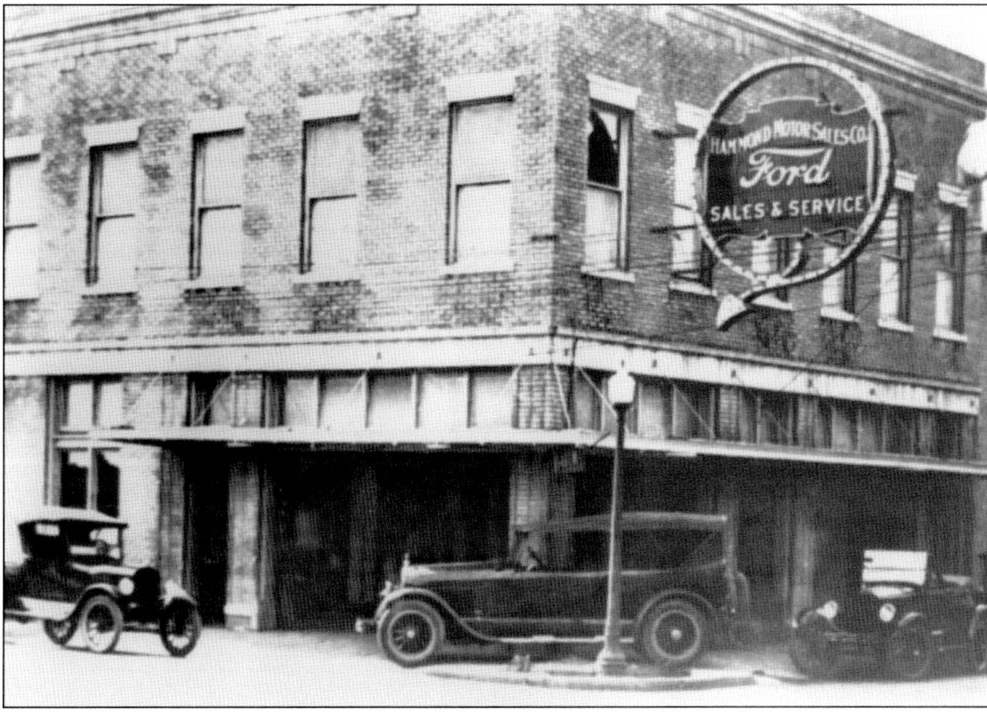

Hammond Motor Sales Company was the Ford automotive dealer in this 1925 image. Located on the southwest corner of South Oak and West Thomas Streets, the Hammond Motor Sales Company replaced a Studebaker car agency. During the Studebaker years, LeRoy McGee owned the building. In later years, the building housed Locascio's Hardware; its current tenant is Bayou Booksellers.

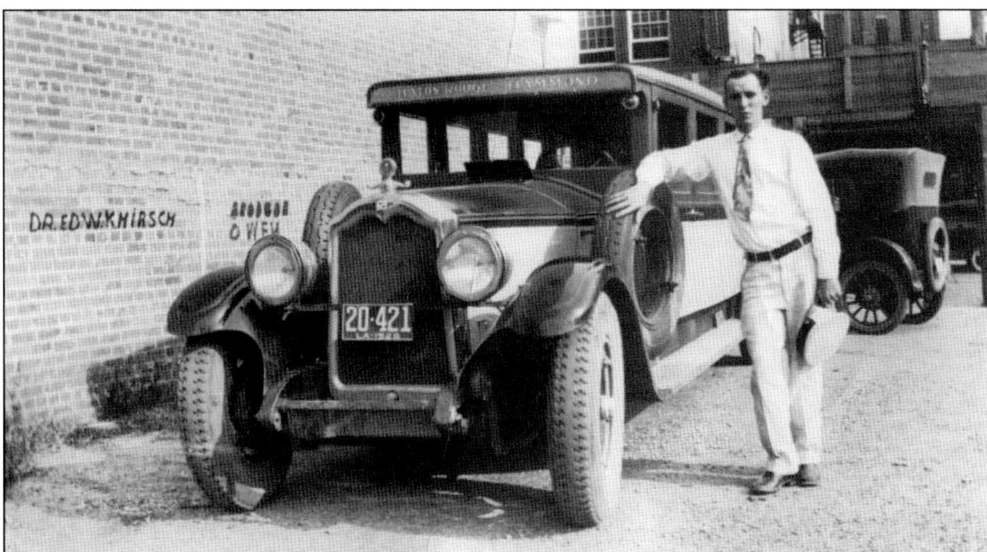

Nelson Penton, owner of a shuttle business that ferried people between Hammond and Baton Rouge, stands beside his shuttle. The Hammond–Baton Rouge route, which took passengers to the downtown Capital House Hotel, was one of the most popular courses. In addition to passenger transportation, the astute businessman offered courier services to businesses, such as banks and merchant stores. Penton's other businesses included several service stations.

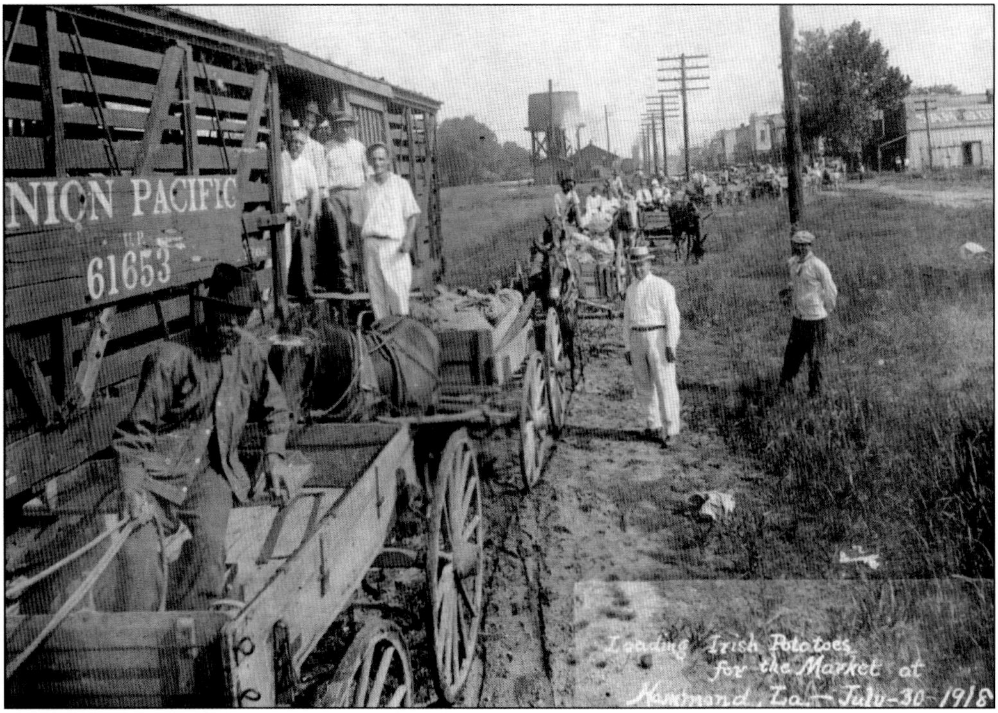

Irish potatoes are being loaded on a Union Pacific car on July 30, 1918, as viewed from South Railroad Avenue to the north. Besides lumber and strawberries, farmers shipped a variety of other vegetables and fruit to northern and western markets and New Orleans. By 1892, over $60,000 worth of vegetables were being shipped from Hammond.

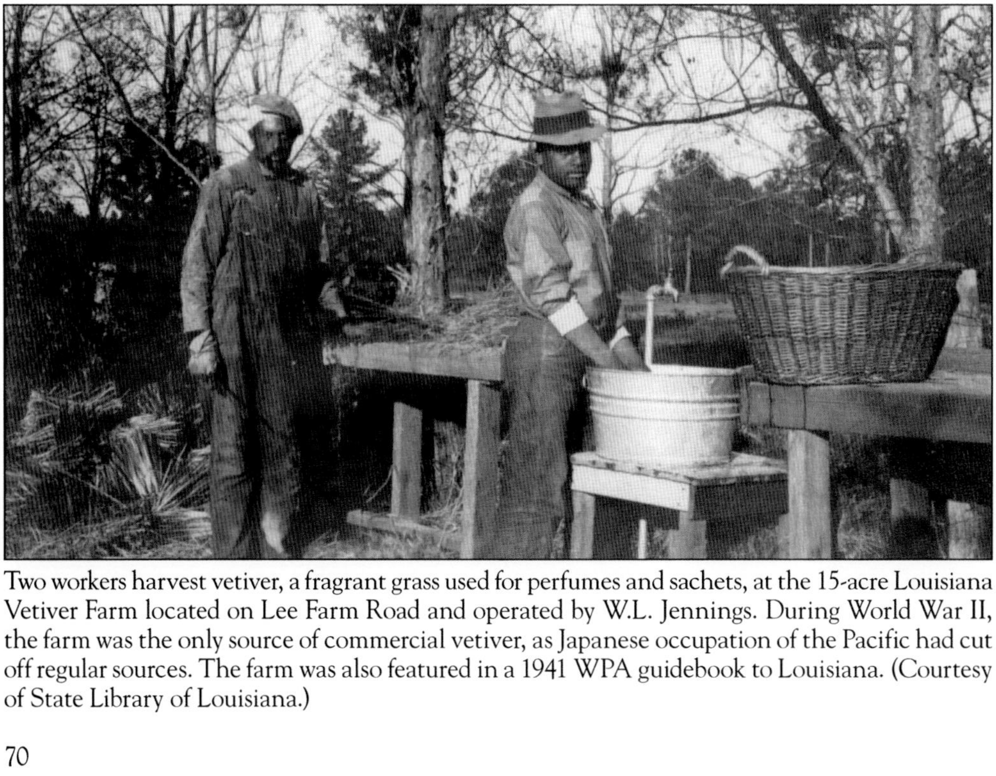

Two workers harvest vetiver, a fragrant grass used for perfumes and sachets, at the 15-acre Louisiana Vetiver Farm located on Lee Farm Road and operated by W.L. Jennings. During World War II, the farm was the only source of commercial vetiver, as Japanese occupation of the Pacific had cut off regular sources. The farm was also featured in a 1941 WPA guidebook to Louisiana. (Courtesy of State Library of Louisiana.)

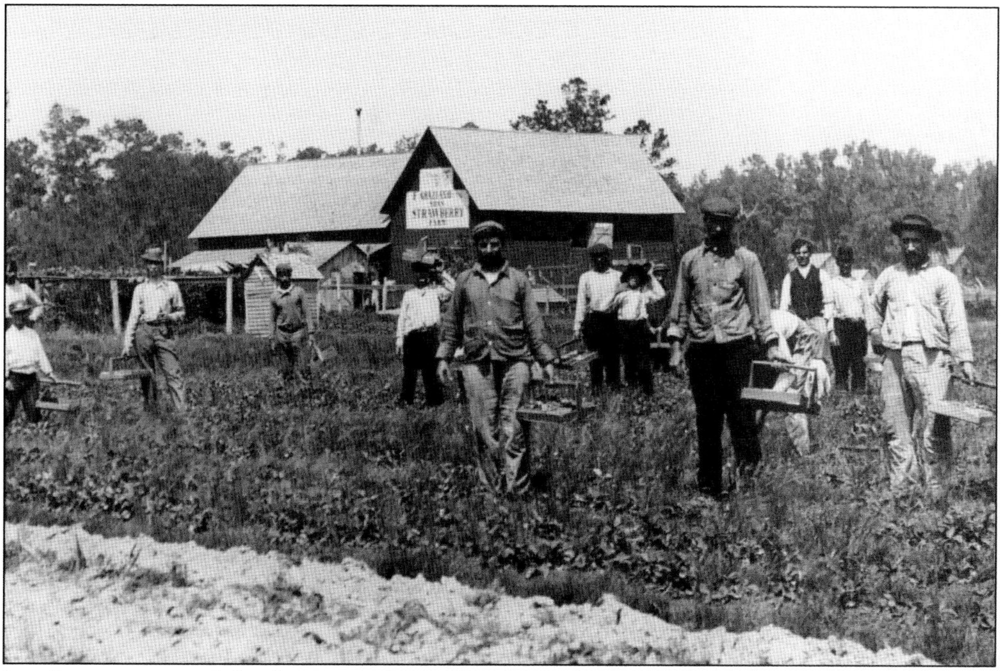

Joe Graziano owned this large strawberry farm east of Hammond, with berries shipped under the JOHN brand label. In 1910, he organized the Hammond Farmers Association, Limited and later incorporated the Strawberry Growers Auction Company and was president of the Italian Agricultural and Supply Company of Hammond. A one-room school for first through sixth grades, the Progressive School, was built on his property.

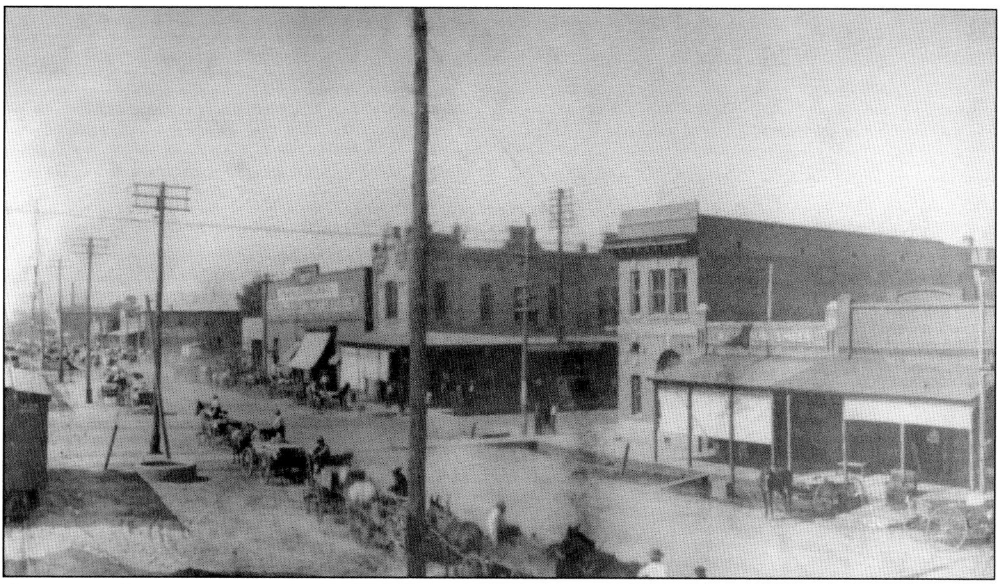

Once strawberries were picked, farmers brought their produce downtown to be shipped by the railroads. In this photograph, wagons are lined up south of Thomas Street along Railroad Avenue, waiting to load their goods at the depot located several blocks away. The General Department Emporium and Boos Building are visible in the center, and an automobile can be discerned by the Boos Building, dating this image to the early 1900s.

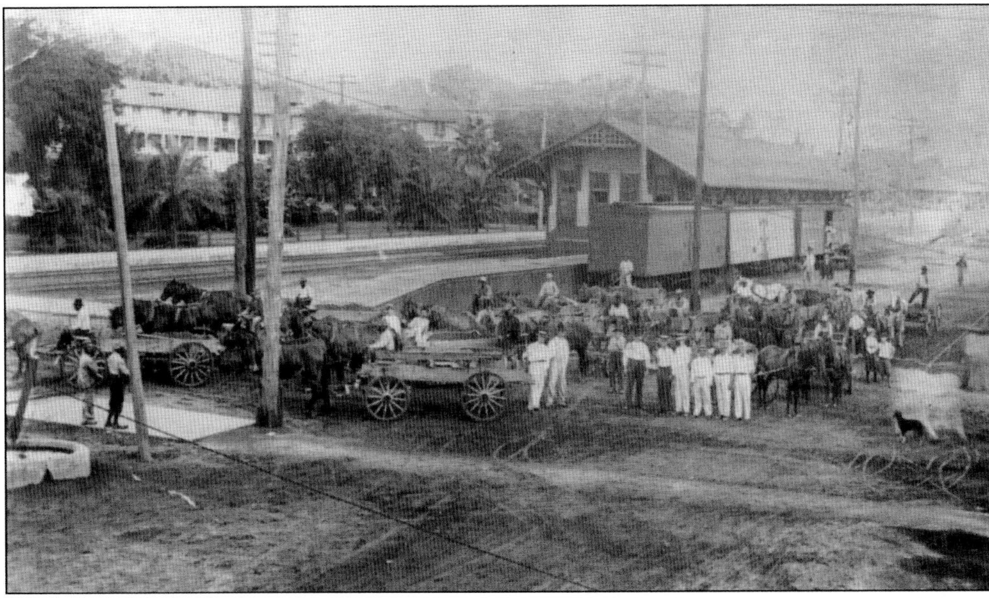

Strawberry season brought about a hive of activity to Hammond and its surrounding towns. Farmers bringing in wagonloads of berries would crowd the streets of the town, and visitors attending strawberry auctions filled the hotels. As the strawberry industry grew, activities such as a Strawberry Festival with a Strawberry Queen would add to the merriment. The first strawberry patch in Tangipahoa Parish was planted in 1876 on the outskirts of Independence (then a village called Uncle Sam, just north of Hammond) by Dr. W.D. Wilson, a railway conductor before he took up medicine. Robert L. Cloud of Hammond made strawberry growing a success by propagating and developing the Klondyke strawberry, a hardy and luscious berry that became the standard crop in the area. Below, a farmer readies his crop for shipping. (Below, courtesy of Library of Congress.)

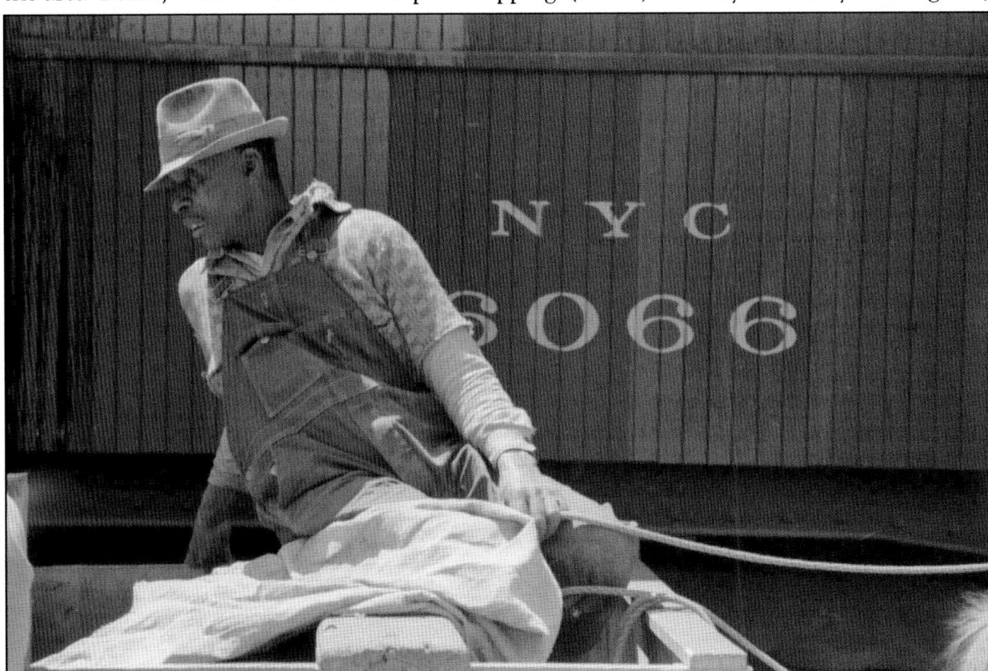

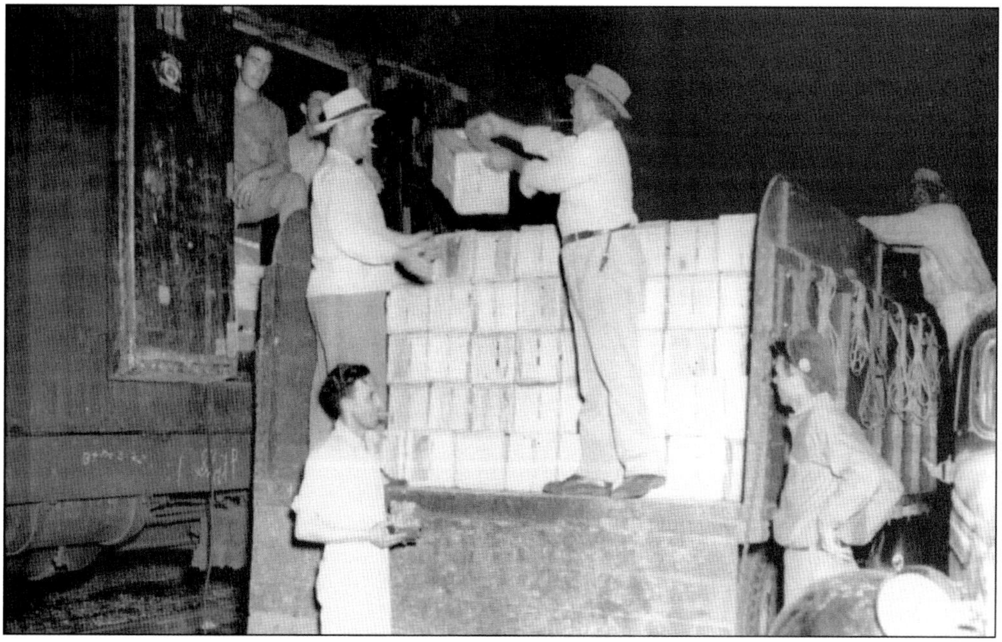

Several men transfer crates of strawberries to an iced railcar, a process that could take from mid-morning until night. The widely known and colorful Sadie DePaula hands a crate to Murphy Bigner for loading into the car. Once in the car, the 24-pint crates will only be stacked four or five levels high, with wood strips between each layer to allow for air circulation. (Courtesy of DF.)

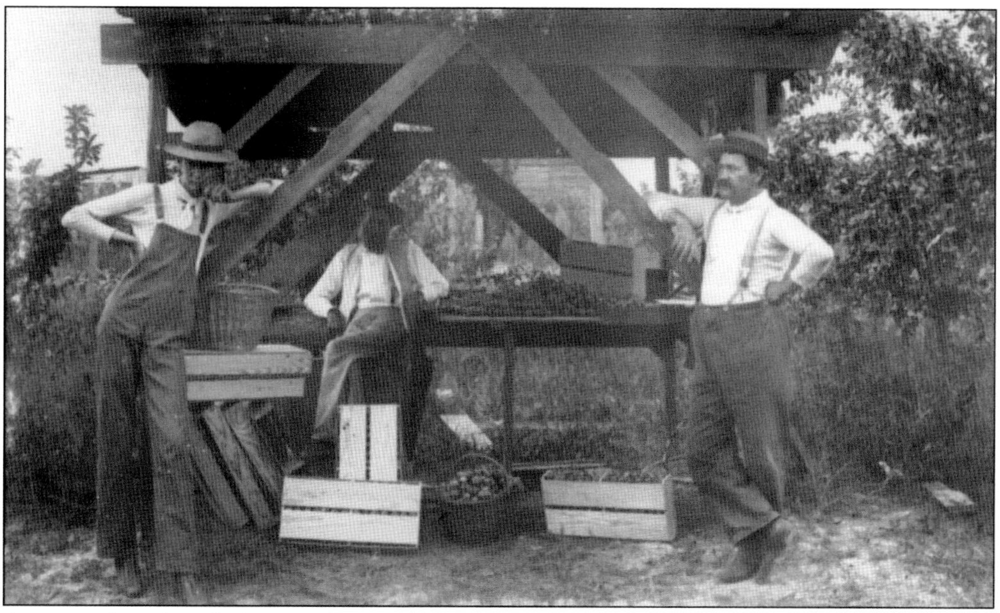

A group of unidentified men sells strawberries in a stand by the side of the road. Roadside stands by local farmers were a common site in the rural areas surrounding Hammond and Ponchatoula and are still seen today. These types of stands are disappearing, as major grocery store chains are able to sell strawberries from California as well as South America during the off-season.

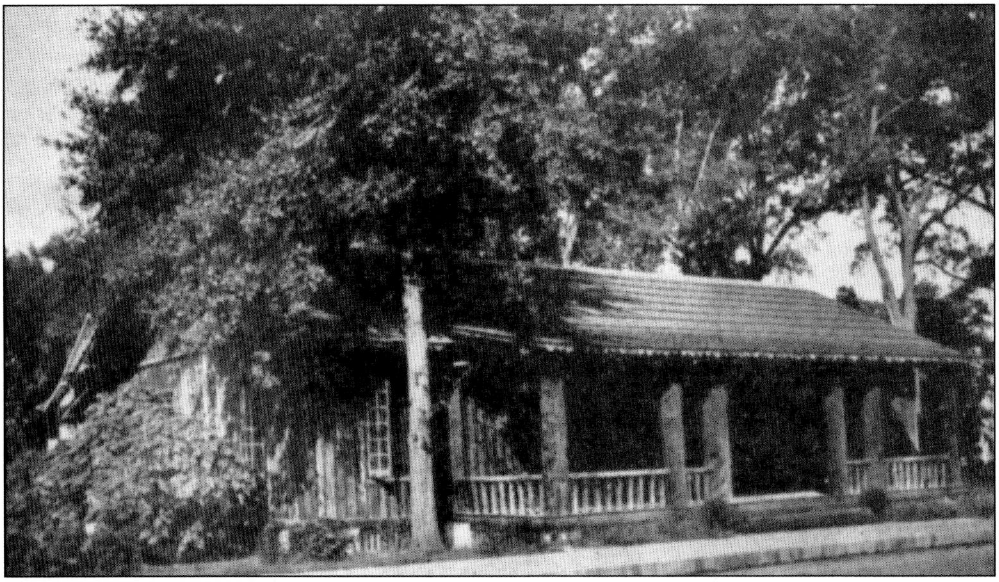

The Log Cabin, located on the northeast corner of the second Oaks Hotel property, was built by William Houlton in 1924, replacing the hotel's Game Room. Houlton was a lumberman from the North who knew about the construction of log cabins; his friend Charles Weinberger, an early promoter of strawberries and icing of train cars, originated the sale of strawberries by auction, vitalizing the industry. The building was 50 feet deep and held two offices, baths, and a large room with rows of stands and an auctioneer's platform. Before refrigerated boxcars, the perishability of the berries necessitated swift auctioning and shipping, and berries picked in the morning were sold by evening. At one time, there were three auctions scheduled each evening around town, staggered so that buyers could attend all three. Below, Billy Stevens acts as auctioneer.

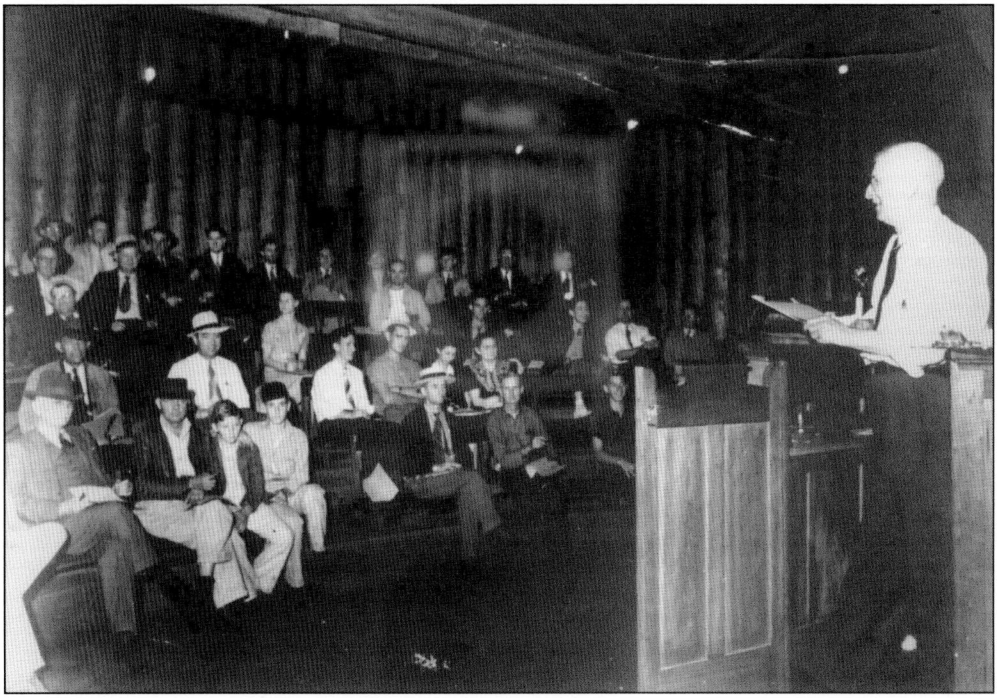

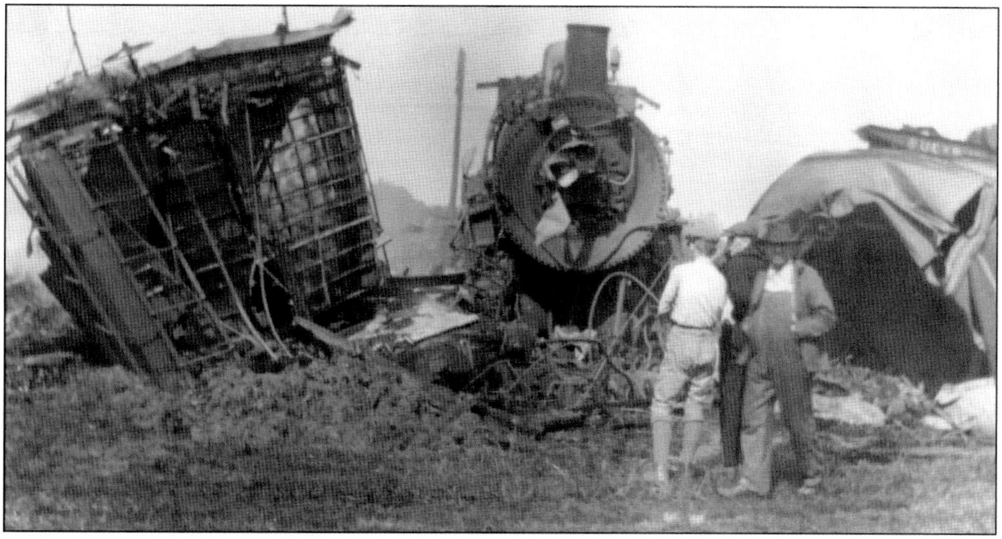

Several men inspect the results of a fatal train wreck that occurred on April 18, 1923, just outside of downtown Hammond, south of the intersection of the railroad tracks and Old Covington Highway. The wreck was dubbed the "coffee train wreck" because a car carrying coffee beans burned, and the town was permeated with the sweet smell of roasting coffee.

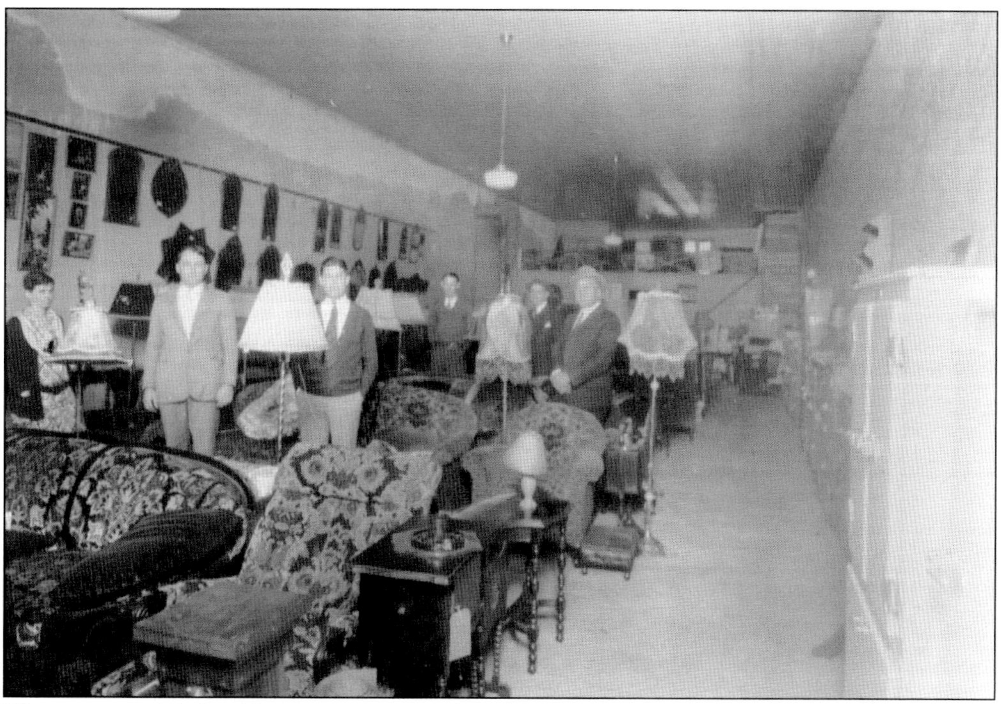

The interior of Forbes Furniture is pictured in the early 1930s. Marie Mitchell Forbes, founder of the store, is on the far left, flanked by co-owner Harold Forbes and employee Cecil Taylor, respectively. An icebox is pictured in the front right. The store operated from 1928 until the early 1980s. The building is now part of the Columbia Theater complex. (Courtesy of H.P. Forbes.)

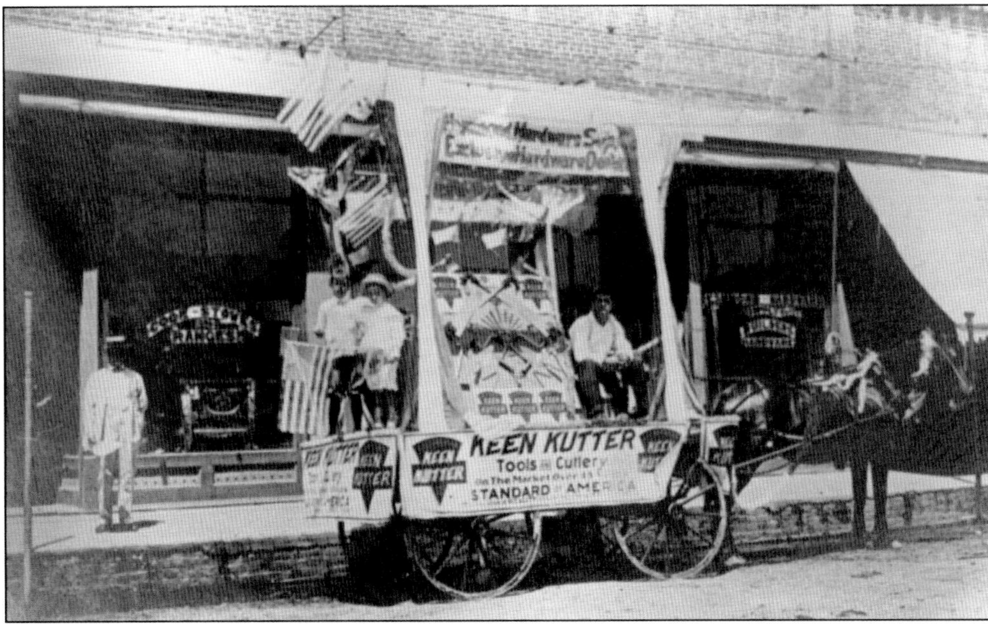

A Keen Kutters Tools and Cutlery cart advertises its wares in front of Hammond Hardware on Cypress Street. The store often featured its products with street displays such as this one. The Keen Kutter trade name was first used by the Simmons Hardware Company of St. Louis in 1880 for high-quality cutlery. The name remained even with changes of ownership, but it was discontinued in the 1990s.

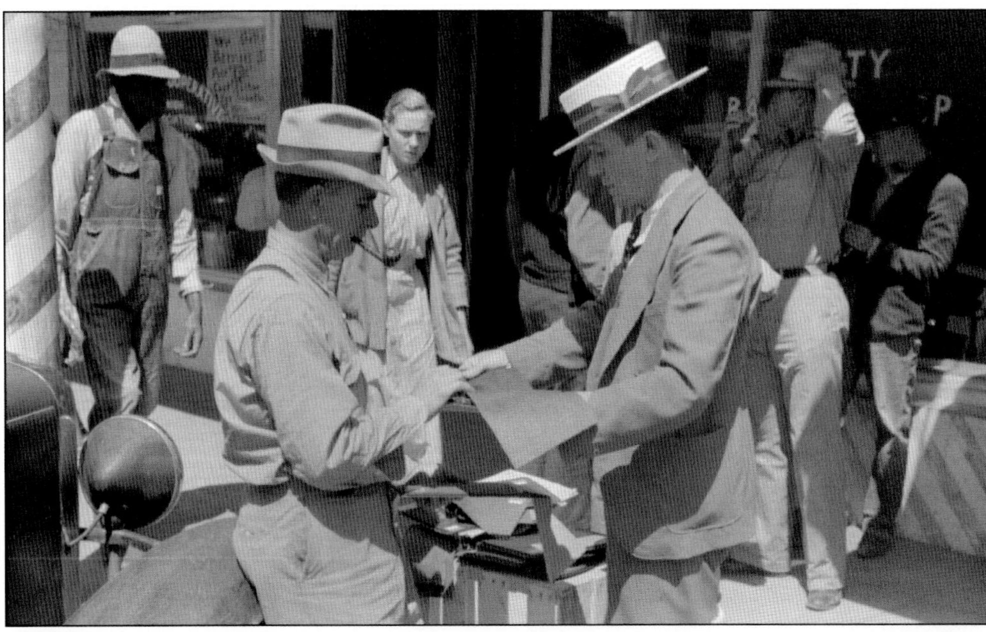

A salesman is shown selling fabric to farmers in front of the City Barbershop and the Strawberry Cooperative on Northeast Railroad Avenue in the late 1930s. Traveling salesmen, such as this one, provided goods that might not be available in local stores. The image was taken by Russell Lee, a noted photographer for the federally sponsored Farm Security Administration photographic project under the FDR administration. (Courtesy of Library of Congress.)

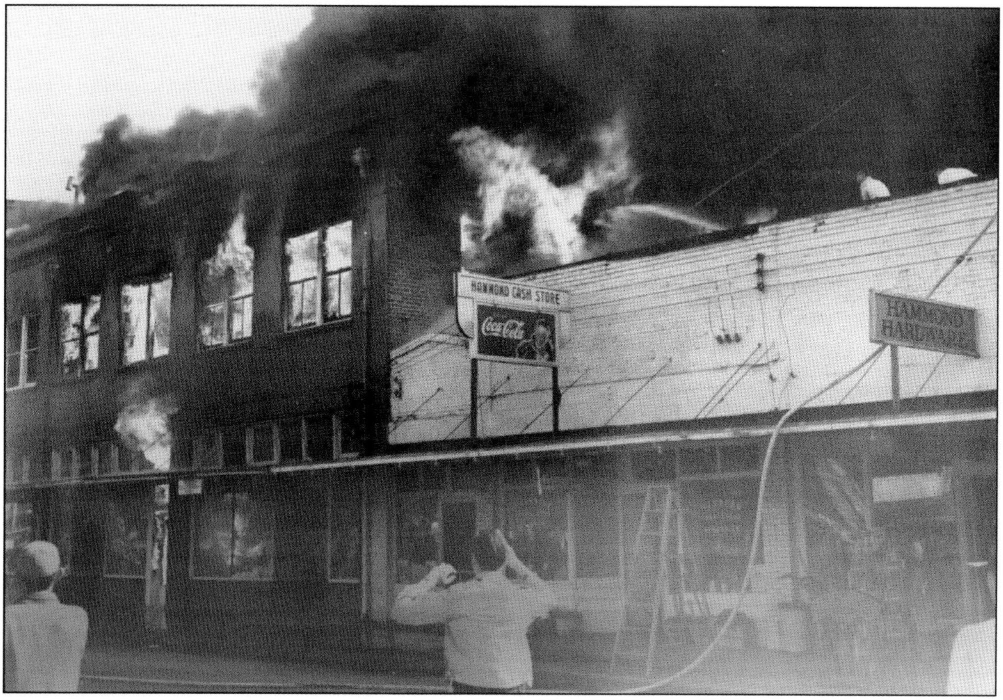

On February 1, 1947, the 1930s building housing the Toggery Shop, a popular clothing store on West Thomas Street that opened in 1922, caught fire. The Toggery Shop and businesses in surrounding buildings were severely damaged. Below, merchandise rescued from the store and surrounding businesses is spread out next to the railroad tracks in front of the police station and jail (shown to the right of the obelisk), half a block from the fire site. The facade of the building was rebuilt, and the shop stayed in business until 2002. The Art Deco neon sign added to the rebuilt store remains as a symbol of Hammond's downtown and has been seen in a number of motion pictures. (Both courtesy of Carlee White.)

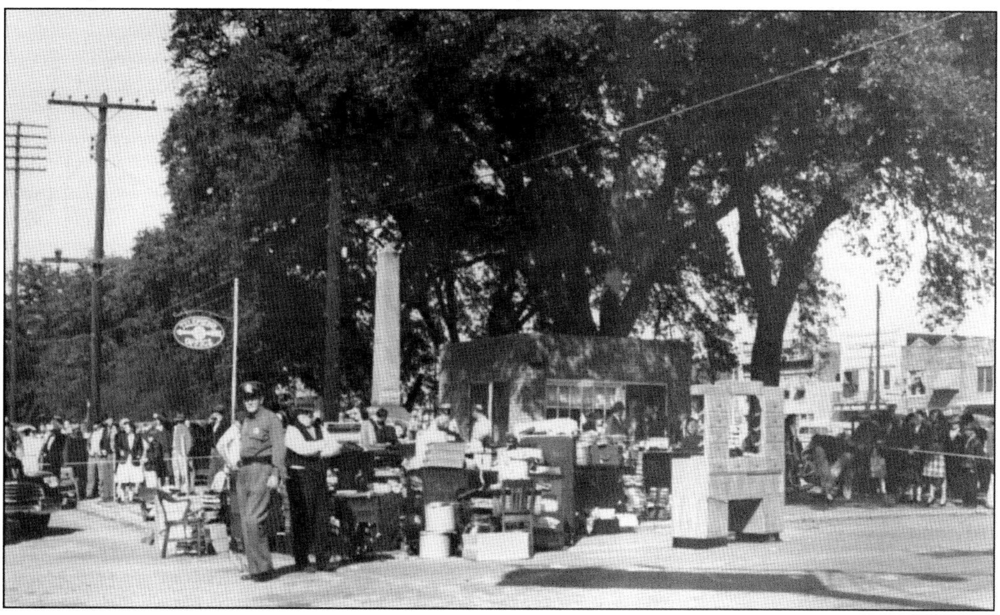

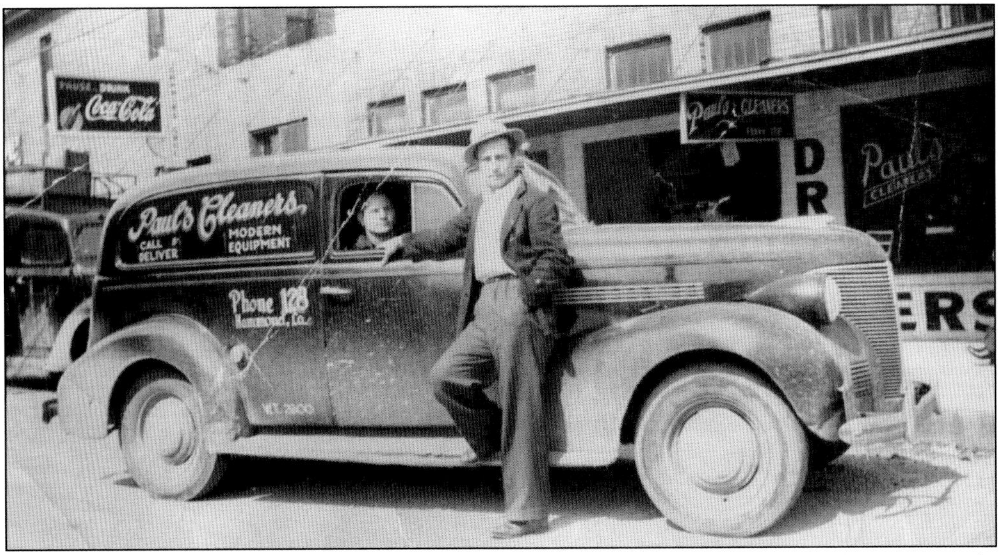

Pete Giannobile (in the truck) and Paul Giannobile chat in front of the family business, Paul's Cleaners. Their brother-in-law Santo Pecora started the business right after World War II. The shop was located on the 200 block of East Charles Street. Pete opened his own business, Pete's Cleaners, which is still located on South Holly Street. Note the three-digit telephone number on the side of the car. (Courtesy of Cecilia Giannobile.)

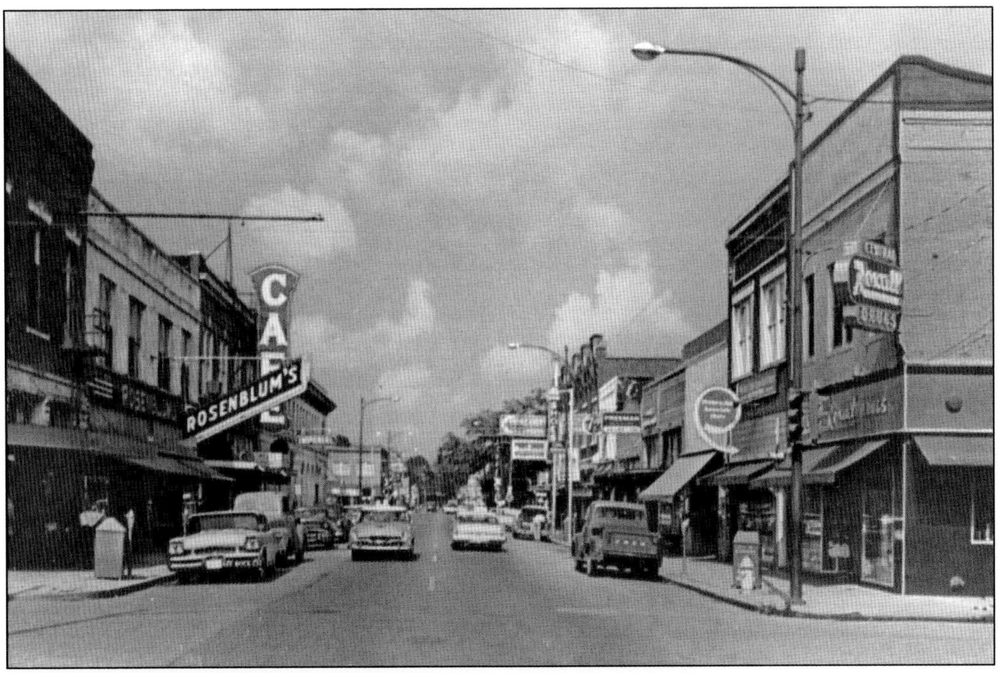

Downtown businesses flourish in the late 1950s in this photograph looking west down Thomas Street. Rosenblum's, a popular clothing store, closed in 1995. The café sign marks the site of several cafés from the late 1900s and early 2000s, including the popular Tropic Café, no longer in business. The building on the right corner has been the site of the Central Drug Store, which was originally across the street, since 1917.

Three

Social Life and Entertainment

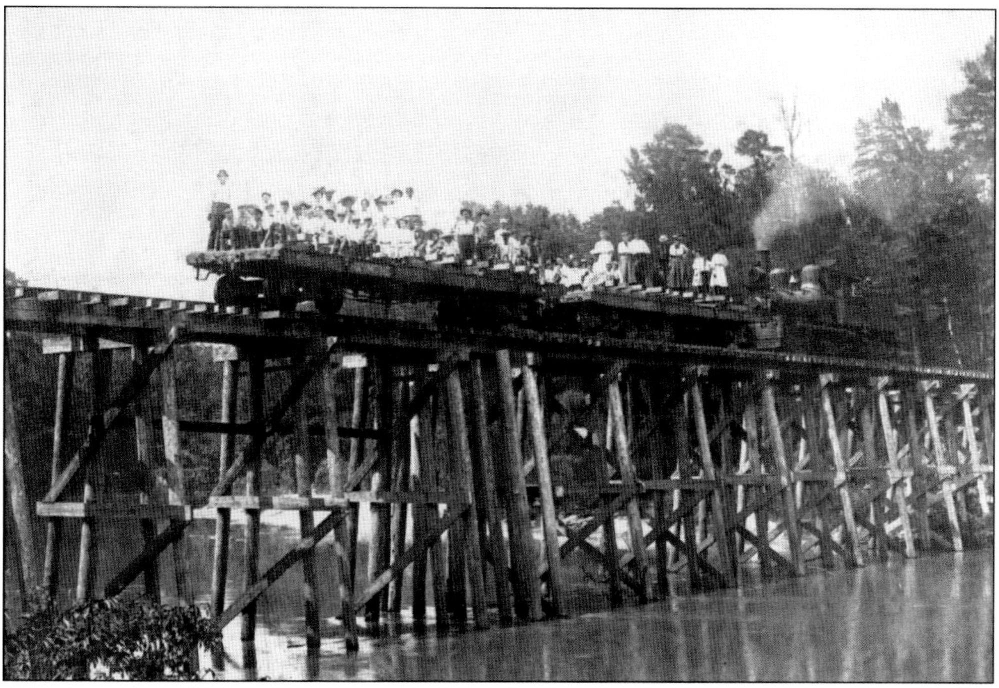

A Hammond Lumber Company "special excursion train," with passengers, crosses the Tangipahoa River. The Hammond and Eastern was a private railroad owned by Hammond Lumber. The company sponsored outings for family and friends of workers. The train also transported the company's baseball team, coaches, and fans to games in St. Tammany Parish. The trestle was located east of the intersection of River and Vineyard Roads.

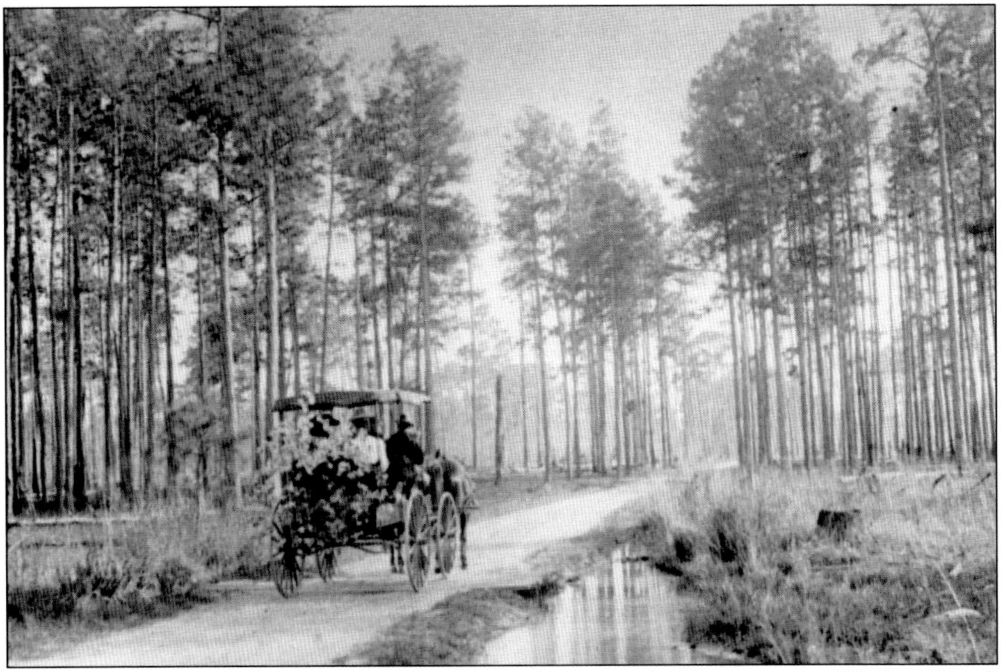

These two photographs appeared in a booklet titled *Hammond, Louisiana—Two Weeks in March 1901* by Florida photographer Allan Pendergrass. The album contained local photographs, which were available for sale at The Hammond Photograph Gallery, operated by Herbert W. Saunders. Above, a carriage brings folks to the countryside for an outing. Excursions such as this were popular, especially on the weekends. Below, women and their driver gather dogwood blossoms. Prevalent in the area in the early 1900s, dogwoods in the past 25 years have been declining and dying as diseases, insects, changes in environmental conditions, and drought stress have decimated the trees.

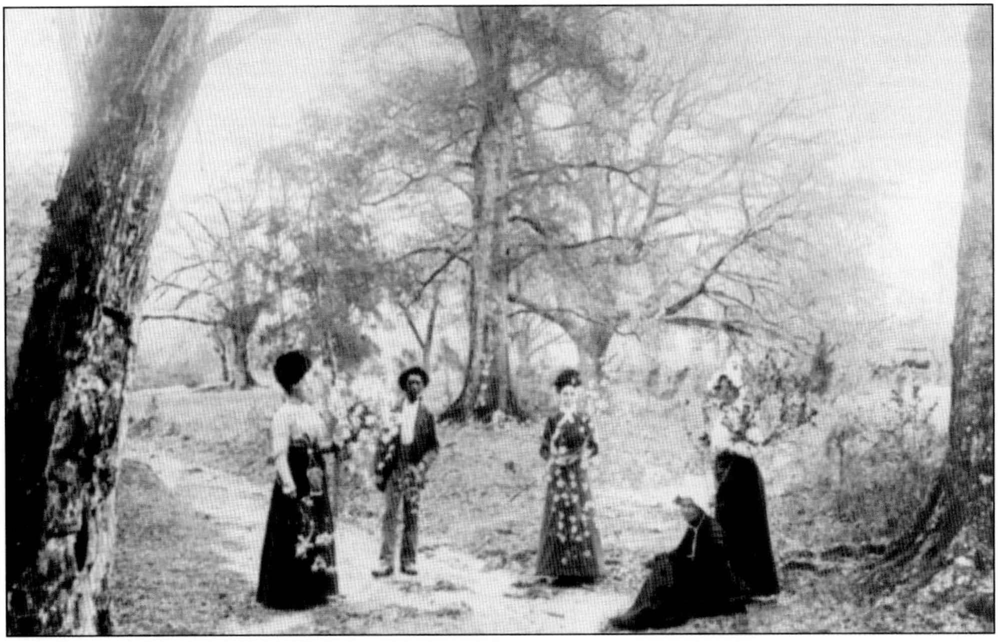

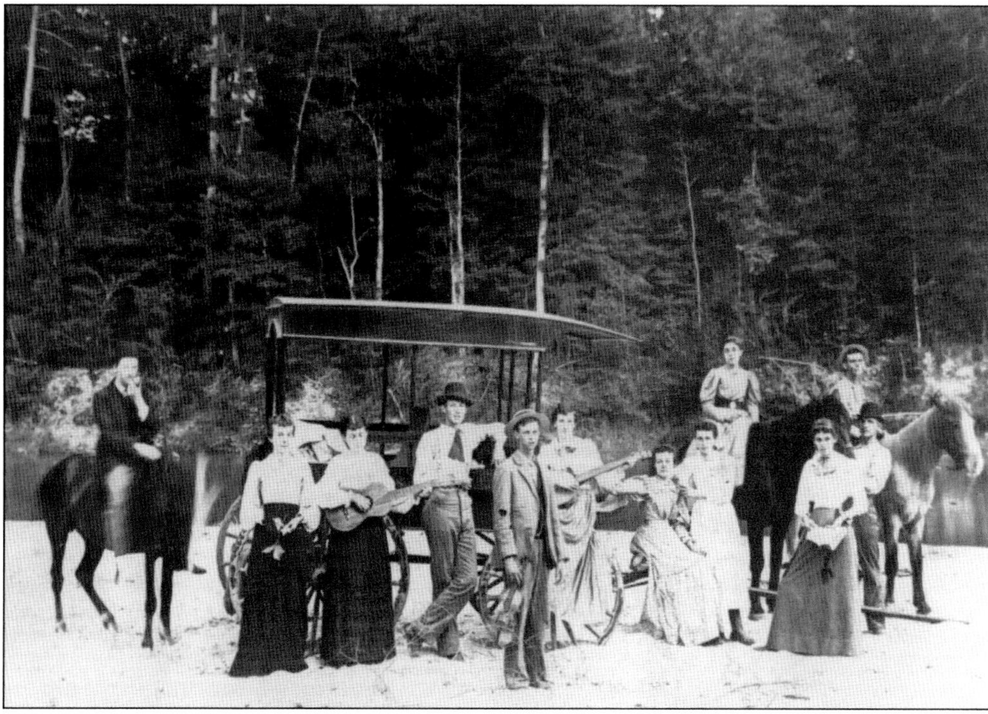

The Carr family and friends enjoy an outing near the chilly waters of Chappapeela Creek east of Hammond. Horses and a carriage, reading material, musical instruments, and sand are available for amusement, but no one seems to be dressed for a dip in the creek. Chappapeela Creek, Ponchatoula Creek, and the Tangipahoa River all provided nearby venues for swimming, fishing, or picnicking during the sweltering summer months.

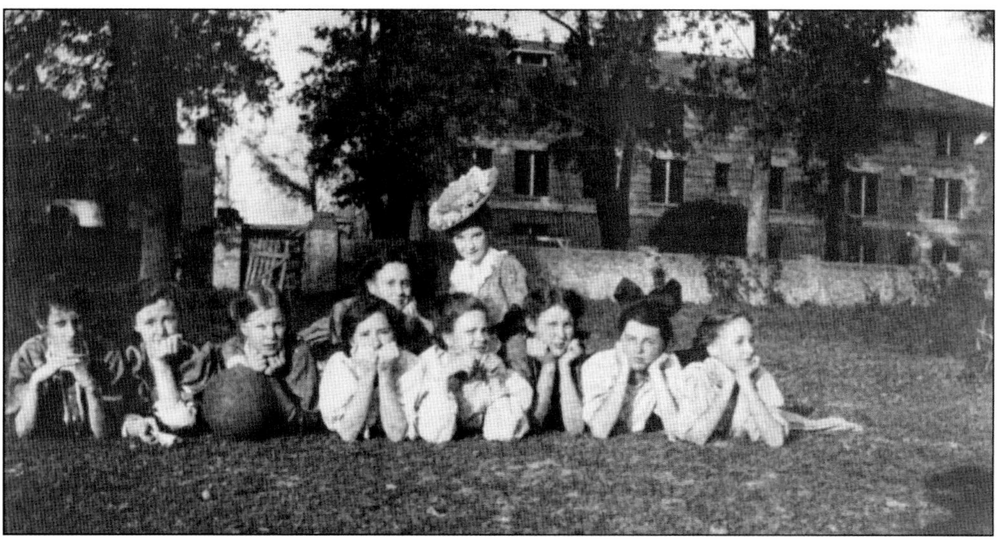

A young women's basketball team takes a break next to the Oaks Hotel. The weathered-looking brick fence behind the girls ran along the hotel property on Oak Street. Mertie Dameron, granddaughter of Charles E. Cate, is pictured on the far right; the others are not identified. The first organized boys' basketball game took place in a YMCA in Massachusetts in 1891, and girls throughout the country began playing soon after.

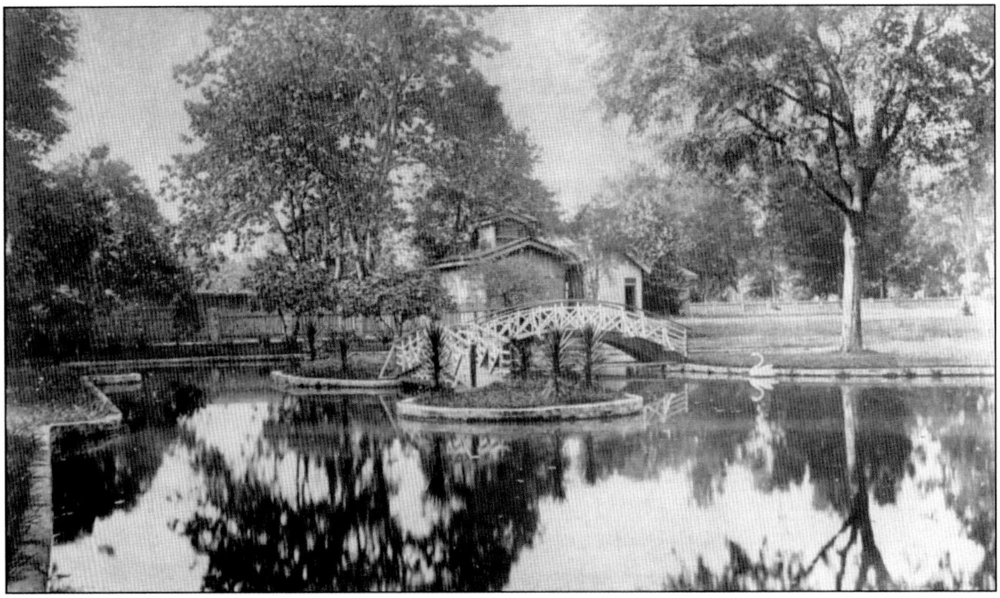

Cate Square was the site of the home of Charles E. Cate, who purchased 300 acres of land and settled in Hammond with his family in 1861. After the Civil War, as Cate and others began planning the town, part of the property was made into a beautiful garden with lagoons, popular for relaxing and boating. In the view above, the carriage house and pigeonniere, remaining after Cate's house burned in 1888, are visible. The Cate estate lost the land for the private park in the Depression. The City of Hammond bought the property in 1942 for $8,000 and made it a park called Cate Square in 1950. A bust of Cate stands as a monument. Below, the ladies on the bridge, are from left to right, Bessie Andrews, Jessie Willis, Edna Potter, and Rose Herbert.

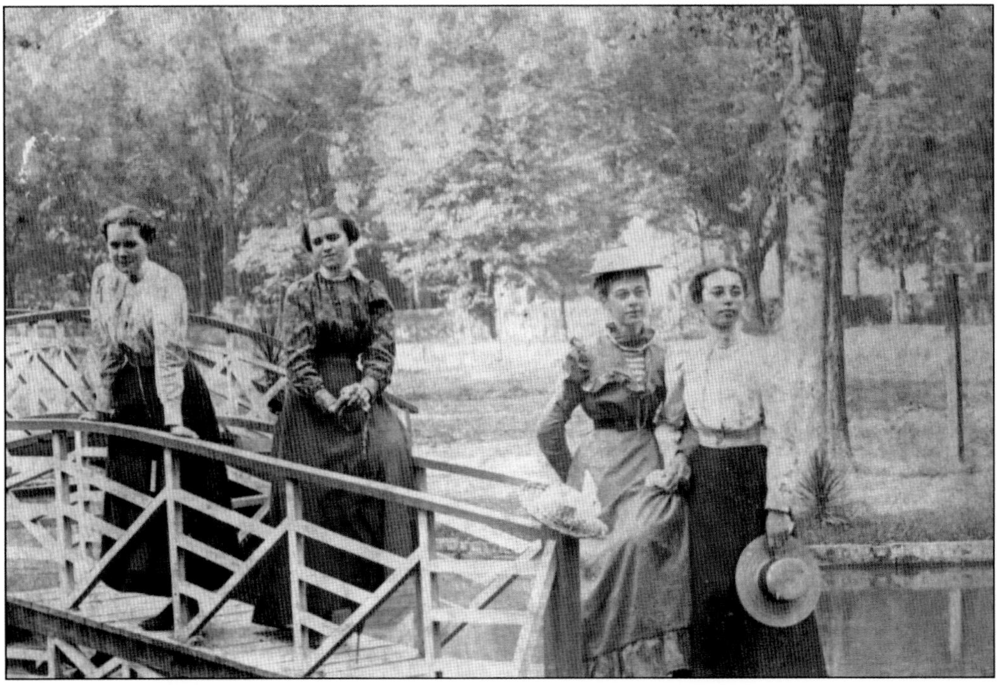

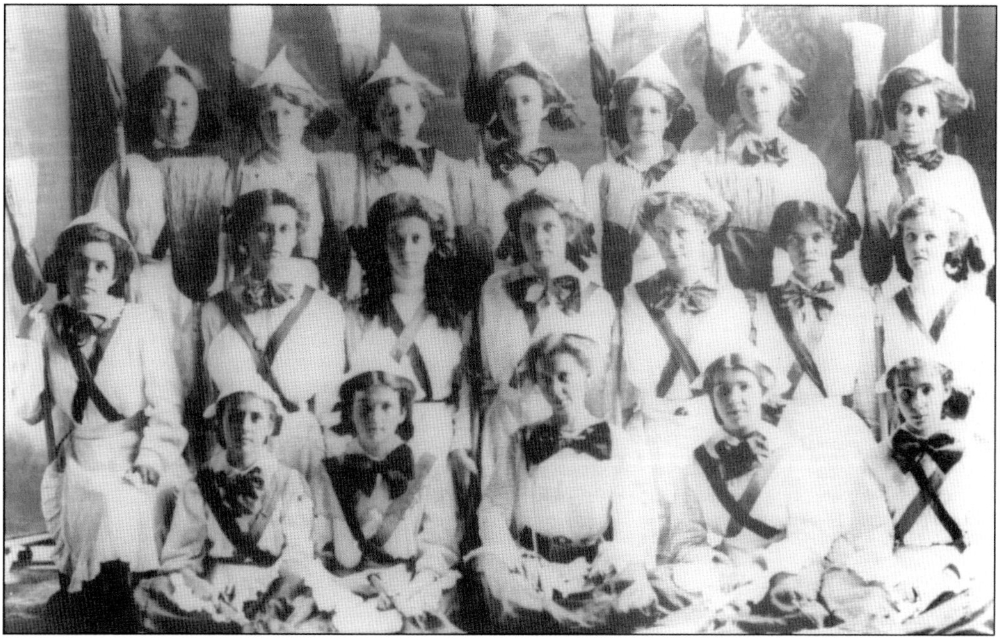

"Broom brigades" were a military style of exercise for women where brooms are carried instead of weapons. In the late 19th century, this type of activity was popular with the young ladies of Hammond. The broom drill was performed in Perry Hall, located over the Imperial Café, and then later in the Baltzell Opera House, just around the corner on South Cypress Street. This photograph was taken sometime after 1890.

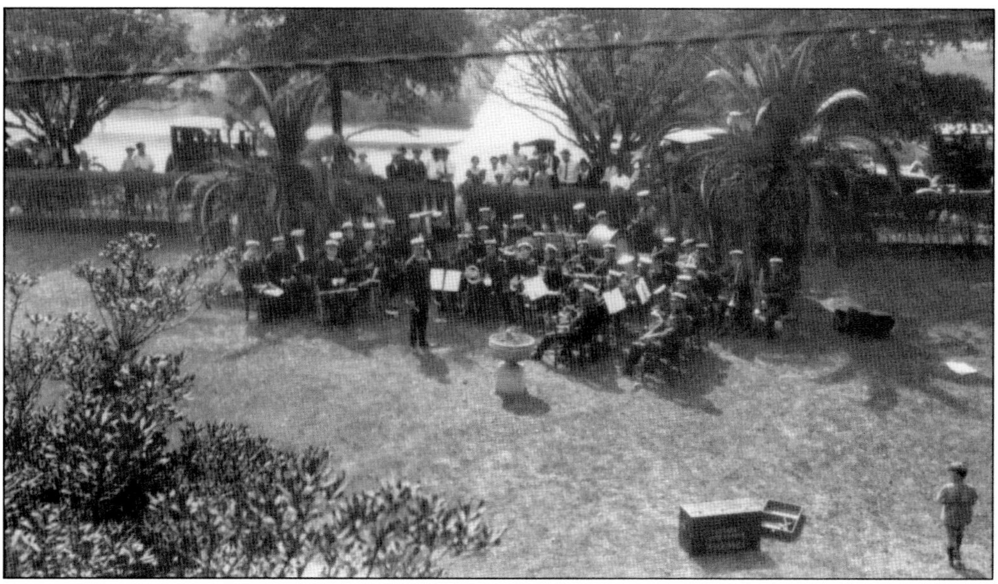

Concerts were held throughout the year in Hammond. In this photograph the Stanocola Band, from the Standard Oil Company in Baton Rouge, provides entertainment on the lawn of the Oaks Hotel. The Stanocola Band performed for many events in the Baton Rouge area, including accompanying Babe Ruth to the state capitol in 1921.

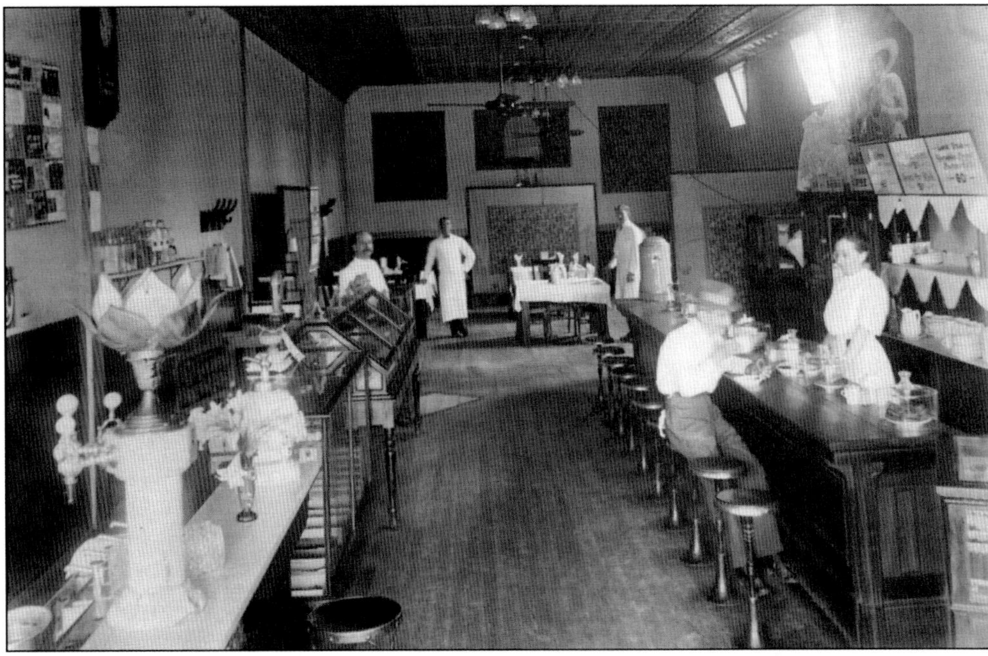

The Imperial Restaurant on the south side of the 100 block of East Thomas Street was a popular eatery operated by Charles E. Norman (left) and Mrs. Lillian Norman (right). The restaurant's motto was "Cleanliness and Promptness." The establishment had been previously operated by J.S. Perry, whose Perry Hall above the restaurant featured lectures and theatrical entertainment.

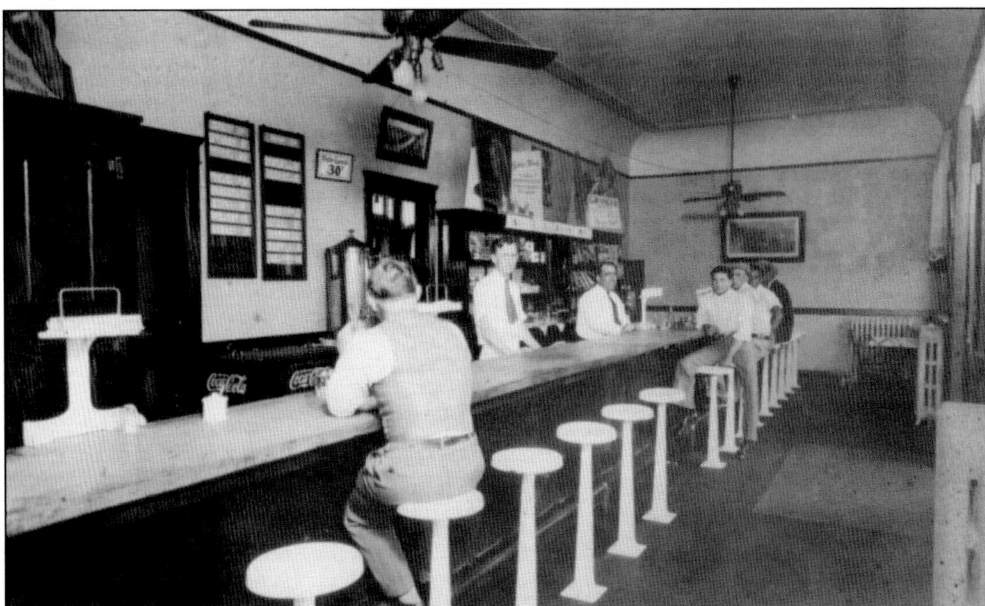

The south end of the 1912 train depot housed the Beanery, a popular 24-hour restaurant operated by the Robinson family, who also owned Oaks Hotel. The name came from the great northern bean, which was always featured in the restaurant's offerings, along with stews, soups, and hamburgers. Longtime residents recall going to the Beanery for a lunch break during high school or for burgers in the wee hours. (Courtesy of LF/TD.)

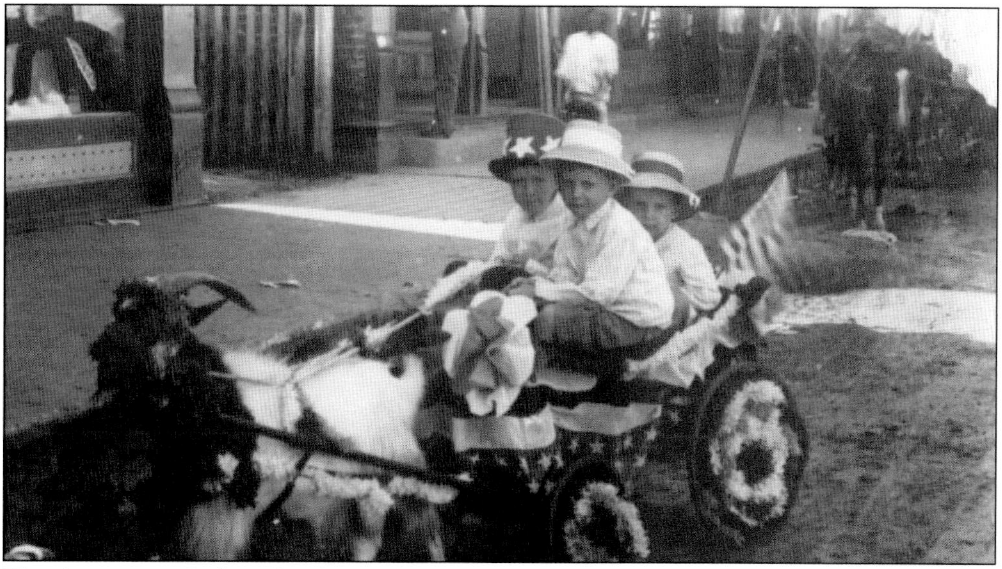

The three young Jackson brothers ride in a goat cart decorated in stars and stripes during the 1913 Fourth of July parade. From left to right are Charles, Joseph, and Harry Jackson. It is hard to tell if the goat cart is part of the parade or an ingenious idea by the parents to contain the brothers during the parade.

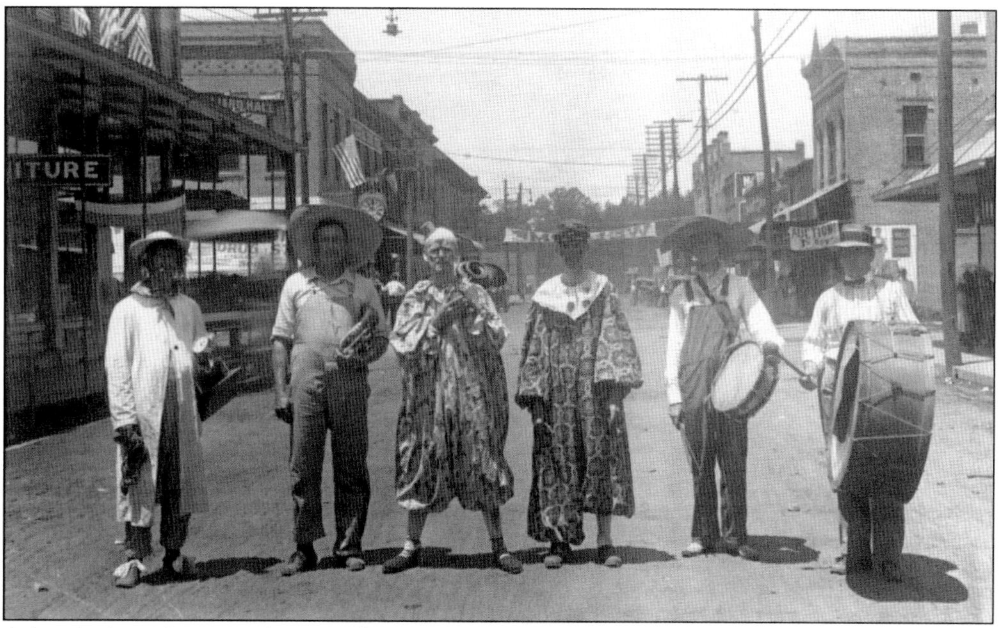

A band of six clowns with musical instruments poses on the 200 block of East Thomas Street around 1910. On the left side of the photograph is the Thomas Furniture Store and Undertaking Parlor. A "welcome" banner is draped across the street in the background. American flags appearing on several buildings may indicate a Fourth of July parade or similar patriotic festivities.

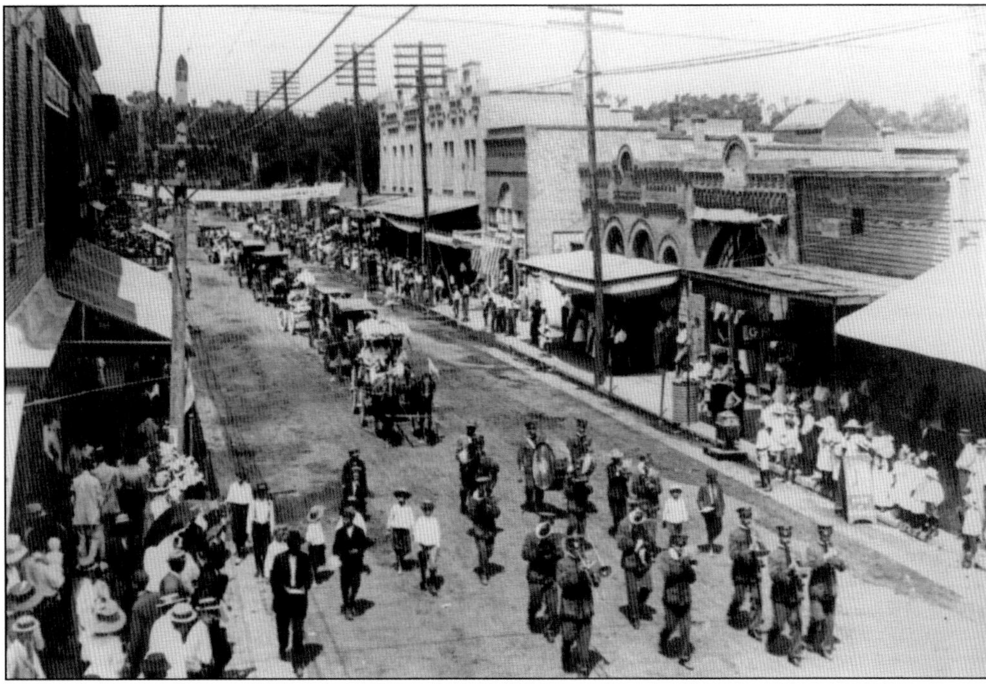

Parades were held to celebrate holidays, the end of World War I, the Strawberry Festival, and eventually Southeastern Louisiana College's homecoming. The Hammond Brass Band leads this Fourth of July parade, sponsored by the Hammond Volunteer Fire Department, down East Thomas Street. A baseball game and other events were held following the parade to raise money for the fire department.

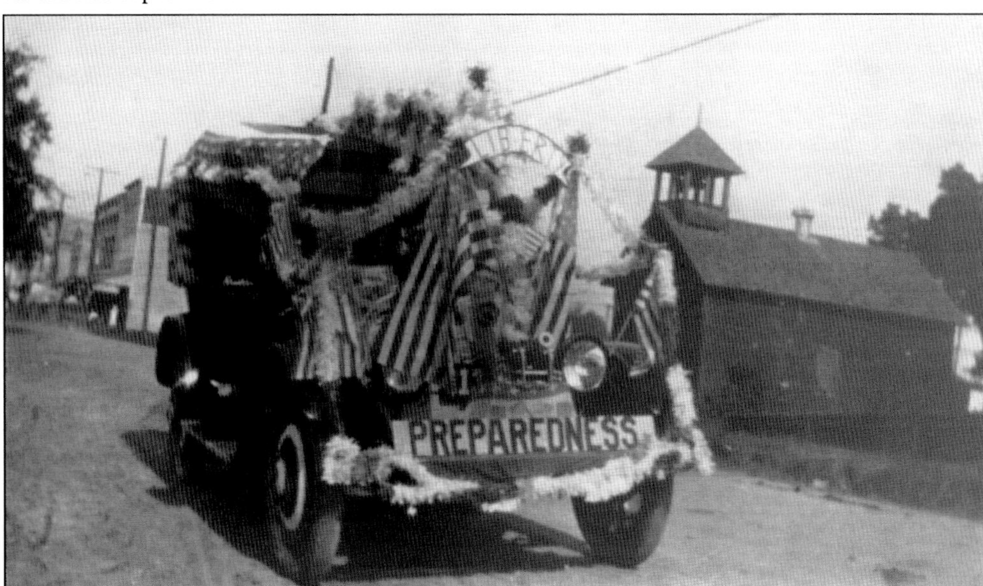

Fourth of July celebrations took on a new significance for the citizens of Hammond while the country and the world were embroiled in World War I. A stray float or perhaps the last float from the 1916 Fourth of July parade, proclaiming "Liberty" and "Preparedness," passes by a fire department hose house. Hammond had two other hose houses placed throughout the downtown area.

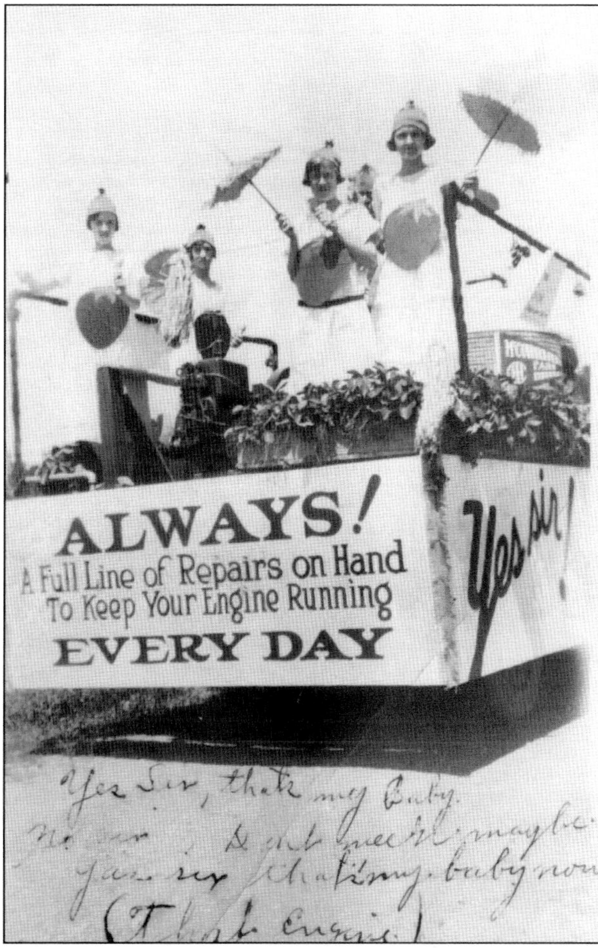

The Strawberry Festival parade was an annual event held in Hammond from 1925 to the early 1930s. At right, the women on the float are, from left to right, Doris Carey, Frances Campbell, Margaret Morrison, and Antoinette Anderson Yokum. The float's logo is handwritten under the photograph. The first African American strawberry festival was held in 1939 at the Greater St. James AME Church. The event received the support of Mayor Jordan, and both blacks and whites were invited. The float below carries festively dressed young ladies in front of V. Misuraca Groceries and Fruits on West Thomas Street. On the sidewalk to the right, young spectators don strawberry caps.

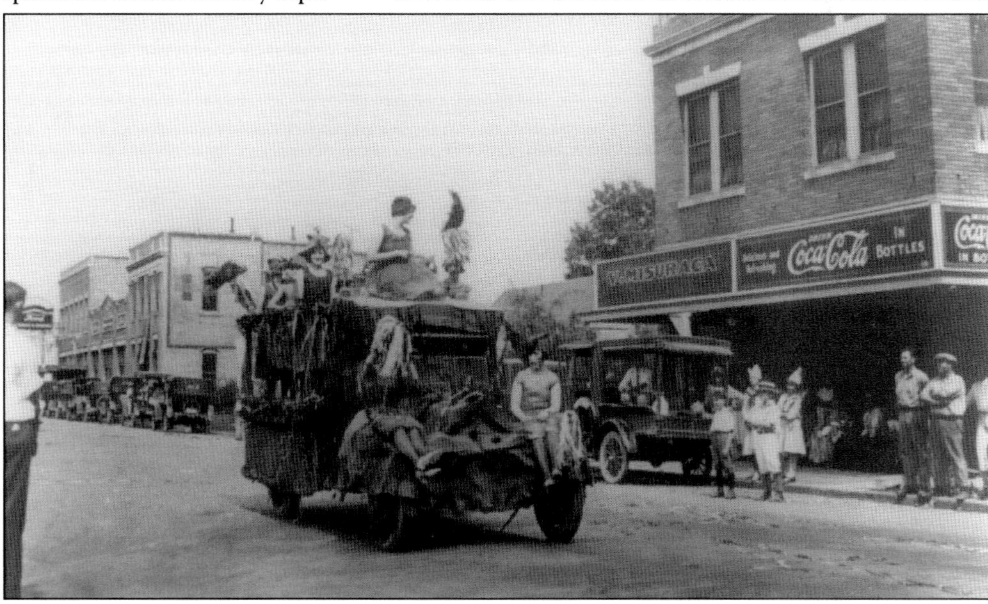

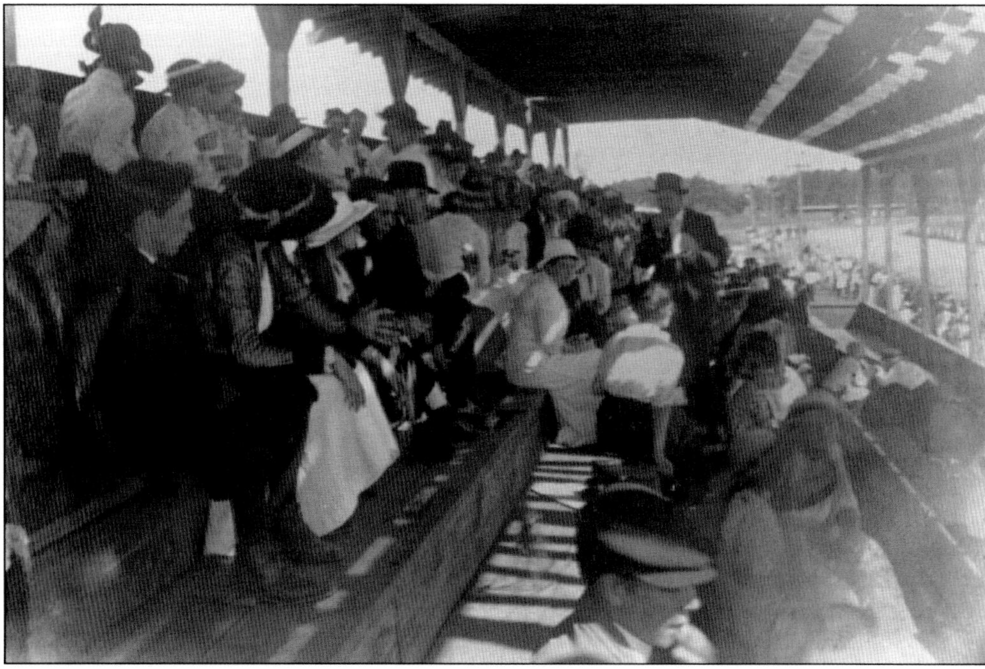

The Old Fairgrounds, located in what is now the Rosewood residential area south of West Church Street, began hosting the annual Tangipahoa Parish Fair in 1910. Events included horse races, airplane shows and rides, dancing in a large entertainment pavilion, and exhibits. The fairs became so popular that in 1921 a new fairground was constructed. Schoolchildren were released from school to attend the fair. The Parish Fair continued in Hammond until 1930, when the effects of the Great Depression and a failing strawberry crop led to a decline of interest and halted it. Above, spectators sit in the fairground grandstands. Below, the 1921 Tangipahoa Parish Fair is seen from the parking area.

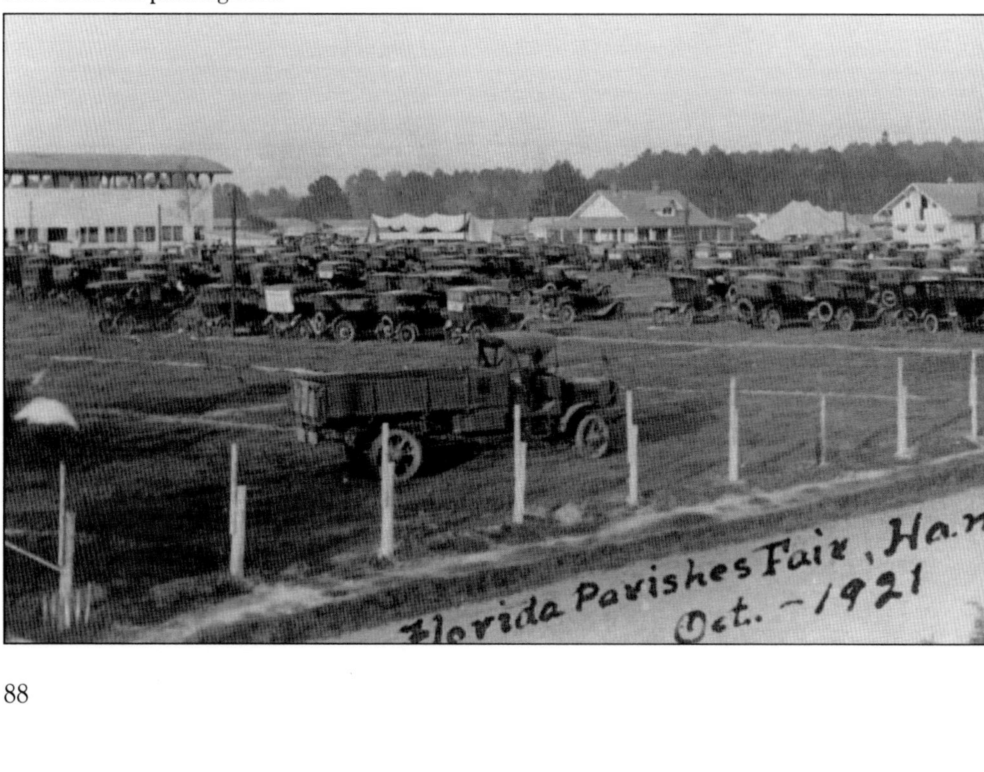

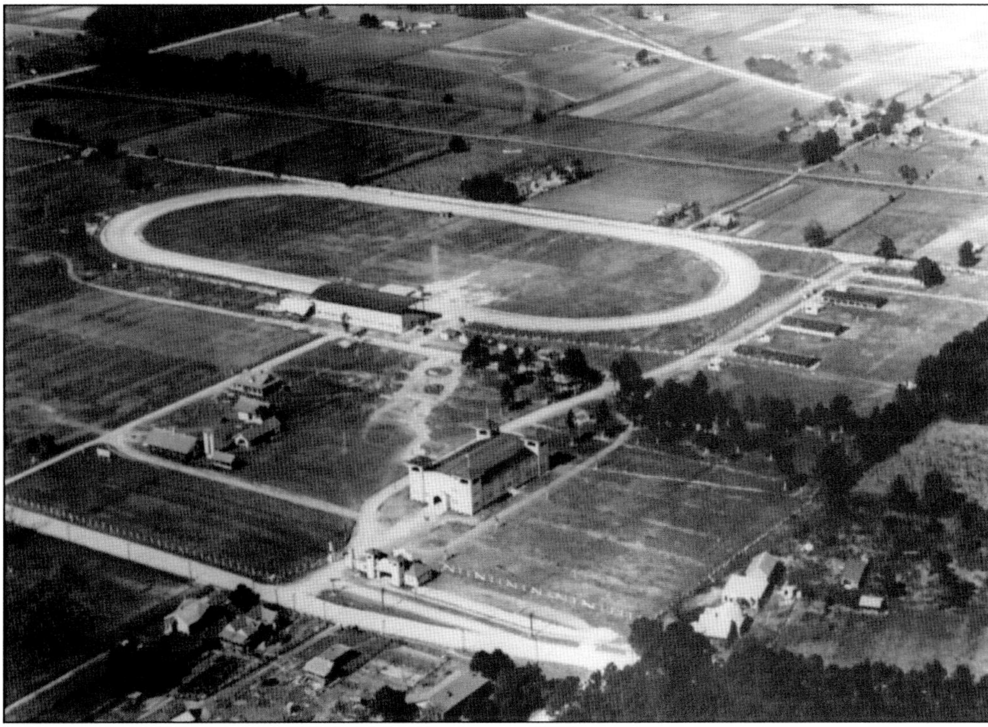

Above is an aerial view of the new Hammond Fairgrounds, which opened on 50 acres with the Florida Parishes Fair in October 1921. The fairgrounds, demolished to create the Rosewood residential area, boasted the grandstand and racetrack, an exhibition hall, the livestock pavilion, and a silo. Over the years, the Hammond Fairgrounds hosted the Tangipahoa Strawberry Festival, Florida Parishes Festival, horseracing, car racing, carnivals, livestock shows, and many other forms of entertainment. Pictured below is the Coliseum, an exhibition hall that was the area's largest indoor venue for public gatherings, livestock shows, concerts, and other events before its demolition.

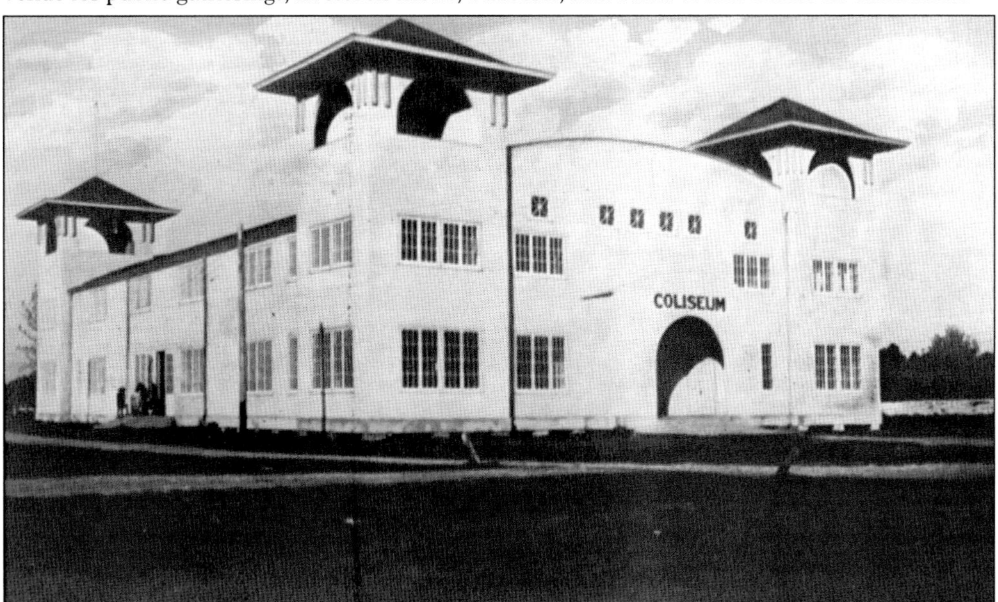

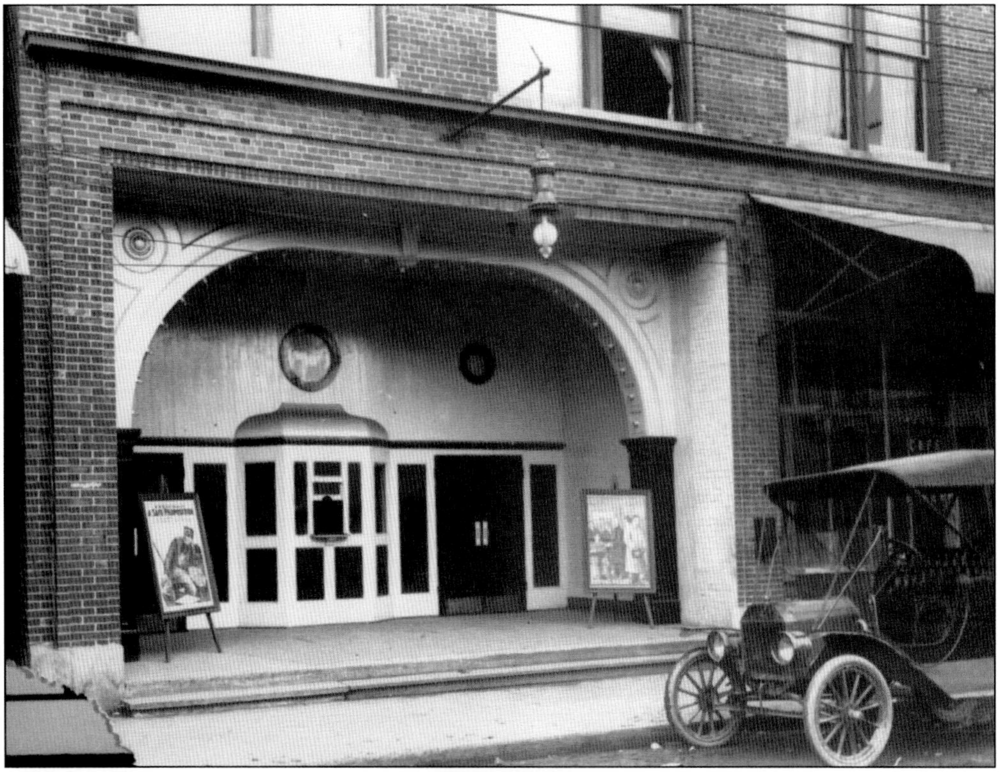

In the early 1900s, the Lomo Theatre, named for operators Charles Lohmann and ? Mollere, showed some of Hammond's first picture shows. Located on East Thomas Street, it offered silent films accompanied by piano music. Children were seated in the front on benches, often next to their dogs. The Lomo Theatre was a favorite of Col. Henry Robinson, owner of the first and second Oaks Hotels.

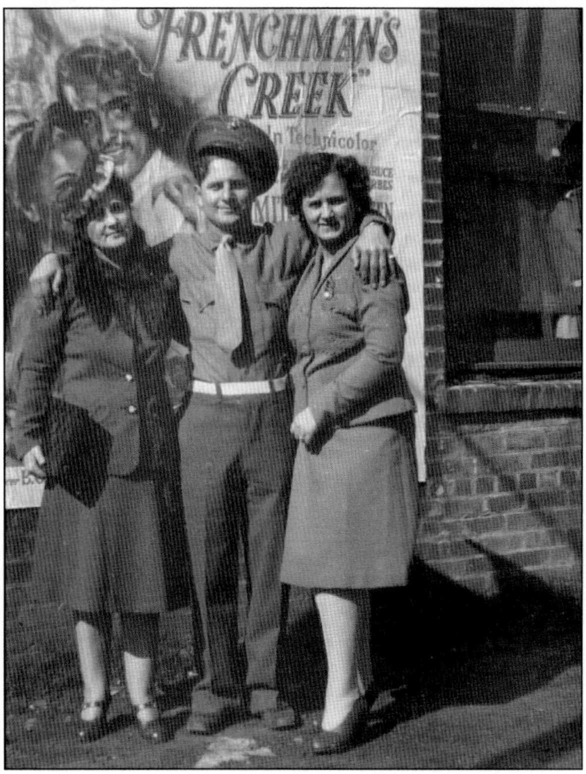

S.Sgt. Pete Giannobile poses in front of a poster for the film *Frenchman's Creek* with his sisters Katie Giannobile Fazzino (left) and Josie Giannobile Pecora at the Rex Theatre in 1944. The theater, built on the first block of Northeast Railroad Avenue the previous year, could accommodate 600 moviegoers. It was demolished in the late 1950s. Today, a restaurant occupies the space. (Courtesy of Cecilia Giannobile.)

Located on the 200 block of East Thomas Street, the Columbia Theatre opened September 1, 1928. Although it was not the first movie theater in Hammond, it was the first one to feature a theater organ and talking pictures. The first "talkie" shown at the theater was *Glorious Betsy*, with Conrad Nagle and Dolores Costello. The Columbia Theatre thrived during the mid-20th century as a respite from the Depression and World War II, and at one time it also included two lady's retail shops: Prescott Style Shoppe and Lucille Hats. During the 1960s, the structure fell into disrepair, and by the 1980s the theater closed. It reopened in 2002, refurbished as the Columbia Theatre for Performing Arts. Other theaters during the 1900s were the Avalon, Lomo, Liberty, and Rialto. Pictured below is the interior of Columbia Theatre in the mid-1900s.

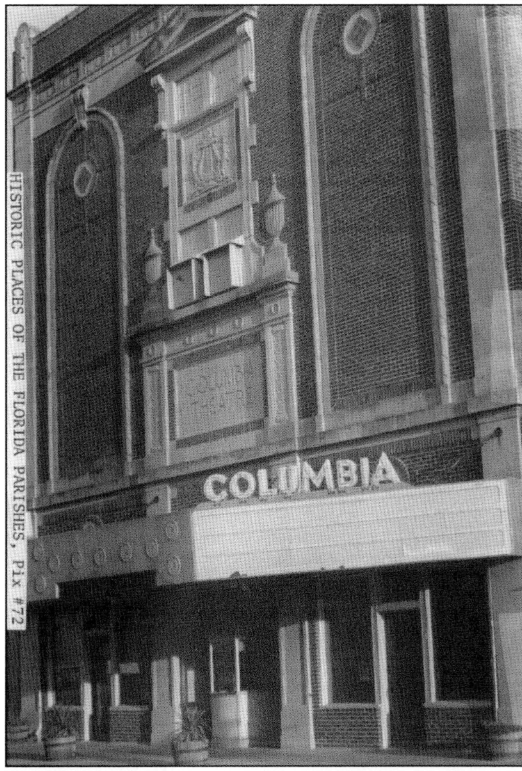

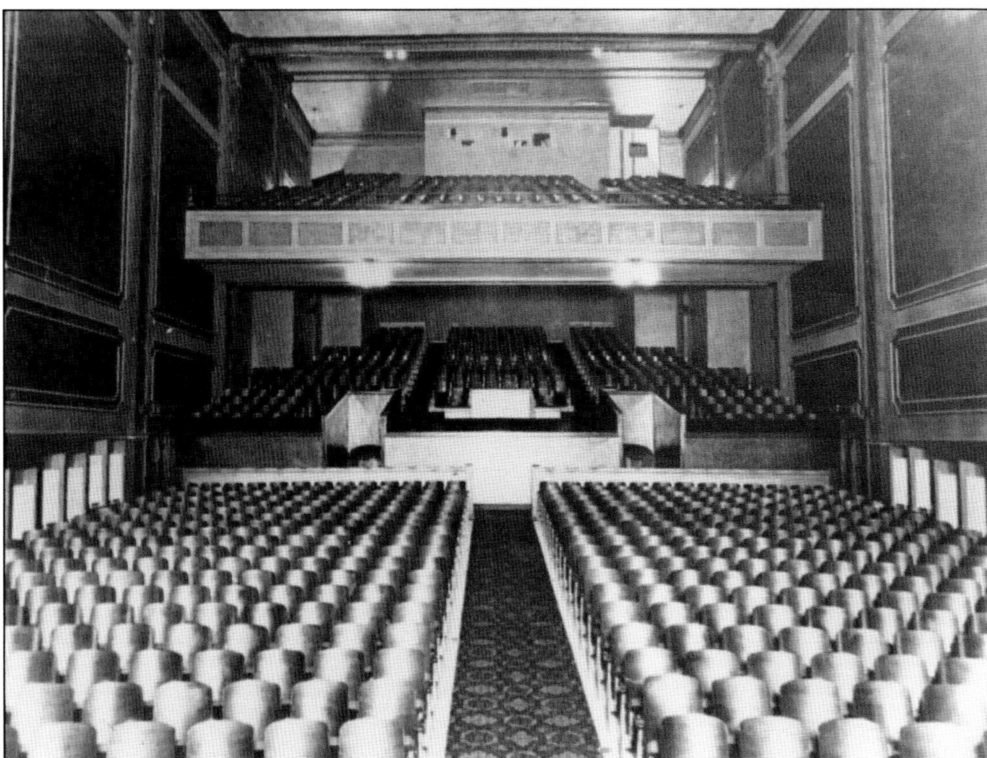

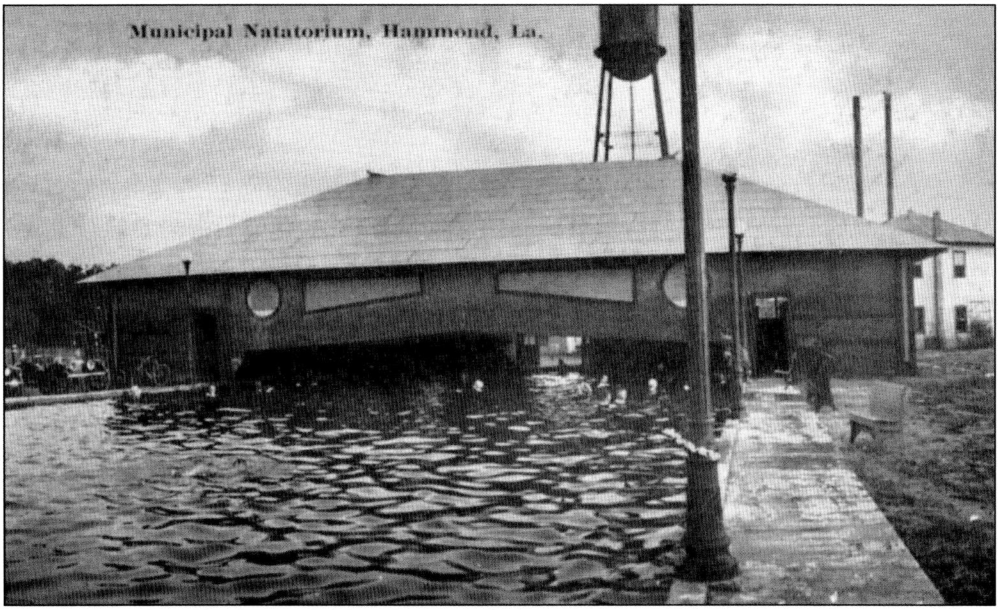

This postcard shows the Municipal Natatorium, located at the east side of South Oak Street at the present-day site of the main fire station. Built around 1916, it was a popular place in the hot months of summer. Percy Kemp and Ned McGehee taught swimming there for a number of years. A new town pool in Zemurray Park replaced the structure.

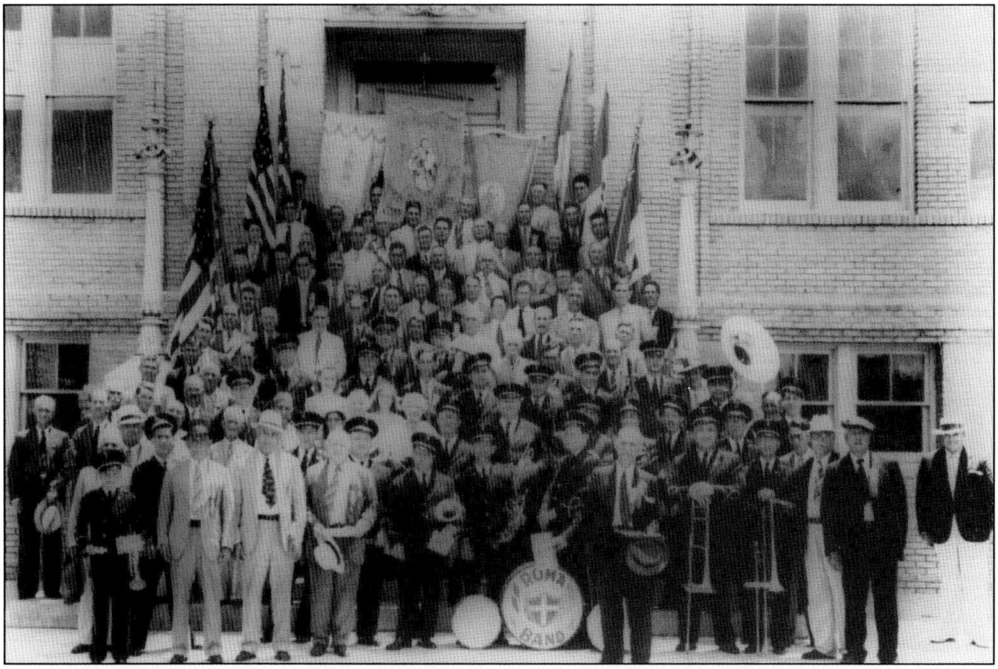

By the early 1900s, Sicilian immigrants were moving to southeastern Louisiana, where they raised strawberries and truck vegetables. The older Italians formed societies dedicated to patron saints. In this photograph, members of Hammond's St. Joseph's Society—which held an annual St. Joseph's Day Festival—and other local societies pose with members of the Roma Band on the steps of the 1914 Hammond High School.

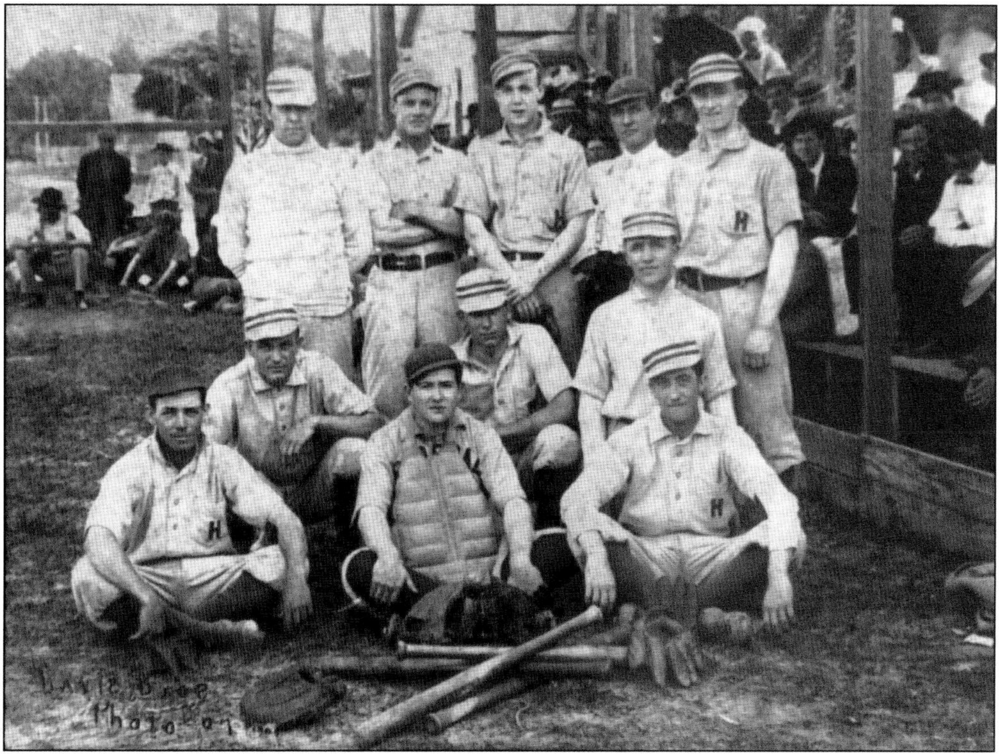

Baseball has been a major source of entertainment for the citizens of Hammond since the 1800s. The *Hammond News* reported that the first organized teams, the Stars and the Pickups, played a three-game series starting in November 1893 and ending on Christmas Day. The two teams had one win apiece, but on Christmas Day the Pickups won the day. With a population of about 1500, there were 350 spectators. Many companies fielded teams and played each other. The image above shows the Hammond Blue Sox of 1907. Thomas G. Kidder is standing on the left, James M. Fourmy is seated on the left, and Joseph W. Robinson is seated in center. Below are the Hammond Berries, who captured the local Evangeline League Championship, Class D, in 1949. Seven other Louisiana teams constituted the league.

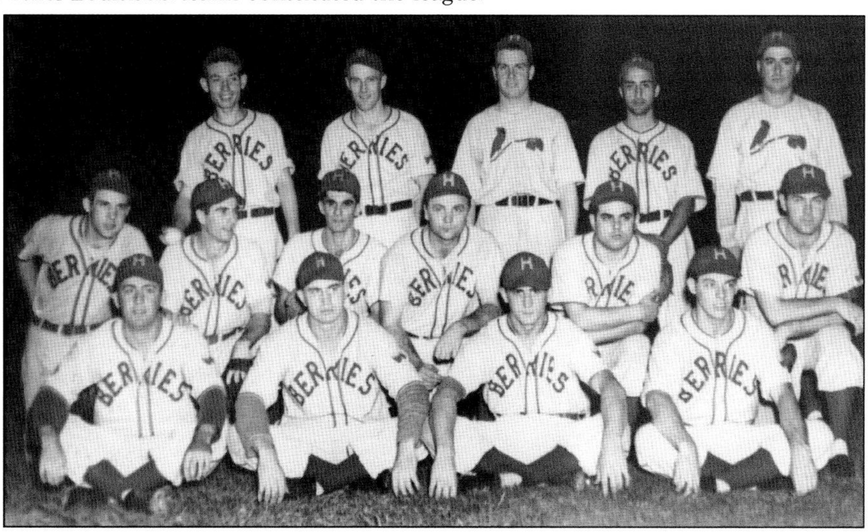

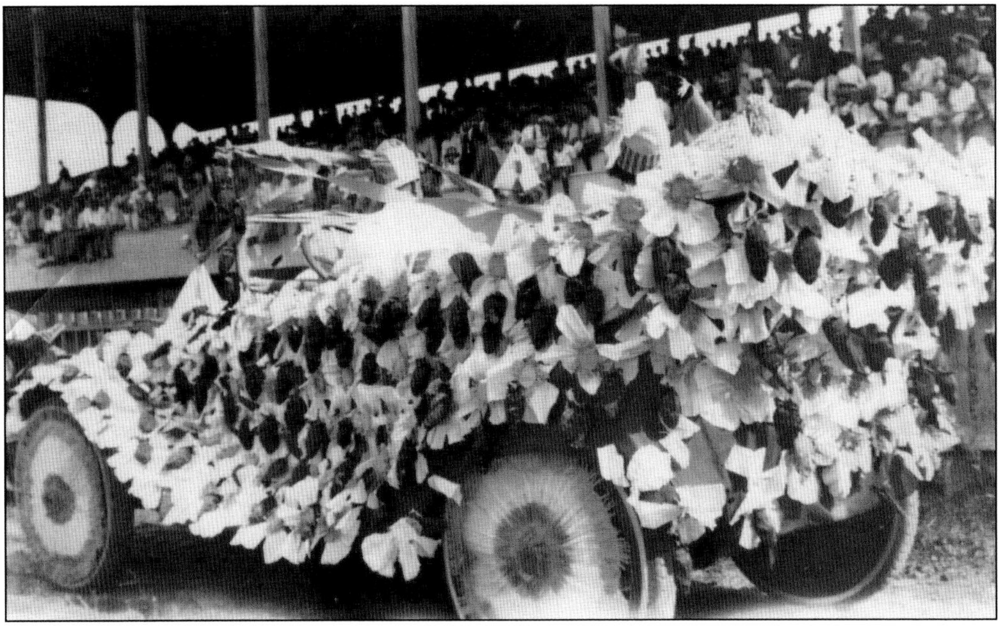

The first Strawberry Festival in Hammond was held on May 22, 1925. Over 80 decorated cars paraded from the fairgrounds downtown and back before circling the fairgrounds for the judging contest. Orris Bradley Nalty was selected as Strawberry Queen of the first festival. She won, among other prizes, a scholarship to Spencer Business College in New Orleans. Entertainment following the parade included songs by local singers and a maypole dance by young girls dressed in white. Above, a car festooned with "strawberries" stops before the judges' stand, while below, in a photograph taken by Albert Tolle, the 1928 Strawberry Blossom float passes the corner of Thomas and Magnolia Streets. Festivals continued for several years following. Since 1972, the annual Strawberry Festival has taken place each April in nearby Ponchatoula.

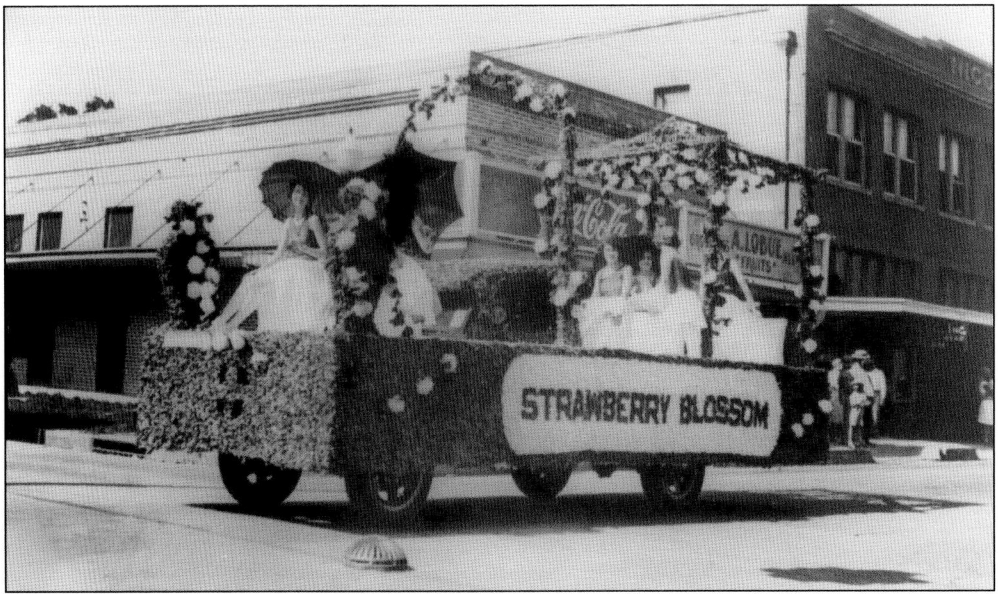

Four

Neighborhoods, Homes, and Churches

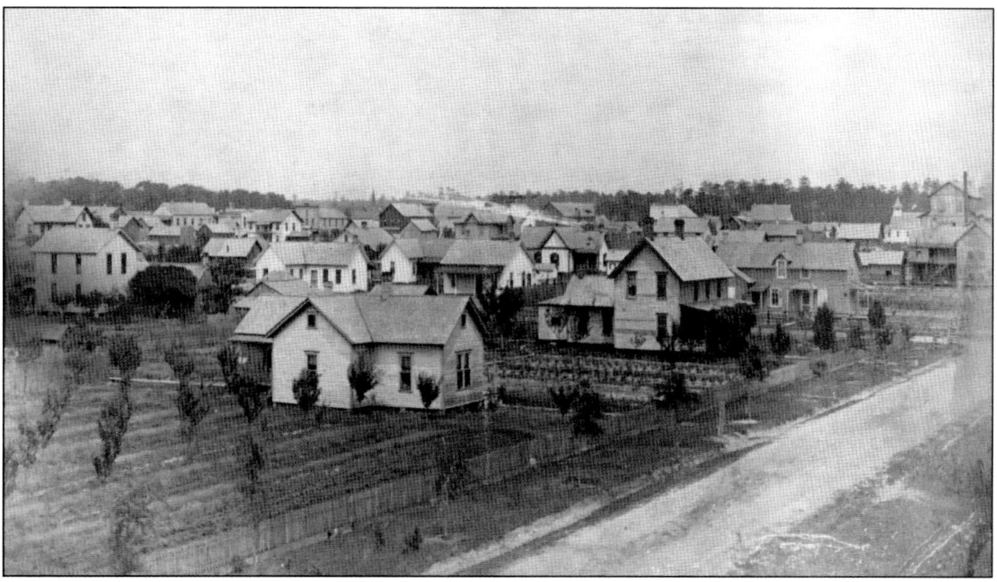

Charles E. Cate and three Iowa businessmen formed a company in 1887 called Iowa and Louisiana Land and Lot Company. In 1906, the company filed a charter of incorporation for its new venture: developing a tract of land in the southeast quadrant of Hammond called the "Iowa addition." The company, with the help of the Illinois Central Railroad, advertised the residential properties throughout the Midwest.

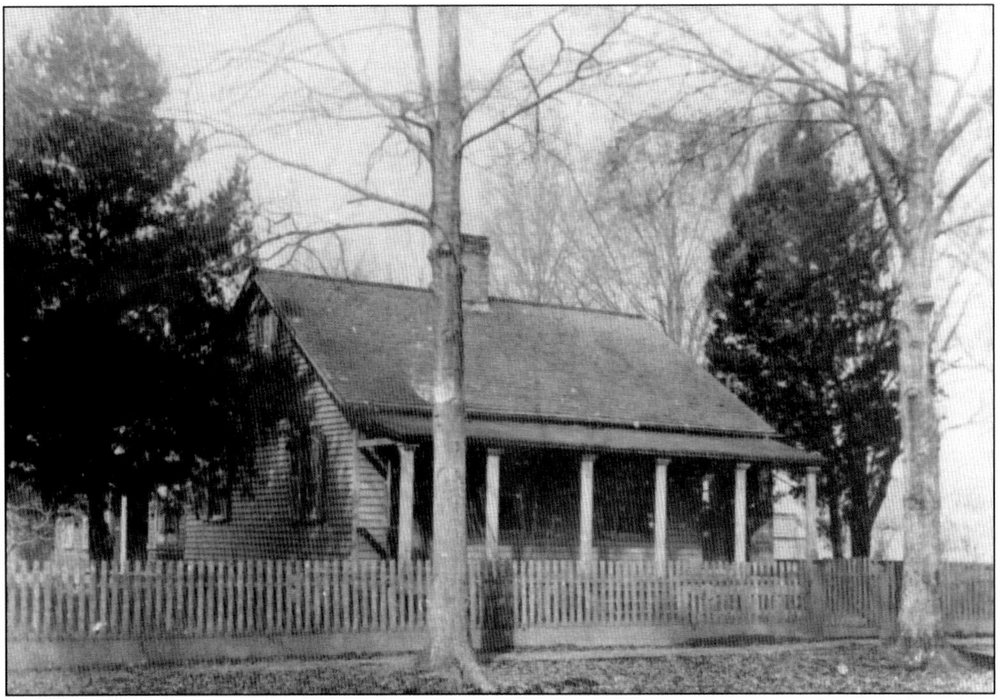

Charles E. Cate's original house stood on what is now Cate Square, facing east and fronted by a fruit orchard extending to the railroad. When the house burned in late 1888 during renovations, Cate moved the detached kitchen to the west of where the house had stood and restored it. Cate's house, Hammond's oldest, still stands at the corner of North Magnolia and West Robert Streets.

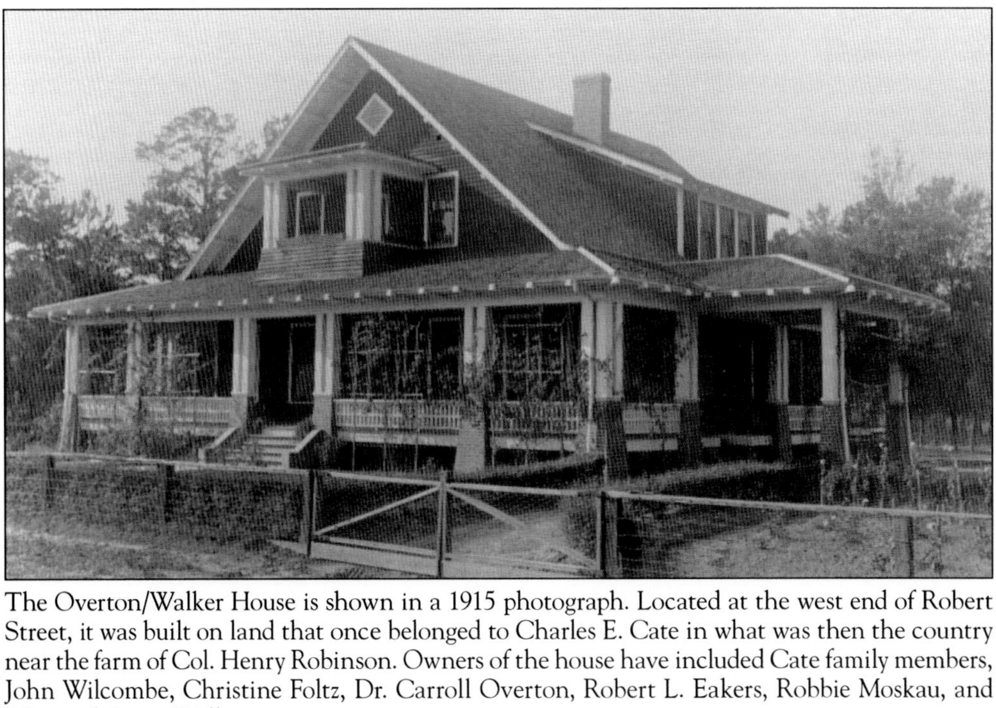

The Overton/Walker House is shown in a 1915 photograph. Located at the west end of Robert Street, it was built on land that once belonged to Charles E. Cate in what was then the country near the farm of Col. Henry Robinson. Owners of the house have included Cate family members, John Wilcombe, Christine Foltz, Dr. Carroll Overton, Robert L. Eakers, Robbie Moskau, and John and Anita Walker.

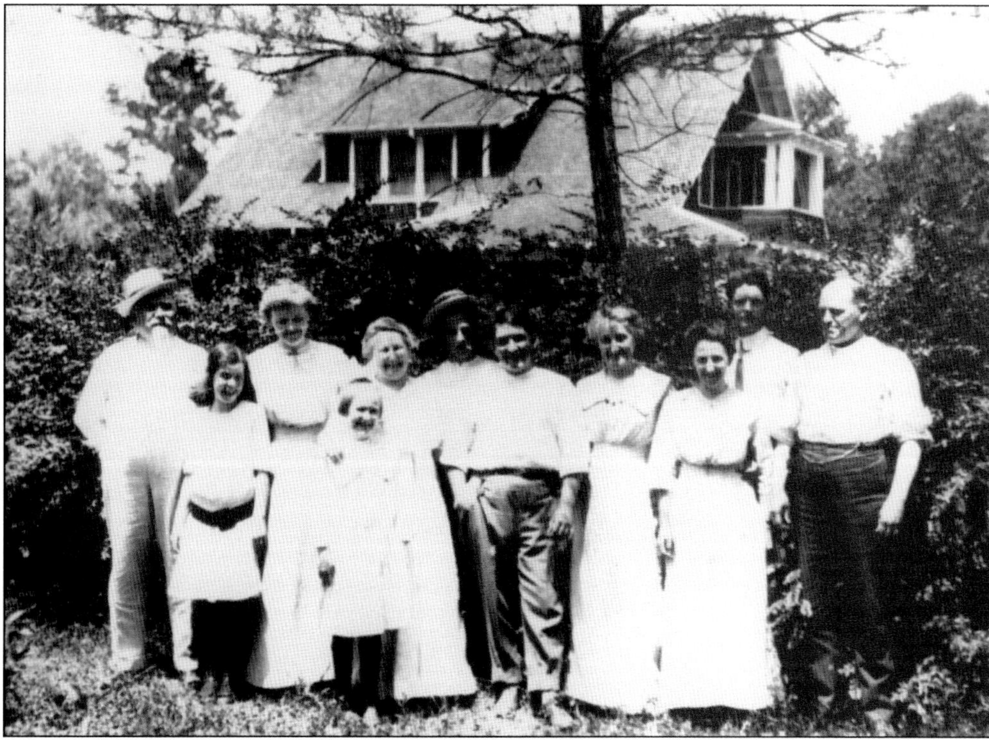

The family of Col. Henry Robinson poses at their farm, "Lazy Lodge," located at the end of West Robert Street, several blocks from their Oaks Hotel. The farm provided vegetables and strawberries for the hotel's dining room. Hotel guests were often ferried back and forth in a horse-drawn carriages and later Robinson's Studebaker for picnicking at the farm. Above, Col. Robinson (far left) and his wife (the second woman from the left) pose with family members and friends. In the photograph below, children cuddle six puppies. A caption on the back of the image states that two of the boys are John M. Robinson and Curtis Richardson.

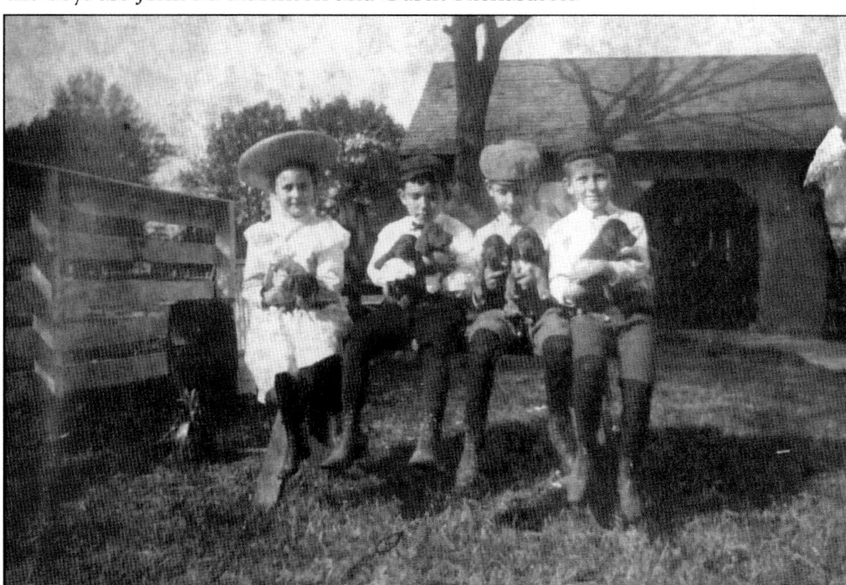

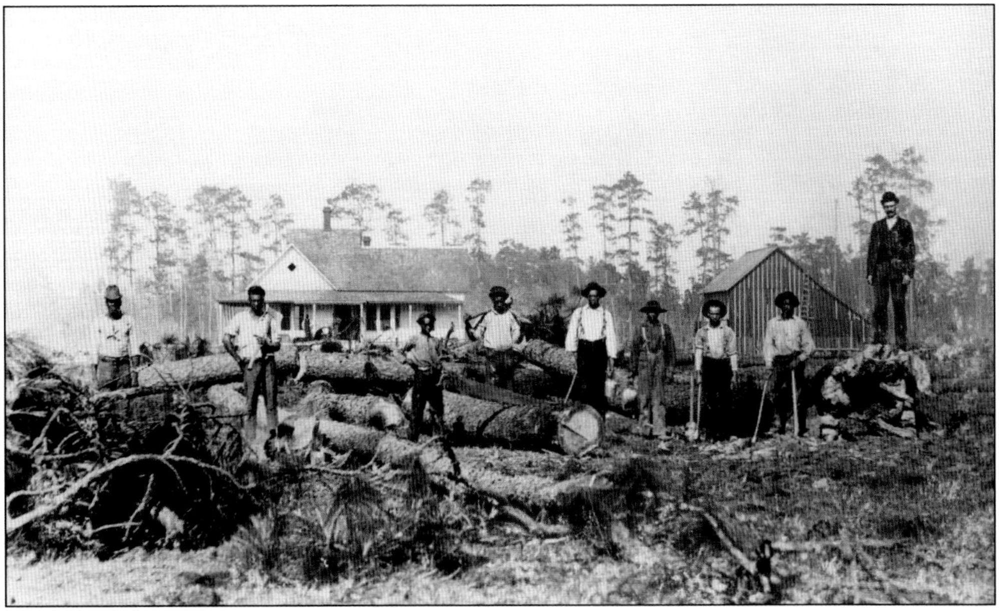

What may be the area known as the Iowa addition is captured in this photograph, taken in the southeast portion of Hammond as the city grew. The Iowa addition was constructed in the first decade of the 1900s, and many of the structures built in the early housing development still stand, although several have been remodeled.

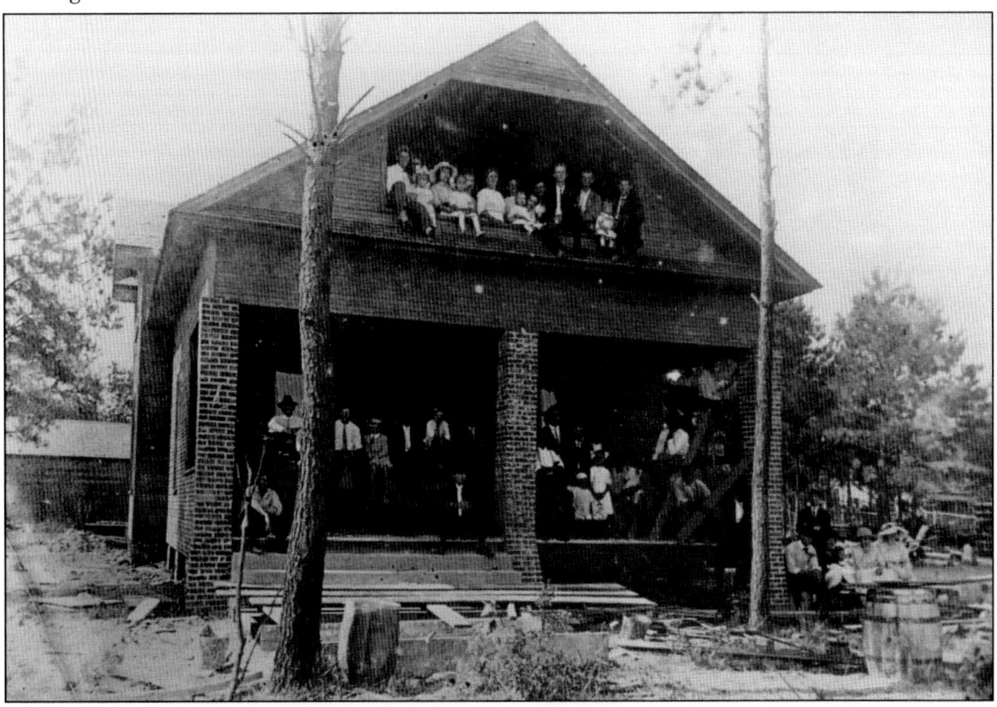

A large group of people poses in a house being built on East Thomas Street in the 1900s. Businesses developed in a relatively small section of the new city, and houses were then built around this central business district. The house later became the boyhood home of future mayor of Hammond, J. Thomas "Tom" Anderson.

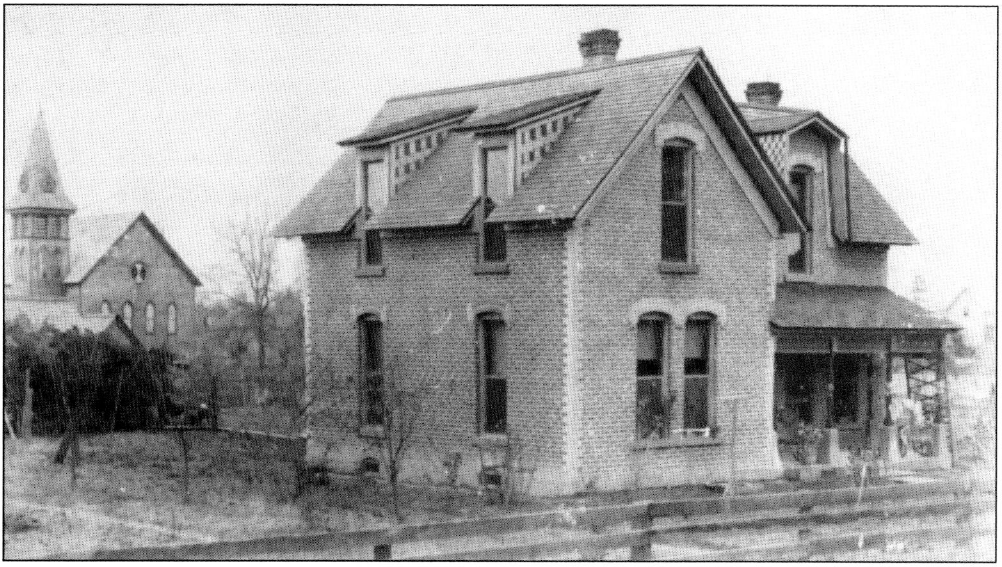

The first brick home in Hammond belonged to the family of Herman A. Kohnke. Kohnke served as mayor from 1898 to 1903, was postmaster, and was elected to the city council numerous times. Later stuccoed, the house stood on the corner of North Magnolia and West Church Streets. In the background and in the photograph at right, the Congregational Church is visible. The church was located on the corner of West Church and North Pine Streets. It organized in 1887 and merged with the Hammond Presbyterian Church to become the Federated Church in 1923, which in turn became First Presbyterian Church of Hammond in 1948. This image of the Congregational Church was taken sometime before 1900, the year that the church burned.

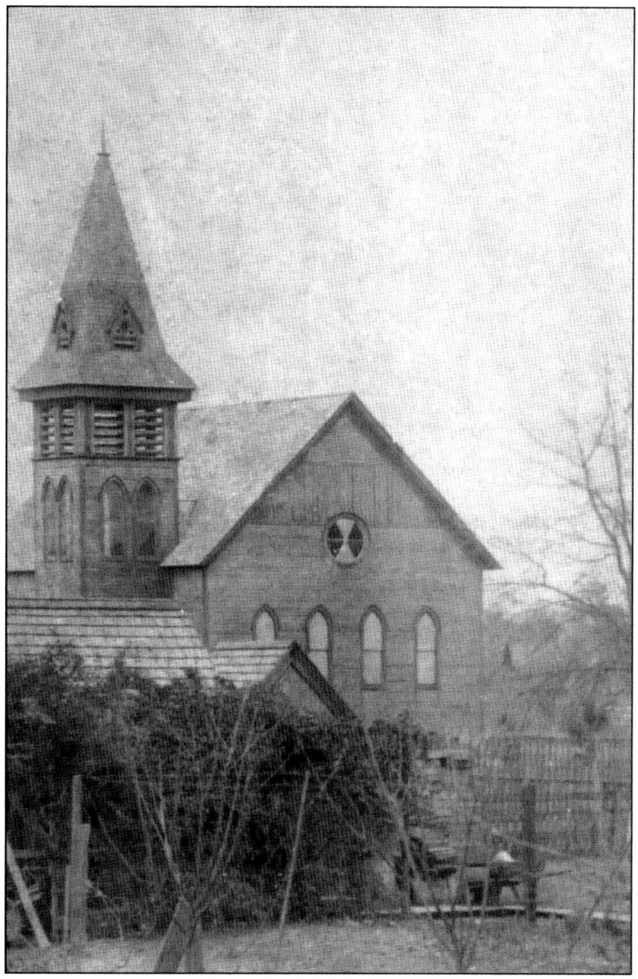

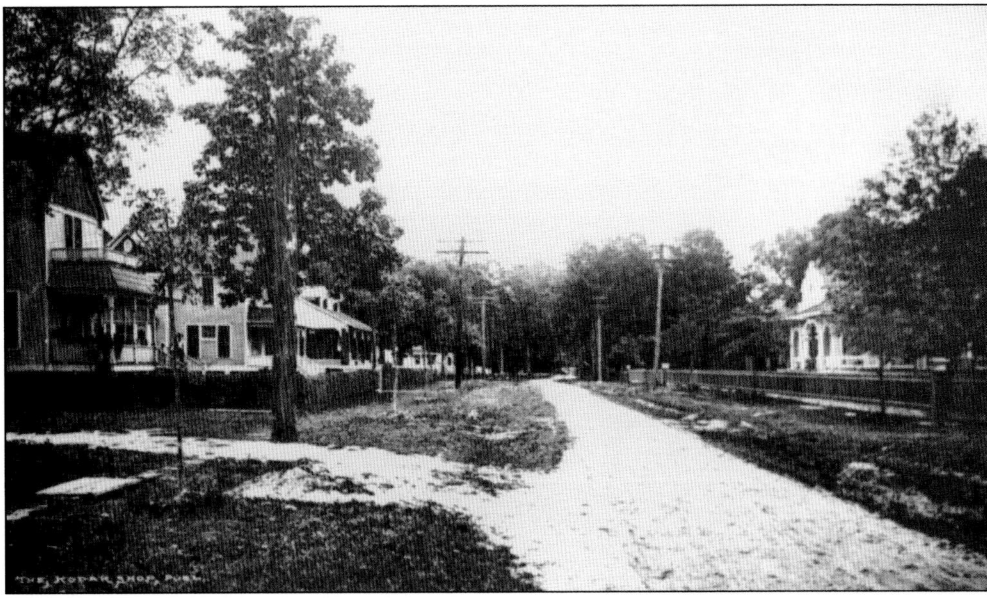

Above, this section of East Charles Street, originally referred to as "Banker's Row," features some of Hammond's most interesting homes. The houses are set back from the street and were built by early settlers. Visible on the left are the homes of the J.E. Muncy family and the Dr. Marquis C. Wiginton family; the latter structure burned in the early 1970s. On the left and below is the Preston House, constructed around 1906. It was the original family residence of Mr. and Mrs. Eli Victor Preston and, in later years, their daughter and granddaughter. The house was copied from a structure on Canal Street that Preston admired. The current residents are attorney and former Hammond mayor J. Thomas "Tom" Anderson and his wife, Donna Gay.

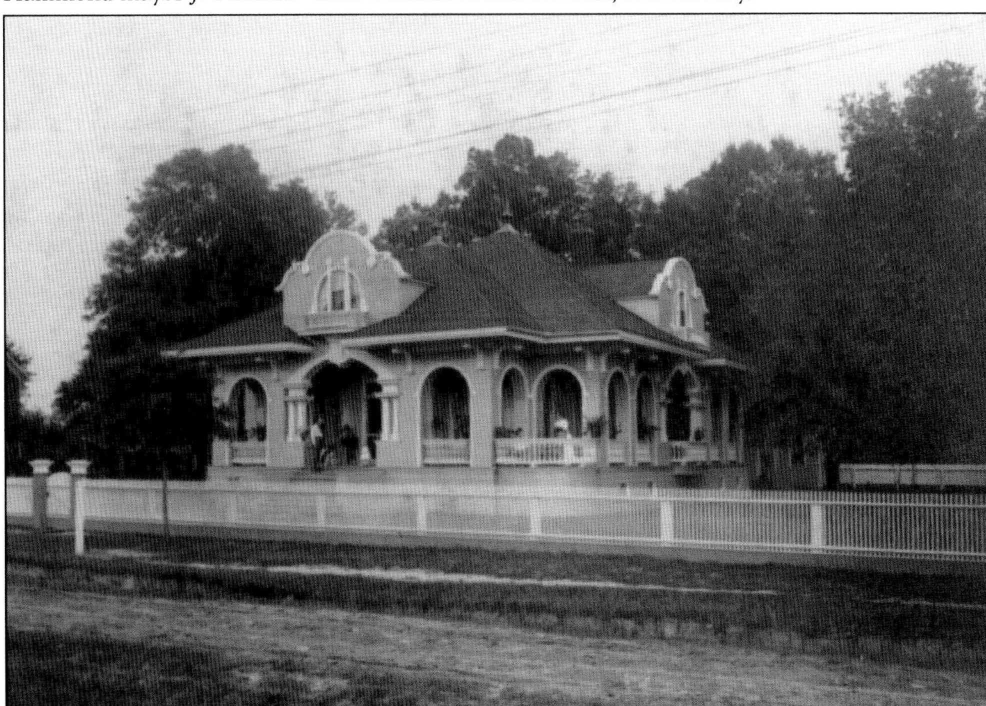

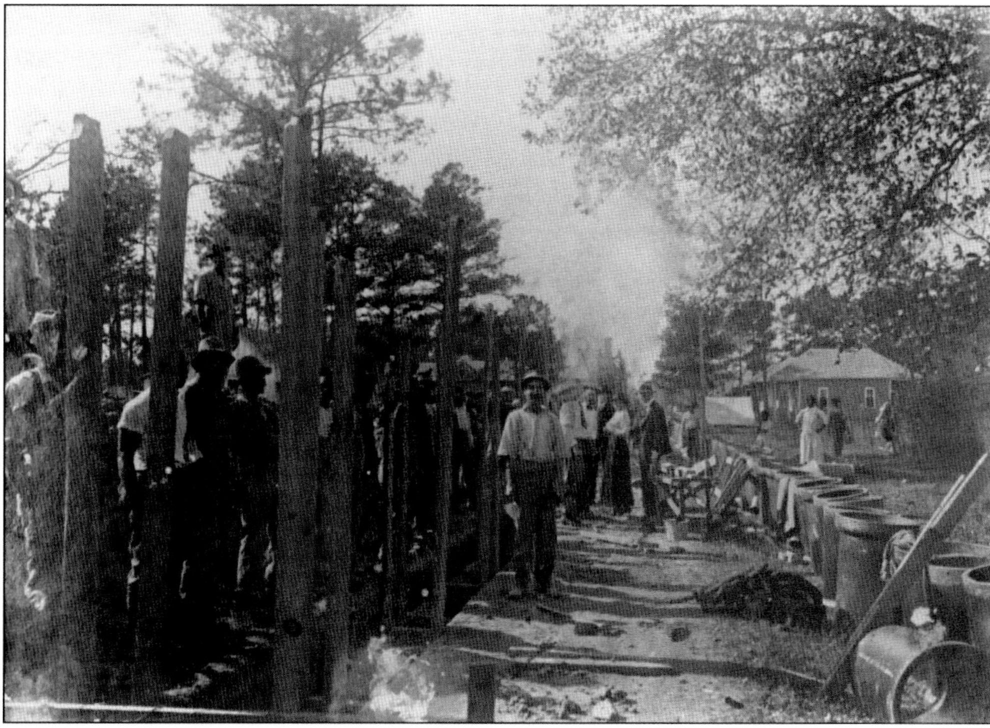

The Hammond water and sewage system is under construction in this c. 1917 photograph looking west on East Coleman Avenue from South Chestnut Street. The Will H. Thomas residence is barely visible in the center background. Thomas was the streets commissioner from 1921 to 1925 under Mayor Charles C. Carter.

The large two-story home of George Neelis and family was located at 501 North Pine Street. Neelis was a co-owner of the Neelis General Emporium with his brothers Frank and John. The Neelis children are seated on the lawn in the early 1900s. The only child that has been identified is Robert Corbin, the boy standing in the back. The house no longer stands.

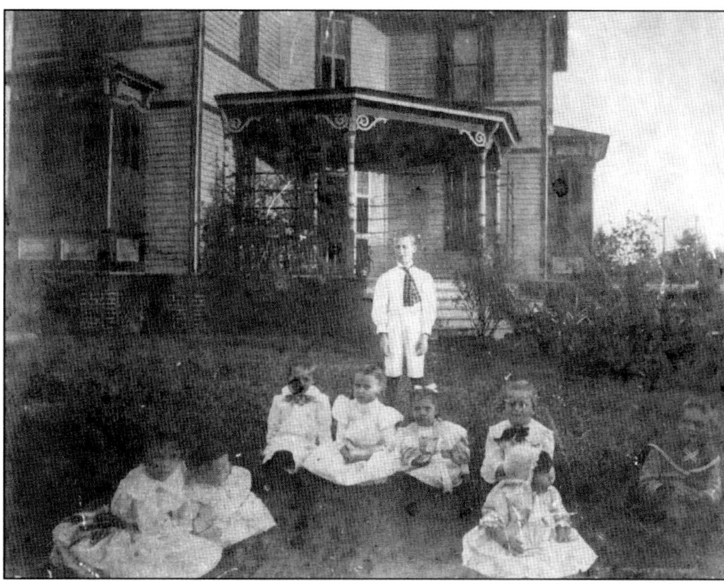

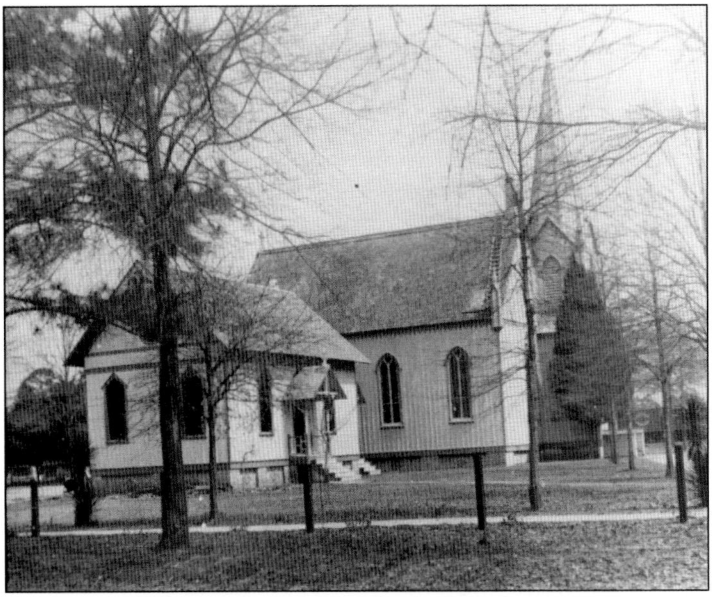

The oldest church building in Hammond, Grace Episcopal Church, was built in 1876 on land donated by Charles E. Cate. The first service in this country Gothic-style church was conducted by Bishop Joseph Pere Wilmer on March 12, 1876. The church was consecrated on October 28, 1888, in memory of Cate's late wife, Mertie. Additional buildings were added later. The Cates are buried in the cemetery behind the church.

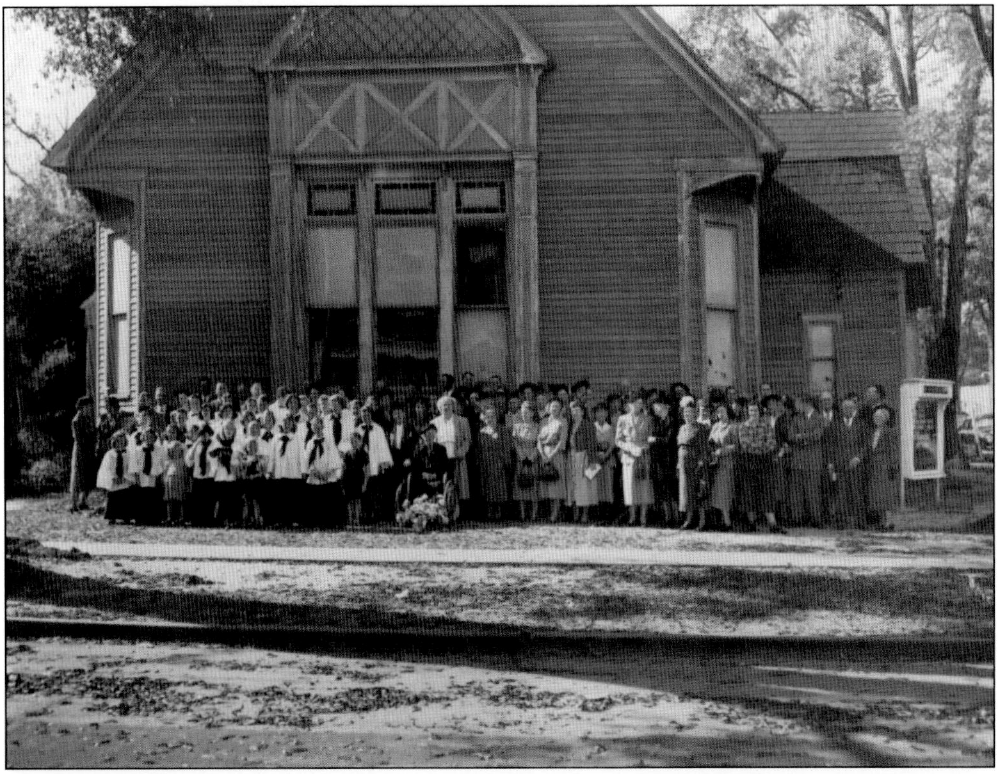

The Federated Church, located at the corner of Thomas and Magnolia Streets, was built by the Congregational Church after its original building was destroyed by fire in 1900. The Congregational Church and the Presbyterian Church, which had purchased property diagonally opposite, held joint services in the building from 1916 until 1950, when the new Presbyterian church for the merged congregations was constructed at the corner of Charles and Spruce Streets.

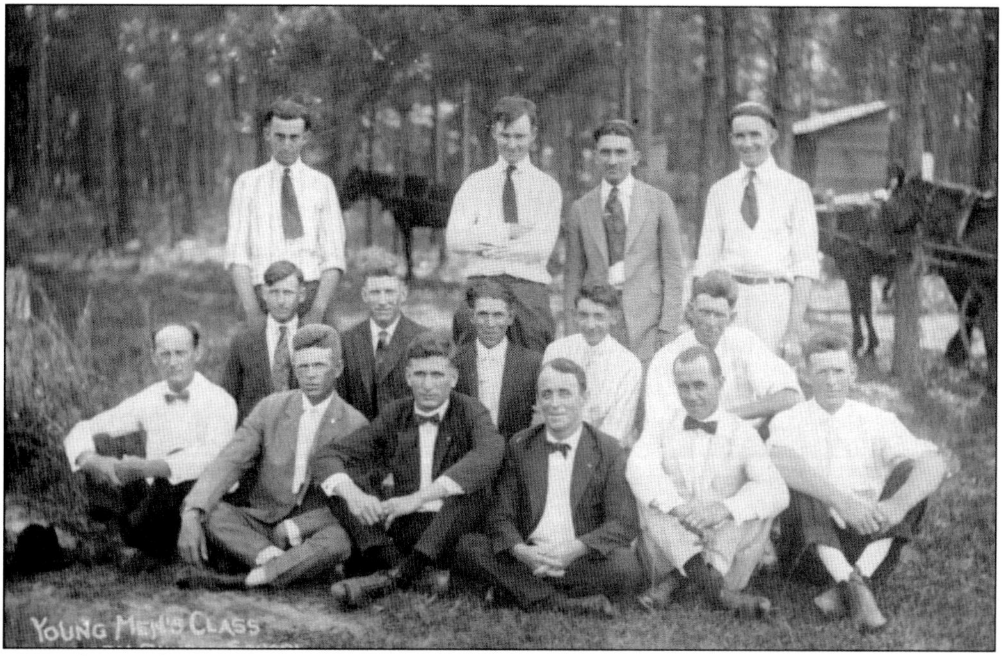

Located on Highway 190 near the airport, the men's Sunday school class of Zenobia Union Sunday School poses outside for a photograph in 1921. Dr. Lucius McGehee is the fourth man from the left, seated in the front row. Although a member of the First United Methodist Church, McGehee enjoyed attending the Sunday afternoon class at Zenobia. He was also one of the founders of Hammond Junior College.

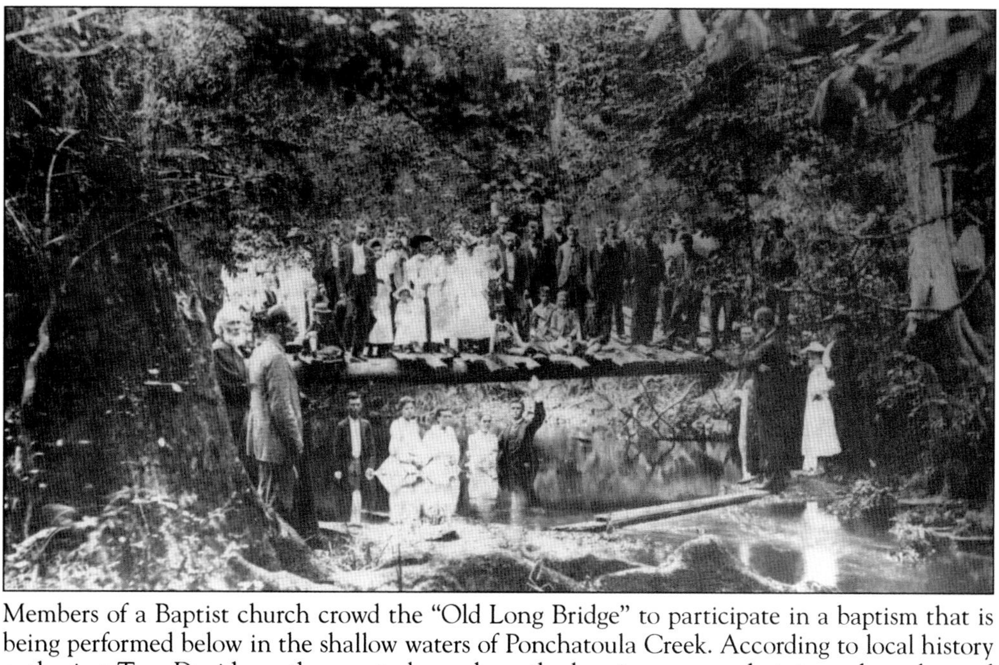

Members of a Baptist church crowd the "Old Long Bridge" to participate in a baptism that is being performed below in the shallow waters of Ponchatoula Creek. According to local history enthusiast Tom Davidson, the exact place where the baptisms were administered was located close to where East Church Street crosses Ponchatoula Creek and was the preferred place for local churches to perform baptisms.

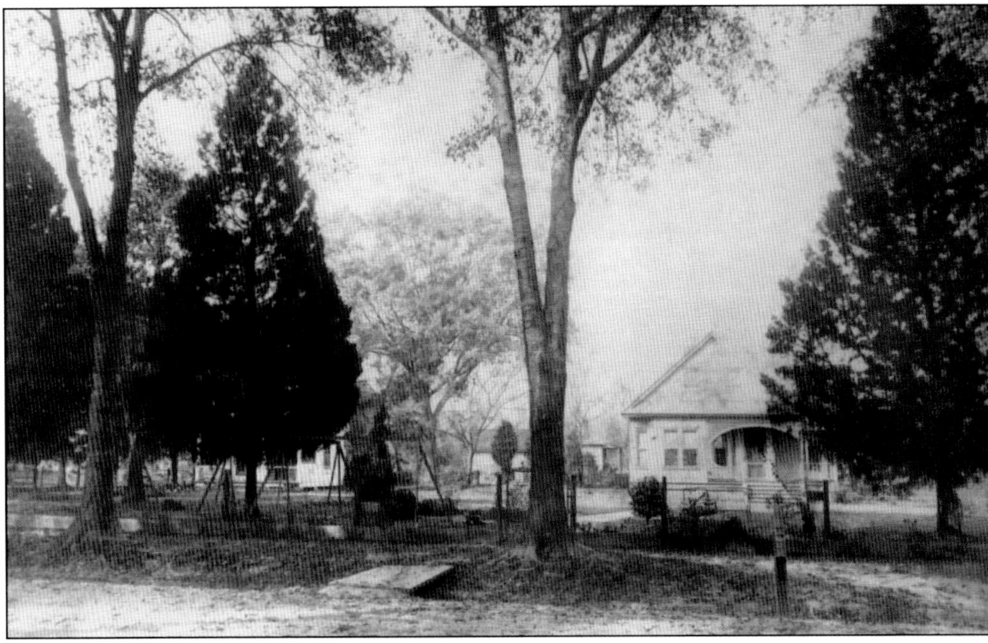

The Robert A. Corbin Jr. house was located in the center of Morrison Square facing West Robert Street. The second house to be built on the square, around 1870, it joined the house on the left, built around 1860, which was occupied by Kentucky settlers Robert Wilson and Henrietta Maria Mann Morrison and, later, their grandson Randolph Corbin. Corbin was married to Katherine ("Katie") Morrison, sister of Benjamin Morrison. Below, the Benjamin Morrison house was built around 1905 on Morrison Square. Benjamin, son of Robert and Henrietta, was a prominent merchant and banker and the father of James, a lawyer and Sixth District congressman from 1942 to 1966. The house still stands on Oak Street, across from Grace Memorial Church. Standing in front is Clementine Gibson with either Sally or Margaret Morrison, the daughters of Benjamin and Florence Morrison.

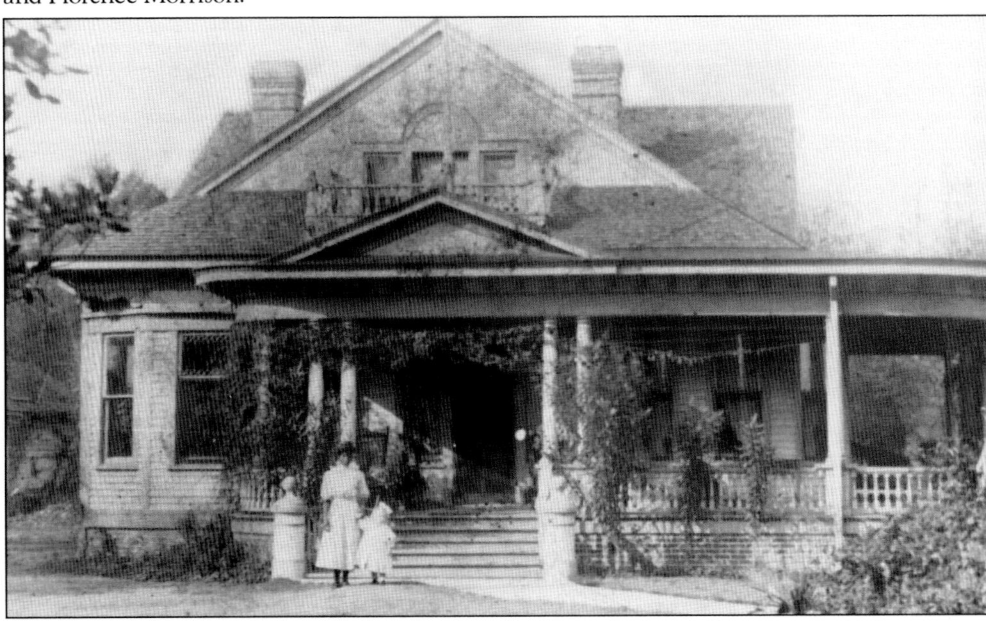

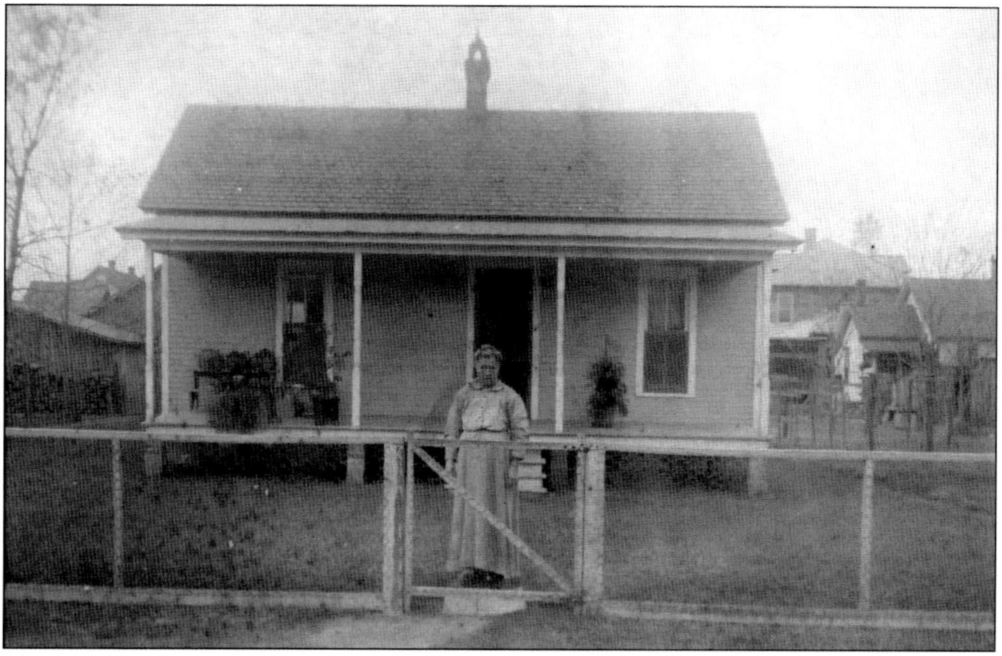

This house, located in the North Holly Street area, belonged to John W. Skinner. Skinner's wife, Clarissa, is pictured at the gate of the modest wood frame home. Skinner served as clerk and tax collector for Hammond during several administrations, beginning in 1893 and ending in 1913 when he was elected mayor of Hammond, until 1917. His wife died while he was serving as mayor.

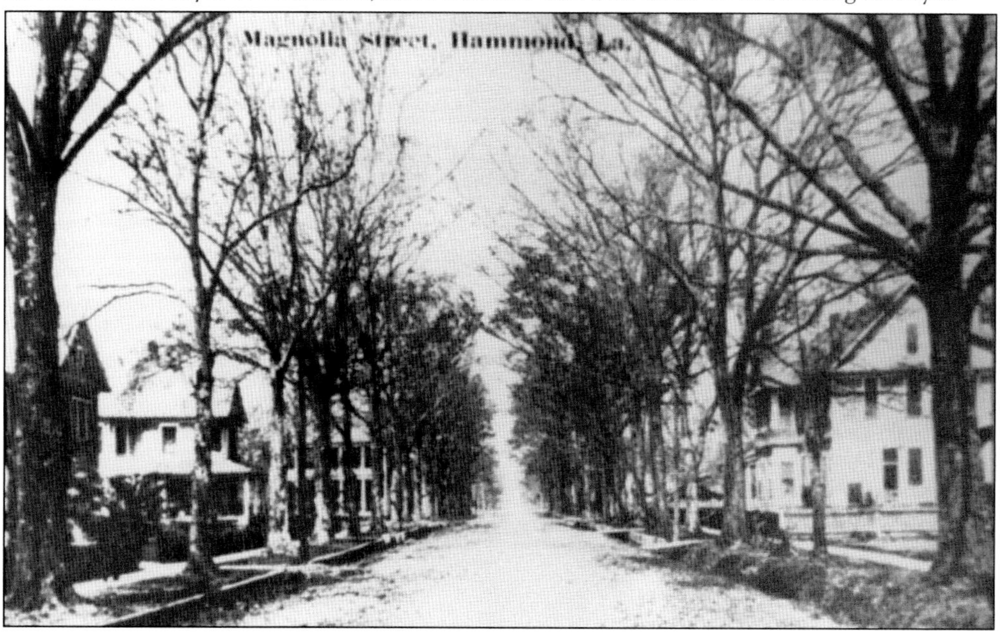

This early view of Magnolia Street looks north from West Thomas Street. The family of Henry P. Mitchell, first president of Citizens National Bank, lived in the first home on the left for many years. The Leon J. Patenotte family at one time occupied the first house on the right. Both houses still stand and have been renovated. Cate Square, though barely visible, is just beyond the Patenotte house.

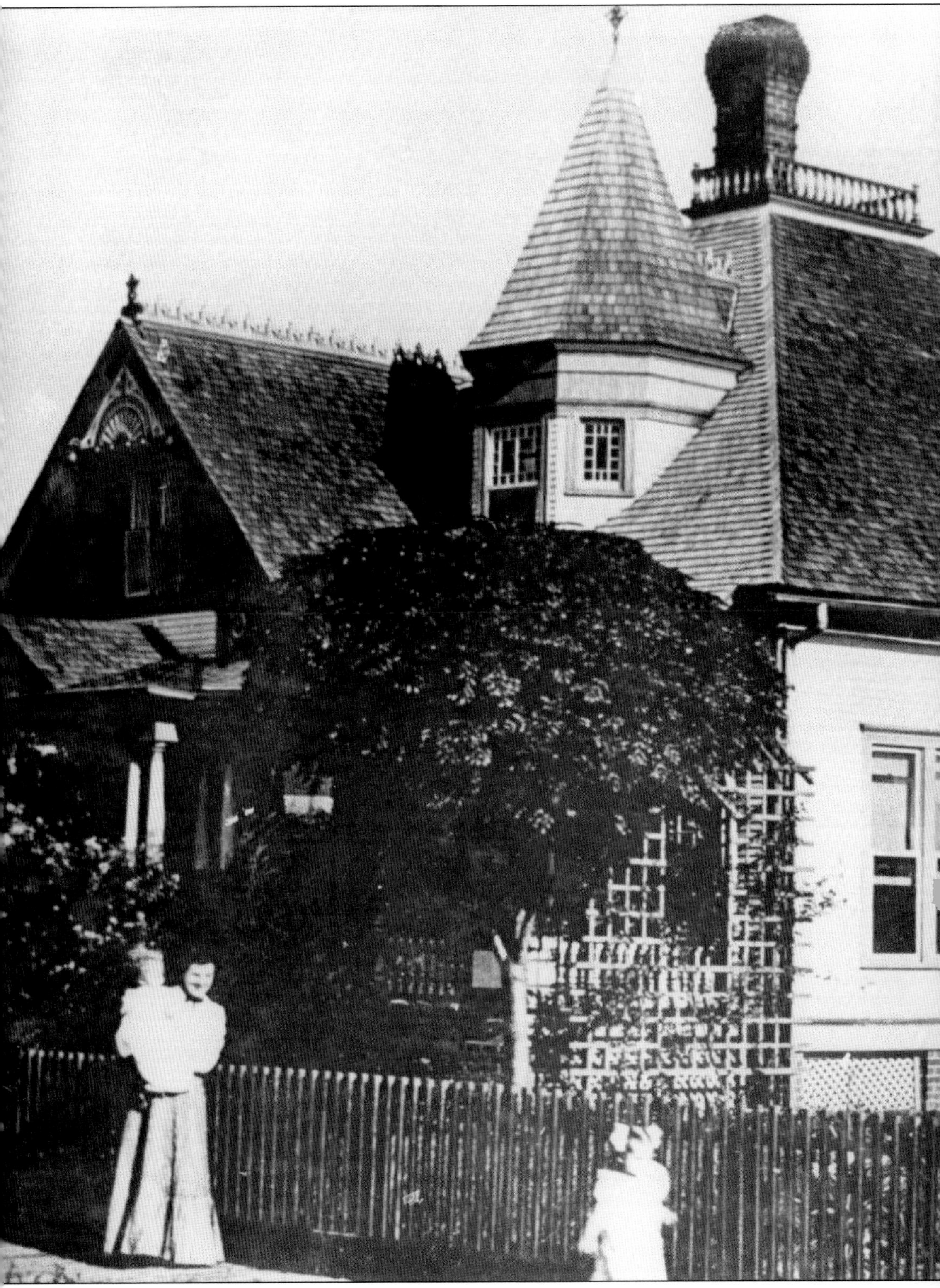

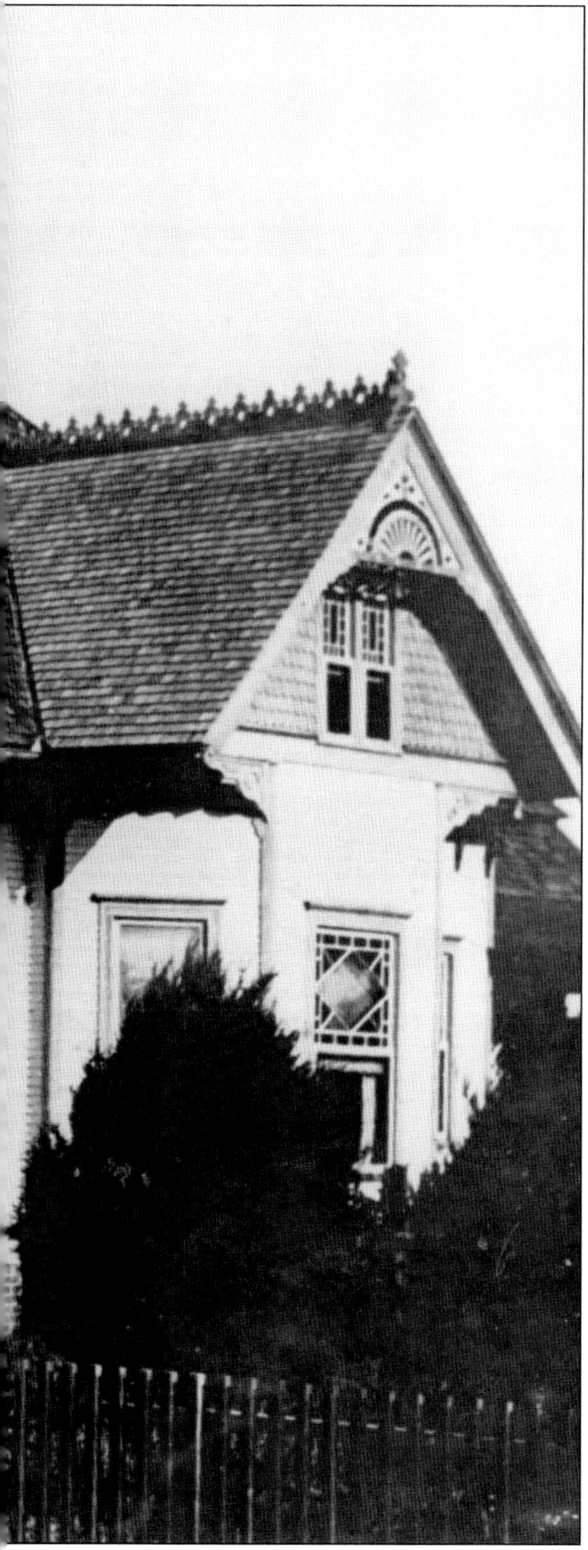

Built in 1895 by Ralph and Harriet June, part owners of Hammond Lumber Company, the June House was located on the 400 block of East Coleman Avenue. The Queen Anne–style house featured a beautiful cupola and hand-carved paneled walls by John Voss, a German master carpenter. One room had silhouettes and initials of the couple carved into the wall paneling. Placed in the National Register of Historic Places in 1983 by then-owners Charles and Barbara Haney, the house burned in August 1986 in a suspicious fire that the fire department ruled as arson. According to the Baton Rouge *Morning Advocate* (February 18, 1987), the owners were suspected of setting the fire but were cleared. Thomas Metz, an acquaintance of Barbara Haney, was arrested in Texas in January 1987 and pleaded guilty to arson in 1989.

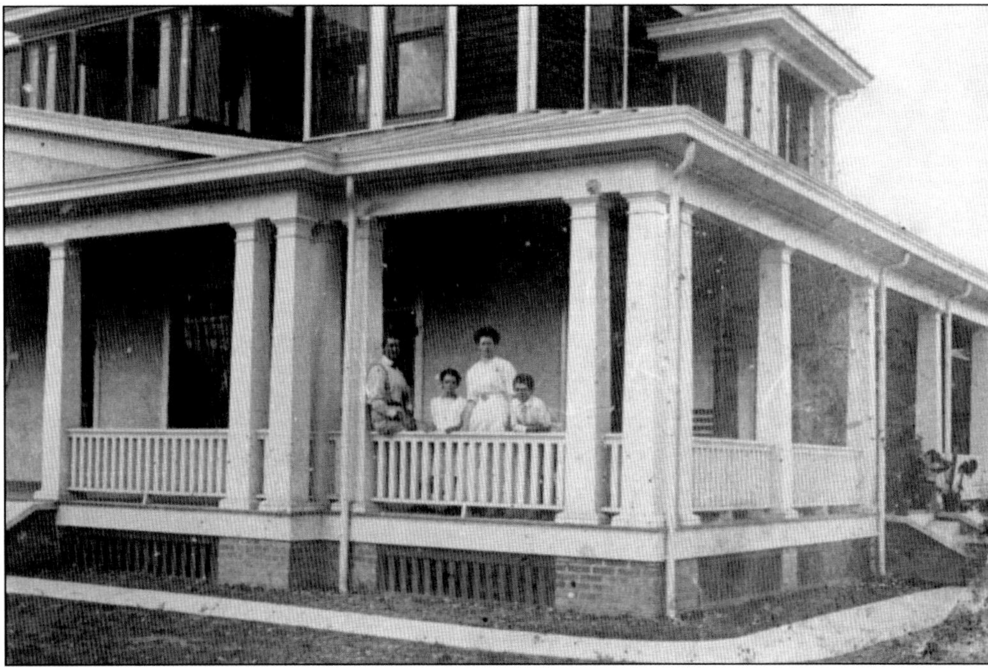

The Michael Seib home, which still stands at 210 North Cherry Street, is shown in this 1904 photograph of Seib, his wife Leona Yokum Seib, and their two children, Wallace and Helen. Seib owned the popular novelty store Noah's Ark. Helen married Andrew M. Edwards Jr., a mayor of nearby Ponchatoula.

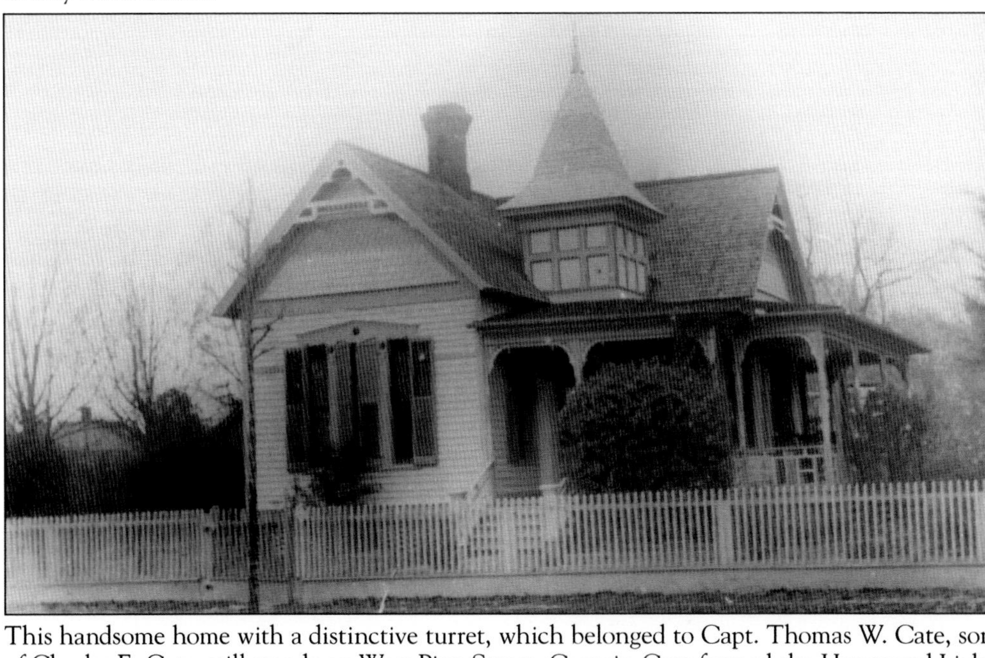

This handsome home with a distinctive turret, which belonged to Capt. Thomas W. Cate, son of Charles E. Cate, still stands on West Pine Street. Captain Cate formed the Hammond Light Guards, who fought in the Spanish-American War. He later became a contractor, was secretary of Hammond's Citizens' Improvement League, and served as mayor in 1896 and as a councilman for several years.

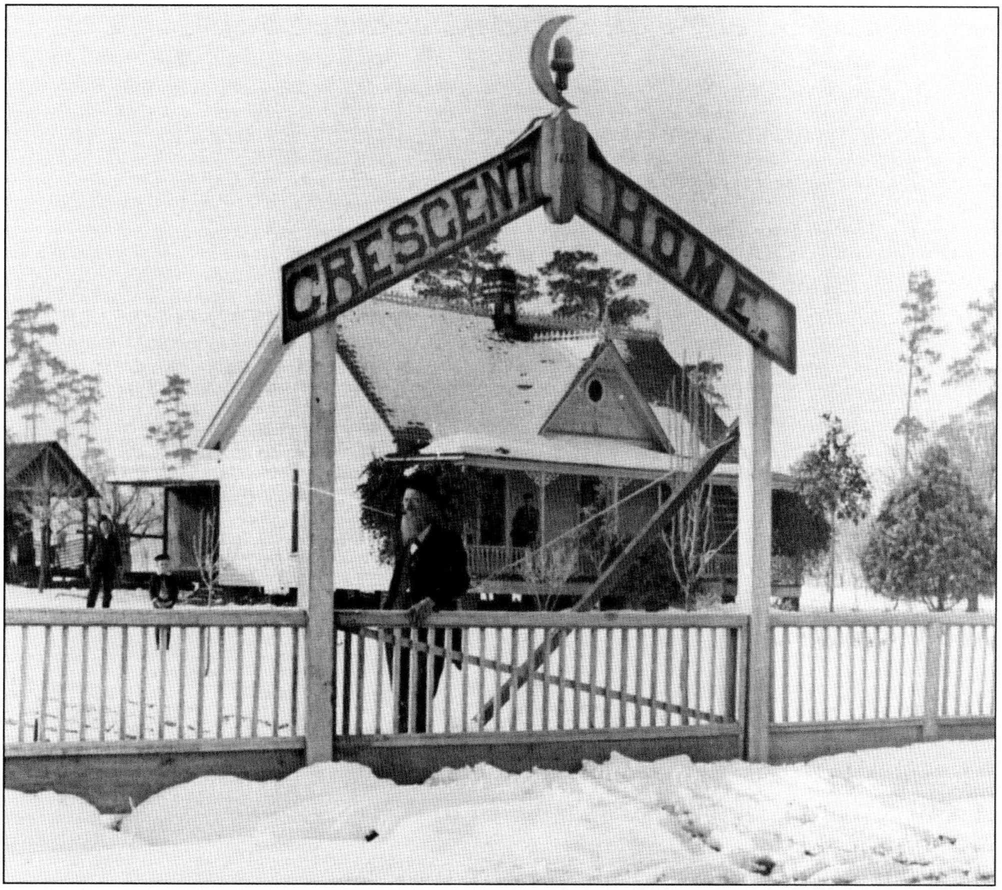

At the foot of South Cherry Street is the Crescent Home, owned by L.C. Reed and, later, Alfred E. Karlton. At one time, the house was supposedly known as the "Old Soldier's Haven," a home for Confederate veterans. The significance of the acorn and crescent moon on top of the gate is not known. Karlton shipped fruit from his orchard and milk to New Orleans. He was killed in the line of duty as a constable in 1917. The photograph above may have been taken during one of the snowfalls in the 1890s. The photograph below offers a panoramic view of the property, with the residence on the right and the barn on the left. The house still stands, but a second story has been added.

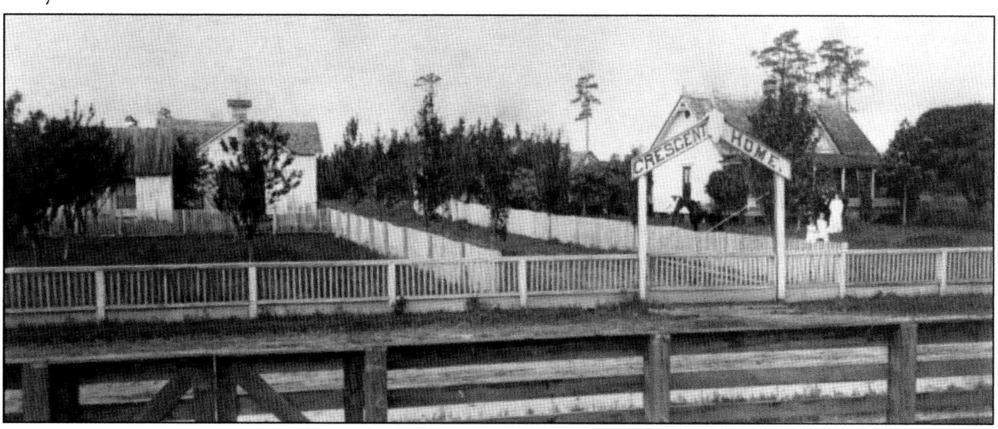

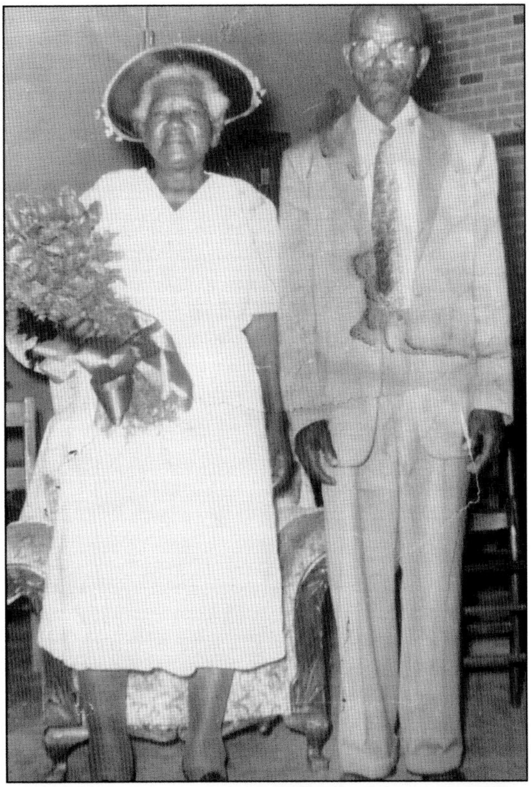

The Greenfield Missionary Baptist Church was built in 1875 on West Coleman Avenue as the Hammond Station Colored Baptist Church on land given by the Cate family. In 1957, the church exchanged land with the Tangipahoa Parish School Board and rebuilt across the street. Shown are the Reverend W.M. Mixon, who became pastor in 1930 and was instrumental in the church's ensuing growth, and his wife, Callie. (Courtesy of Cathy Martin.)

Christian Church Sunday school participants pose in front of the Christian Tabernacle on South Oak Street. The church later moved to the corner of Cherry and Charles Streets in a building sponsored by Frederic Reimers and his wife, Fay, who was director of music and Sunday school superintendent from 1916 to 1961. The original tabernacle became the Harmony Baking Company, operated by J.H. Meyers, who was famed for his Butter-Nut Bread.

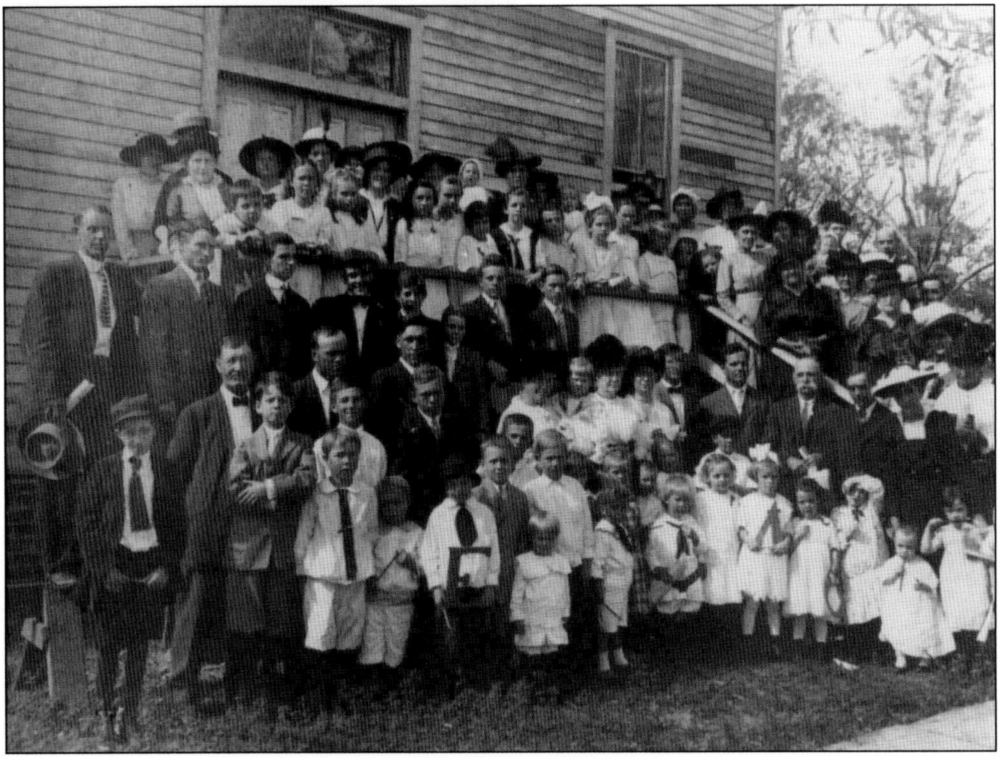

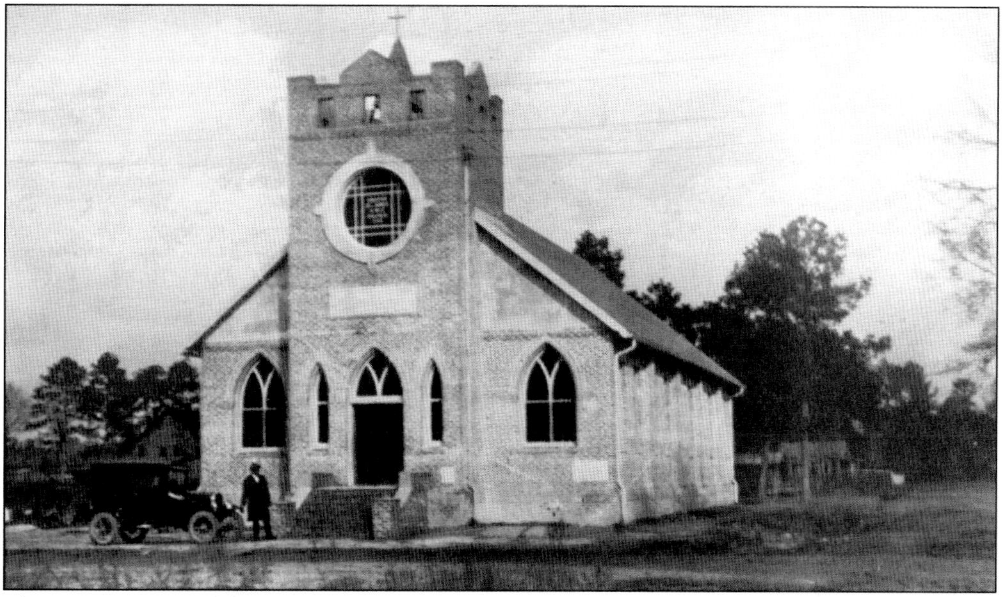

The congregation of the Greater St. James AME Church was organized in 1867 by Rev. Charles Daggs and worshipped in various venues until a church was built on the 400 block of East Thomas Street. The church depicted here was erected in 1925 to replace the Thomas Street church and still sits at the corner of East Michigan and North Holly Streets.

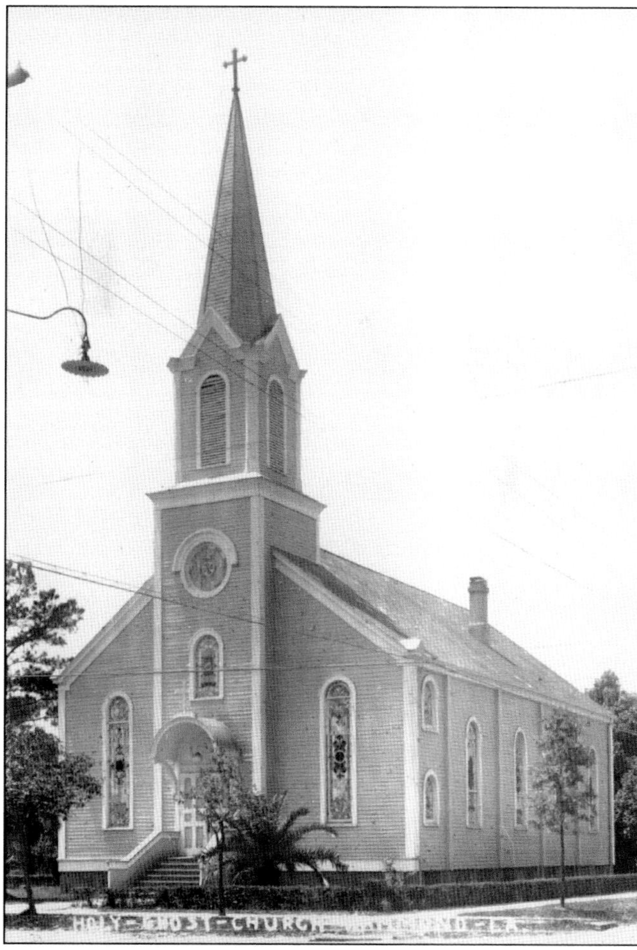

Fr. Leander Roth performed the first Catholic Mass in Hammond in 1890. Services took place in the home of John Neelis's widow, Susanna. After years of worshipping in the Neelis warehouse, the new Holy Ghost Catholic Church was dedicated on November 23, 1902. Since the congregation had outgrown its 1902 building, this 1930s photograph reflects changes made before a renovation doubled capacity in 1937. (Courtesy of Holy Ghost Church.)

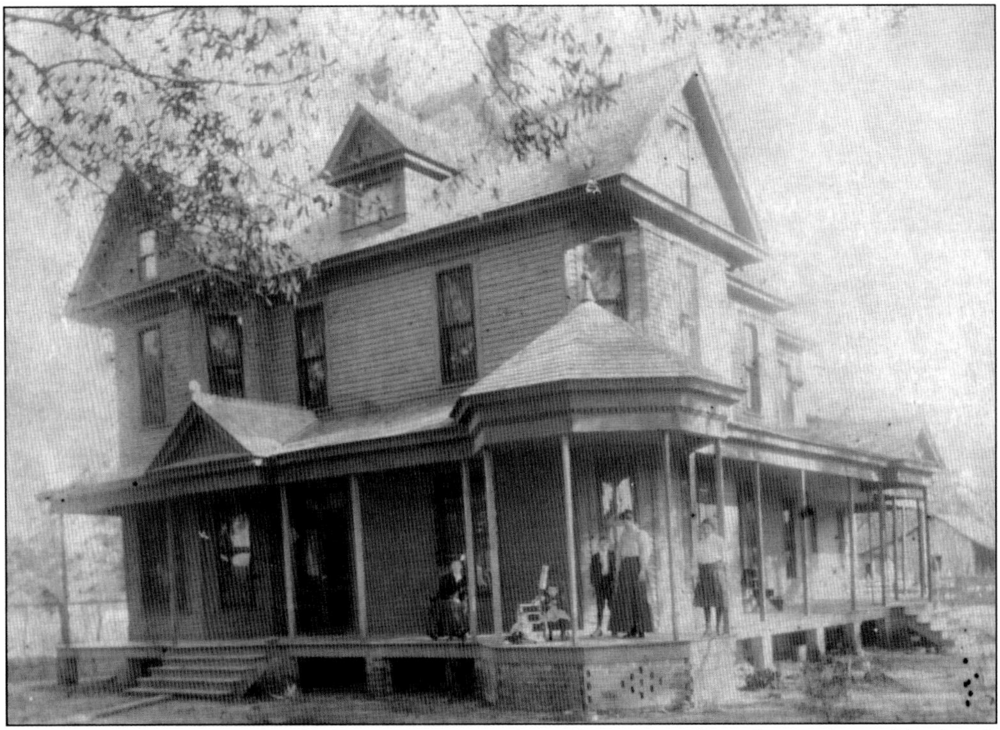

The Queen Anne–style Hughes House, at 300 North Holly Street in the Adams-Lily neighborhood, was built at the turn of the century by Jefferson Davis Hughes, grandson of Peter Hammond, to accommodate his extensive family. The house remained in the possession of the Hughes family for 100 years and is currently operating as a bed-and-breakfast.

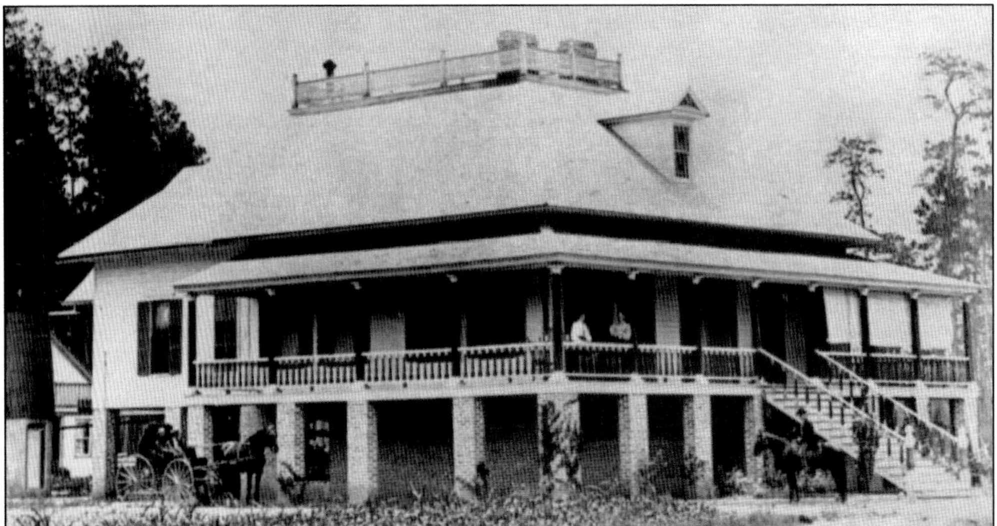

Capt. F.A. Stinson of Bath, Maine, settled in Hammond and built his home, "Villars," which was named for the family of his wife, Marie. The house was constructed in 1896 on land that would later become the Hammond Airfield. Stinson had traveled all over the world and was in command of several ships, including the *Prussia* and the *Scotia*. The house, which featured a widow's walk, was used for an Enlisted Men's Club and later demolished.

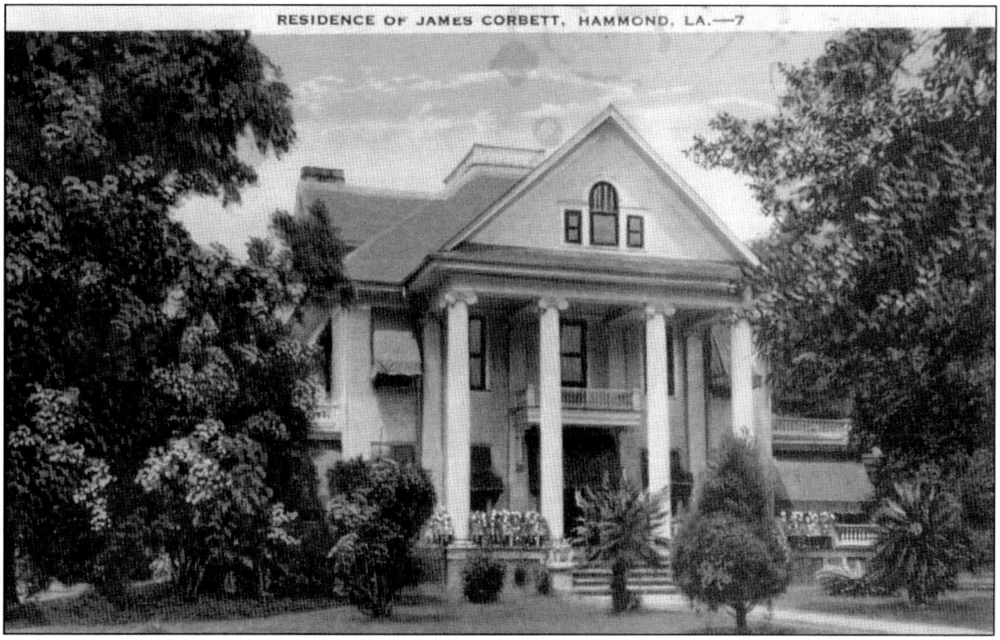

This stately home on West Thomas Street was built in 1900 by lumberman E.P. Denkman, originally of Rock Island, Illinois. The house was constructed of longleaf pine lumber in the Southern Colonial style and features grand columns and balustrades covering the porch. The house was later owned by James Corbett, John W. Patenotte, and Hans and Marietta Reimers Schneider, niece of Denkman.

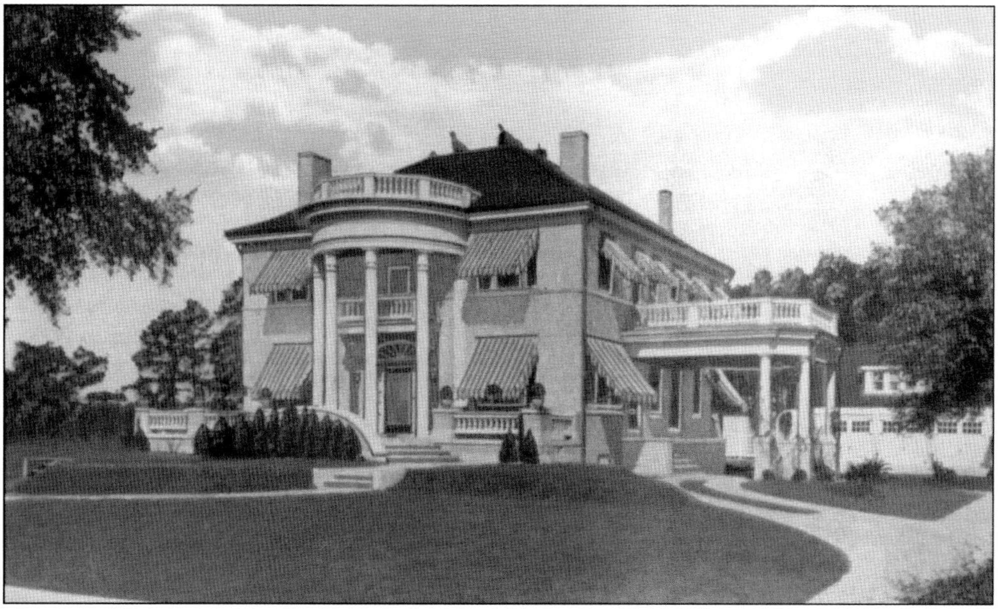

The grand home of the John B. Nalty family, located on the corner of West Church and North Hazel Streets, graces a Hammond postcard. Nalty, owner of Hammond Lumber Company, built the house, which was designed by local architect Albert E. Tolle, around 1906. Nalty's son Raymond later lived in the house. The Wiley Sharp Jr. family purchased the house in the 1960s.

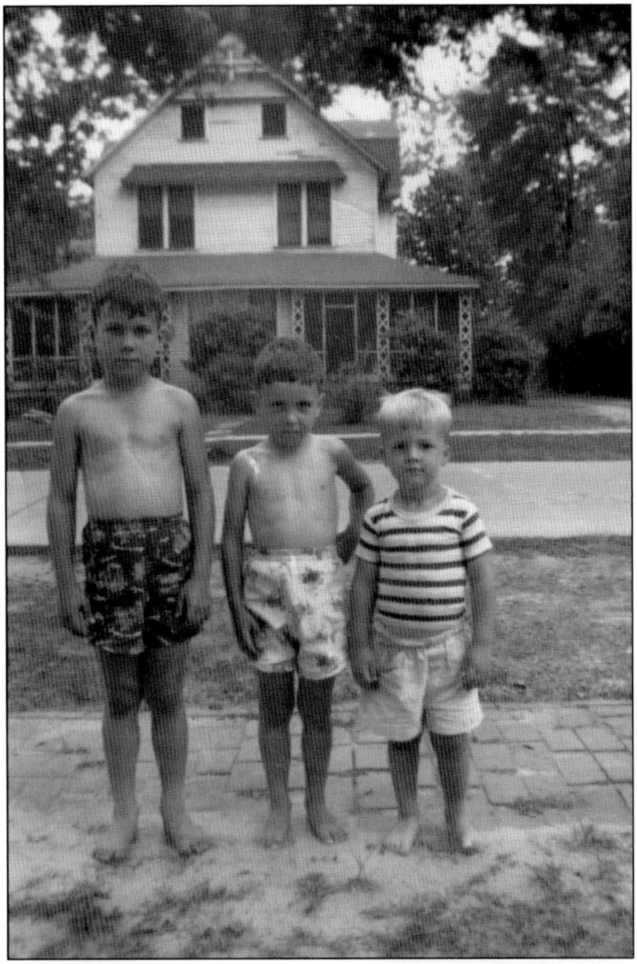

From left to right, Rodney and Brian Kidder and their cousin Hall Starnes Jr. pose in Cate Square with the Starnes home behind them in the late 1940s. The house, located on the 200 block of West Robert Street, was a "double," with two families occupying the house. The homes on that block of Robert were demolished and replaced by a large apartment complex. (Courtesy of Hall Starnes.)

Hall Starnes Jr. swings in Cate Square around 1948. The second home of Charles E. Cate and family can be seen directly behind the child. The park, originally part of Cate's property, has provided many hours of enjoyment for the citizens of Hammond and is still an integral site for community gatherings, such as caroling in the park at Christmas and numerous concerts and fairs. (Courtesy of Hall Starnes.)

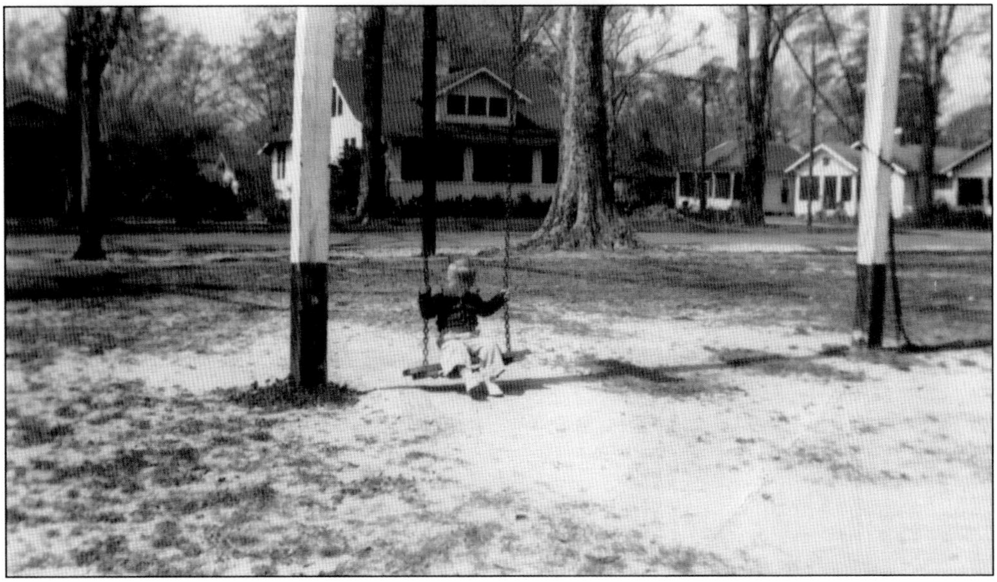

Five

Education

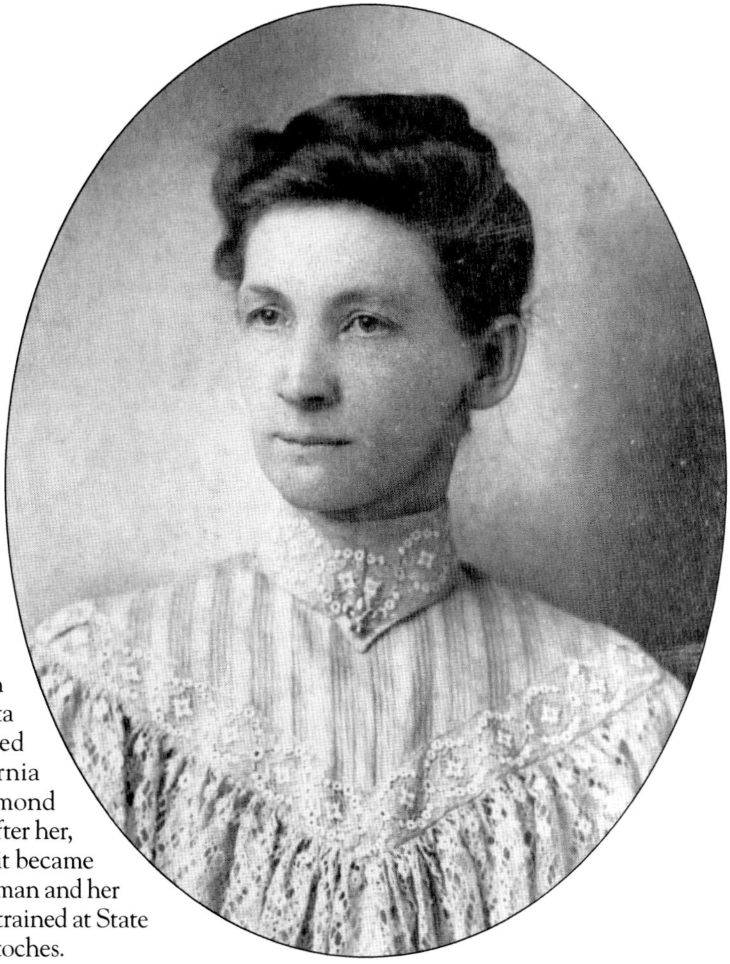

One of Hammond's "legends" is Annie Eastman, a devoted teacher who was born in Maine, lived in Minnesota and Missouri, and moved to Hammond via California in 1889. The new Hammond High of 1924 was named after her, retaining her name when it became an elementary school. Eastman and her younger sister Zylpha were trained at State Normal School in Natchitoches.

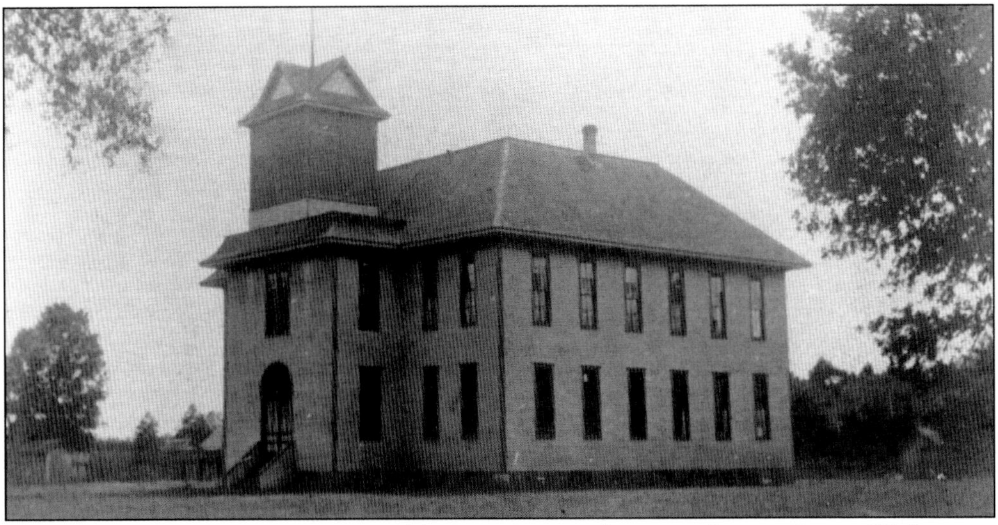

Around 1866, Charles E. Cate arranged for Mary Louise, the sister of writer George Washington Cable, to come to Hammond as a teacher. She remained until around 1885. She taught in a private home and then in a building shared with a store, post office, and freight depot. As the population increased, this classroom was replaced by a one-room home, then other temporary venues, and finally a schoolhouse in 1876. In 1893, the city built the Hammond School, which included primary through high school students, on West Morris Avenue between Magnolia and Pine Streets. The first senior class graduated in 1897 and consisted of six young women; by 1909, the school had grown to 87 high school students. Below, Hammond School's Class of 1903 is pictured with teacher Annie Eastman (seated in the center). The building was moved to Coleman Avenue for African American students.

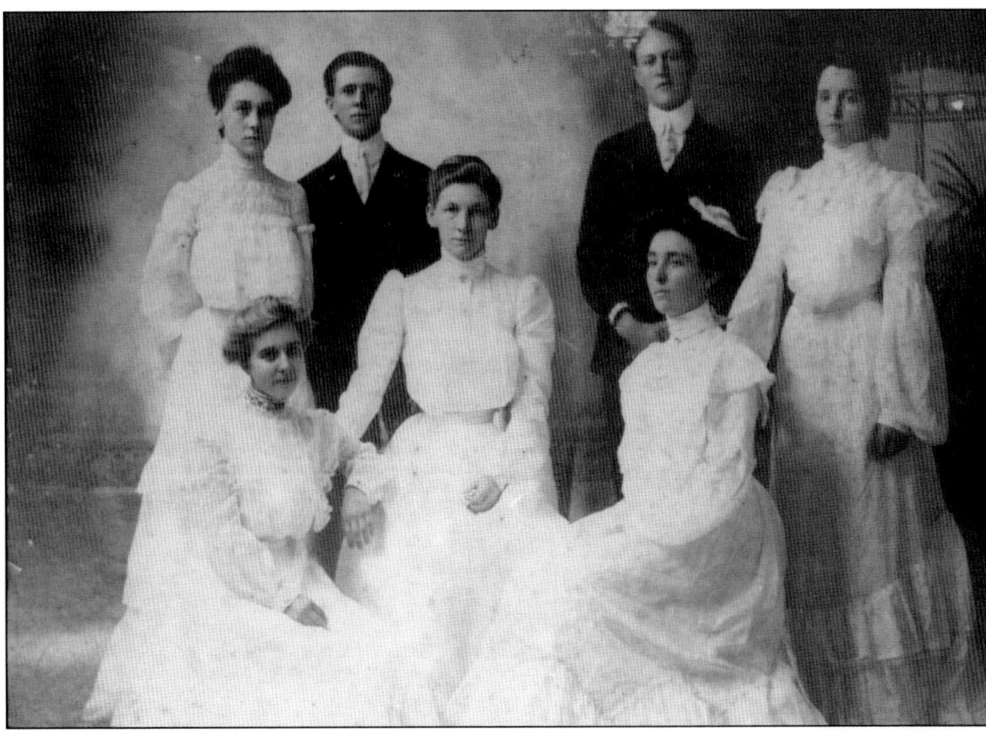

The first teacher at the Hammond School was Nettie Mann Morrison, who taught regular classes as well as piano and dancing. She retired and was replaced by Kate and Ella Waterman and Etta Fermley. Here, Hammond's school teachers pose for a c. 1900 photograph. From left to right are (first row) Ida Van Patten, ? Crandall, and Lucy Braselman; (second row) Zylpha Eastman, Hattie Williams, Annie Eastman, and Lizzie Walker.

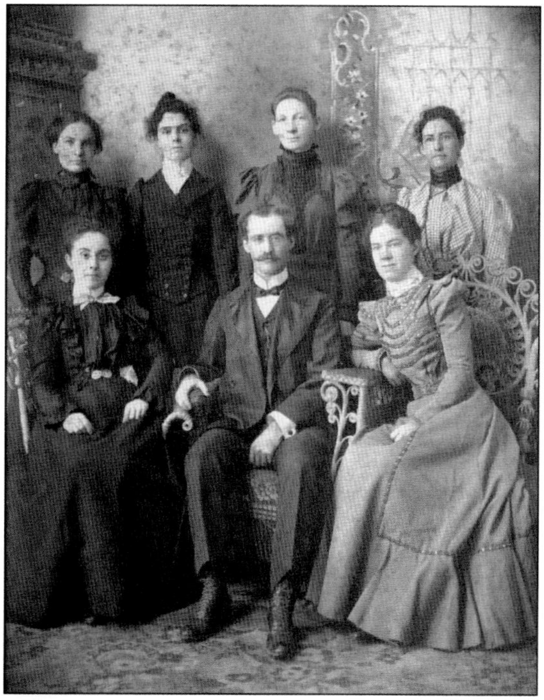

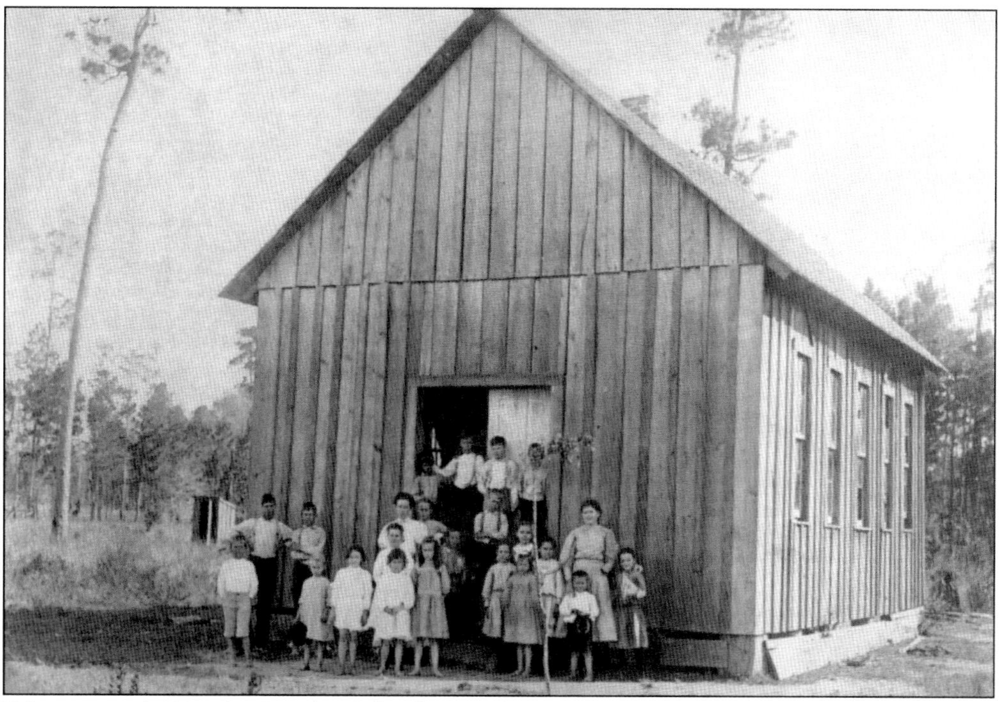

Taken around 1914, the Zenobia School, one of several one-room rural schoolhouses, operated east of Hammond on what is now Highway 190. Other rural schools of the era included Happy Woods School and New Beulah School, both located west of town. The first African American school, known as "The Colored School House," was donated by the St. James AME Church, and its first schoolteacher was Lizzie Booth.

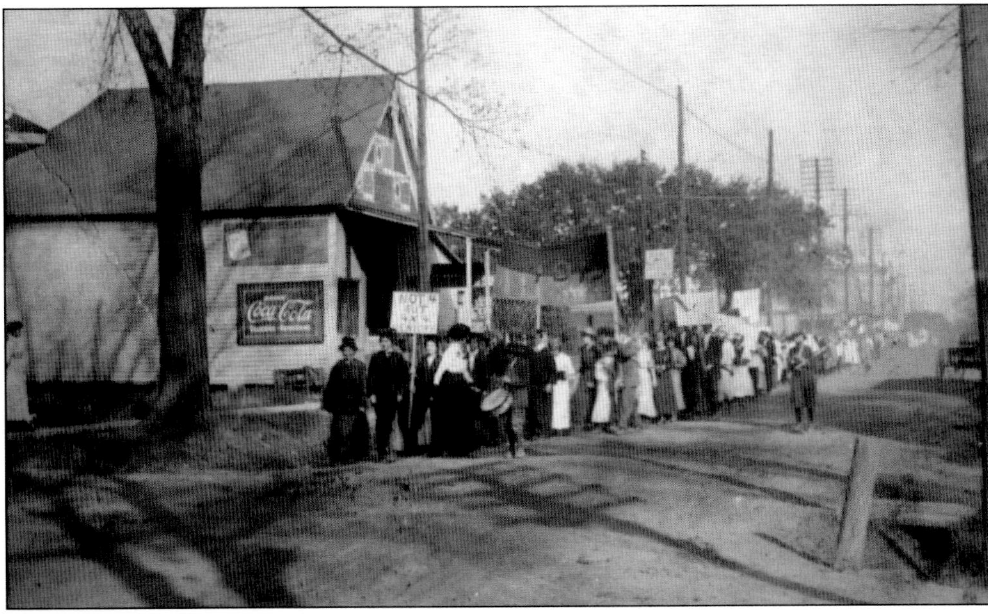

Hammond High students march in a parade advocating a new school around 1907. By 1909, 508 students were enrolled in the Hammond School, and a four-room annex—containing three elementary classes and a domestic science department—was added to address overcrowding. By 1912, there were 610 students enrolled, and a bond issue and property tax provided a new school in 1914 on South Holly Street.

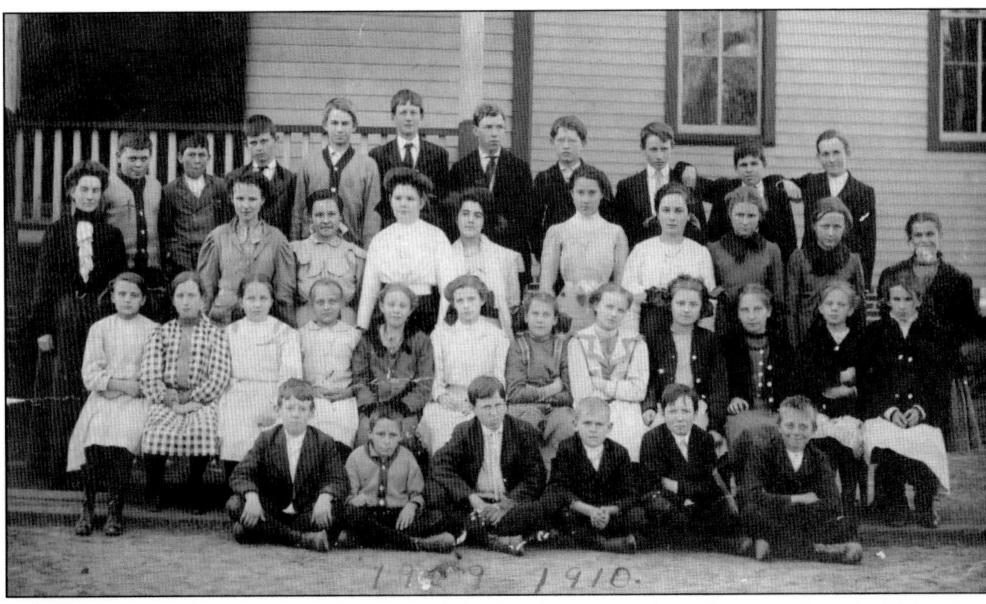

Zylpha Eastman's classes during the 1909–1910 school year pose for a photograph at the Hammond School. Zylpha, a member of the school's first graduating class of 1897, was the sister of Annie Eastman and, like her sister, a lifelong teacher. She lived on South Cherry Street with Annie and died in 1962.

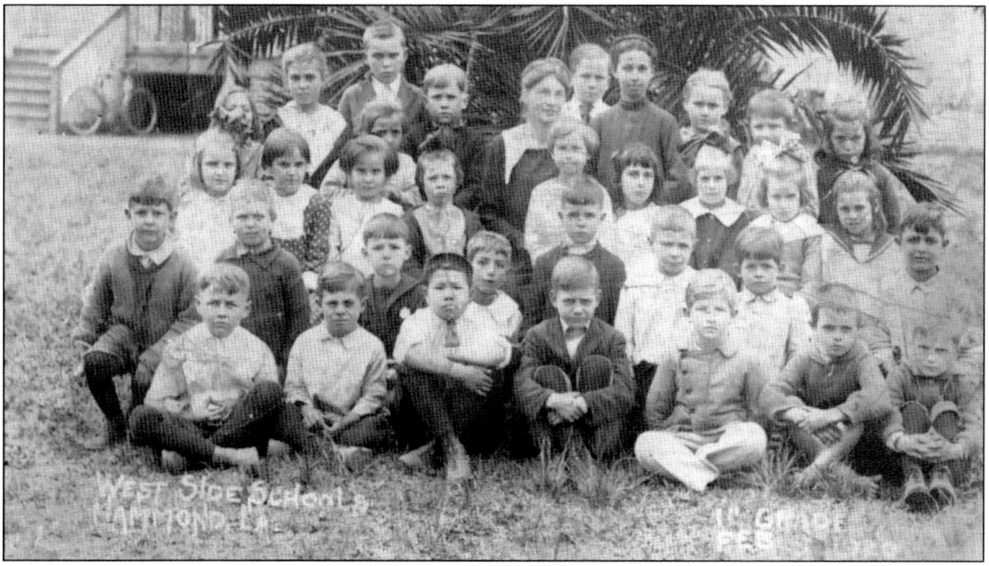

A February 1920 portrait of this first-grade class, consisting of 35 students, is labeled "West Side Schools." The teacher in the center of the fourth row appears to be Zylpha Eastman. It is not clear which schools constituted the "West Side Schools" or where the image was taken.

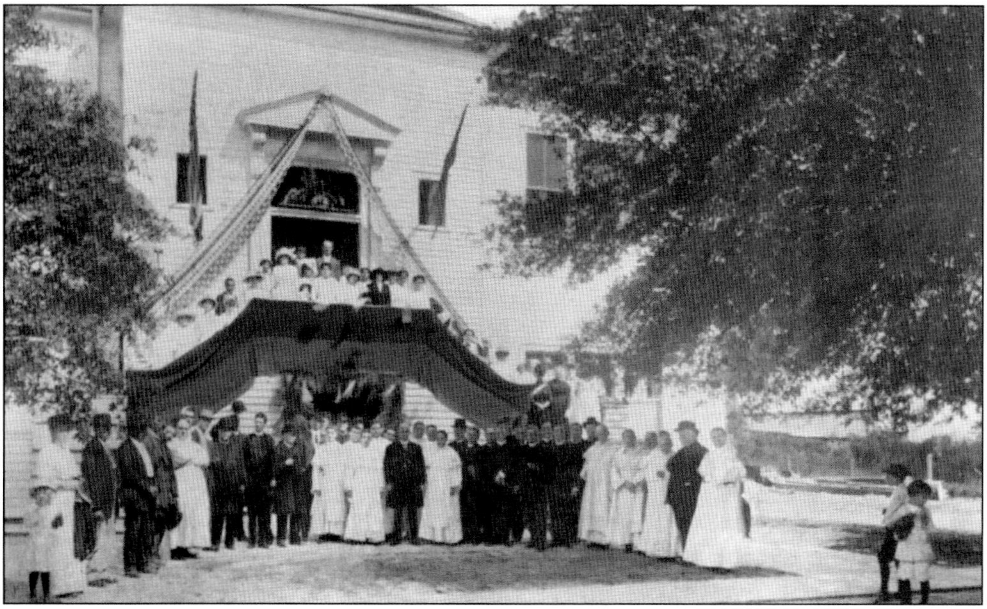

A crowd gathers at the 1913 dedication of St. Thomas Aquinas School. Located in the convent, the original school opened in October 1912 with 30 students in first through eighth grades. The cramped quarters meant that upper grades were taught in the parlor and lower grades in the dining room. The school's name was changed to Holy Ghost School in June 1949, when new buildings were constructed.

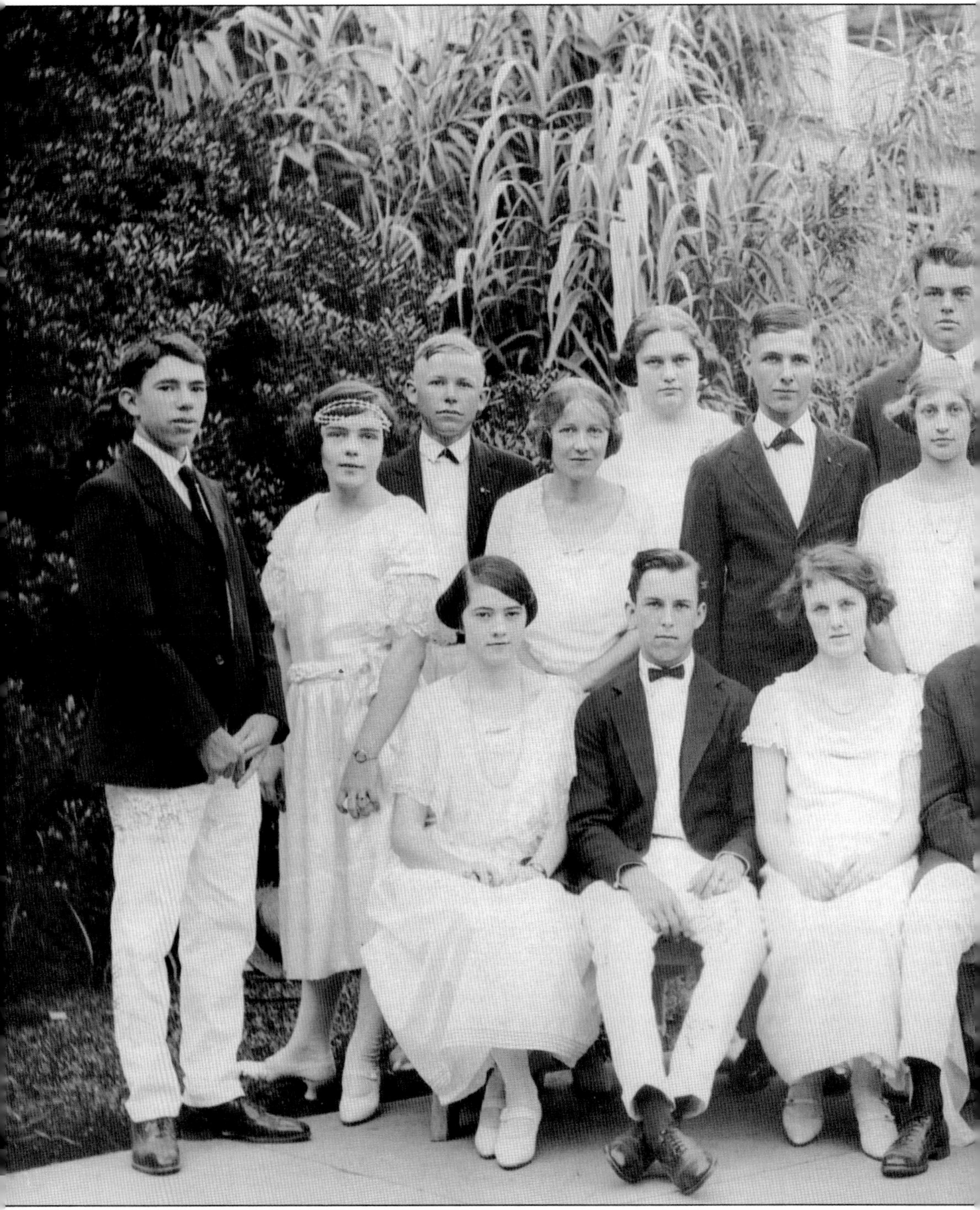

The Hammond High Class of 1923 poses in front of the Oaks Hotel. This was the last class to graduate from the high school when it was located on Holly Street. The valedictorian of the class was future Pulitzer prize–winning journalist William Hodding Carter Jr. (standing, fourth from the right). After graduation, Carter attended Bowdoin College in Maine and studied journalism at Columbia. Carter wrote for several newspapers, as well as United Press and Associated Press.

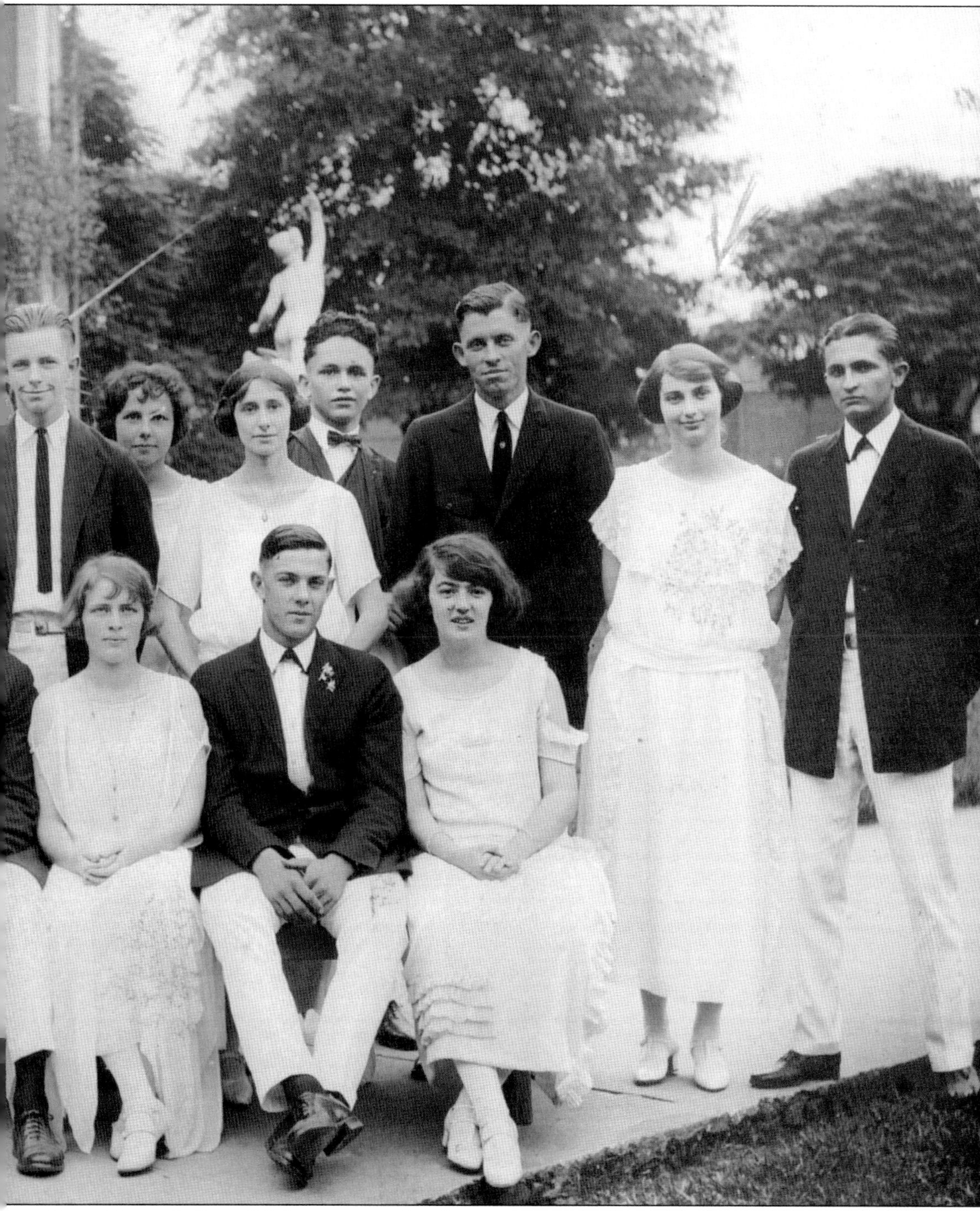

He and his wife, Betty Werlein, returned to Hammond, where they started the *Daily Courier*, an anti–Huey Long newspaper, before moving on to other endeavors. Carter is known for his writings about civil rights and was awarded a Pulitzer Prize was for his coverage of Japanese treatment of American prisoners of war. (Courtesy of Marion Ruth Chandler.)

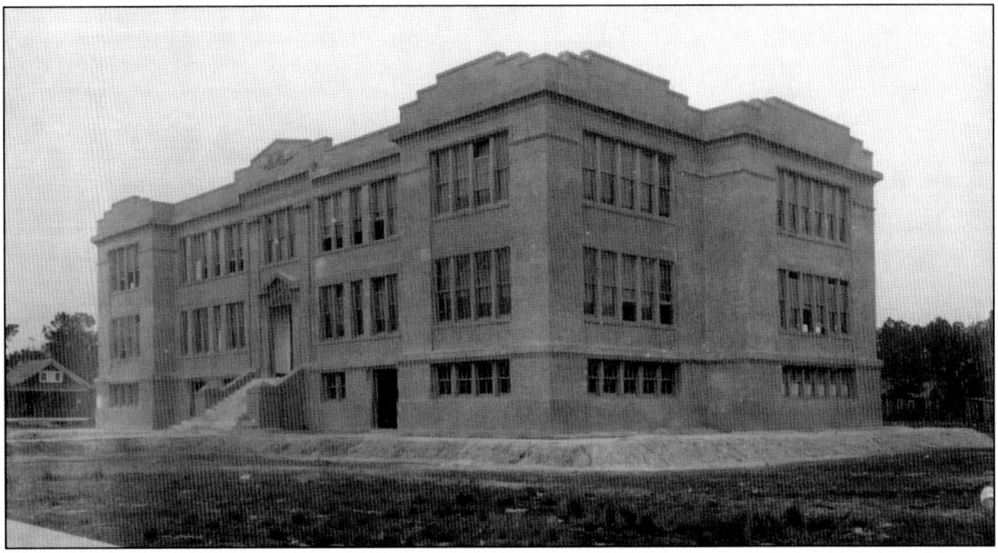

Built in 1914 and opened for the following school year, Hammond High School (above) was designed by Albert Tolle and located on the corner of East Thomas and Orange Streets. The elementary grades occupied the first floor and the high school was on the second floor. J. Caldwell was principal, and Annie Eastman was assistant principal. Eastman would remain in this position until 1939. Within eight years, the building was already inadequate for the number of students, so another building was funded and constructed in 1924 on West Morris Avenue. Annie Eastman High School (below) usually referred to as Hammond High School, added a gymnasium, track field, and football stadium in 1929. After school desegregation in 1969, the school became Annie Eastman Elementary.

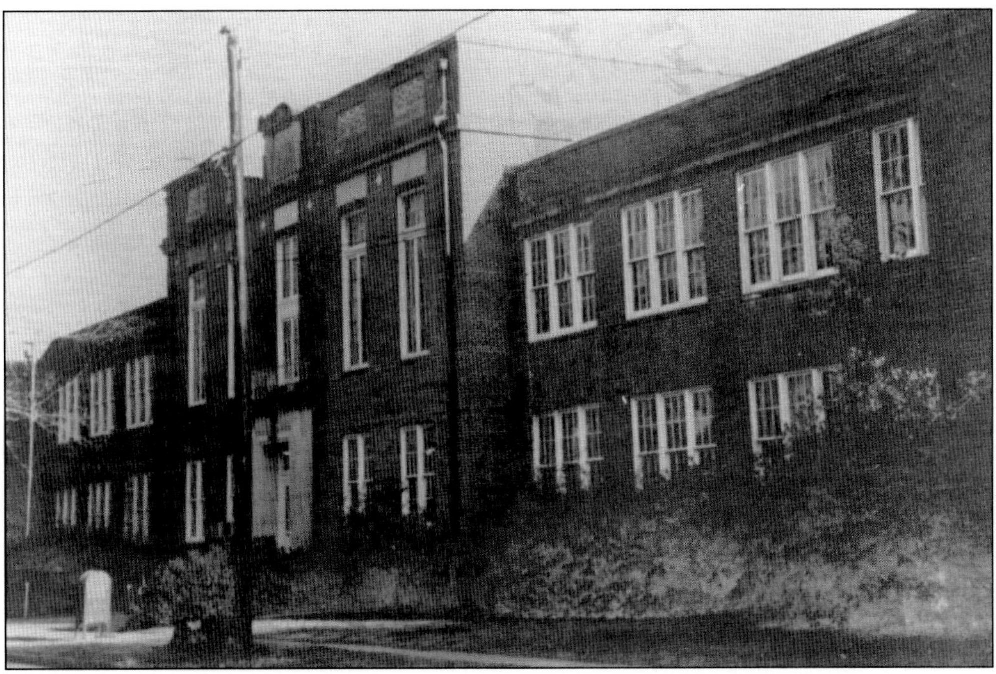

Hammond High principal Linus Sims, at right, was instrumental in the establishment of Southeastern Louisiana College, which became Southeastern Louisiana University in 1970. Hearing that the state wanted a junior college system, Sims petitioned Dr. Lucius McGehee and Oscar Donaldson, president of the chamber of commerce. With the passage of a one-mill tax, Hammond Junior College opened in fall 1925, holding classes in the high school for three years. Five faculty members taught 40 students the first year: Walter S. McKay, science and psychology; Joseph Perry Montgomery, education, mathematics, and sociology; Marie del Norte Theriot, French and history; D Vickers, English, speech, and civics; and Ione Duncan, music and art. Below, at a 25th anniversary reunion with alumni of the Class of 1926, are Theriot (front left), Vickers (back center), and Montgomery (back right).

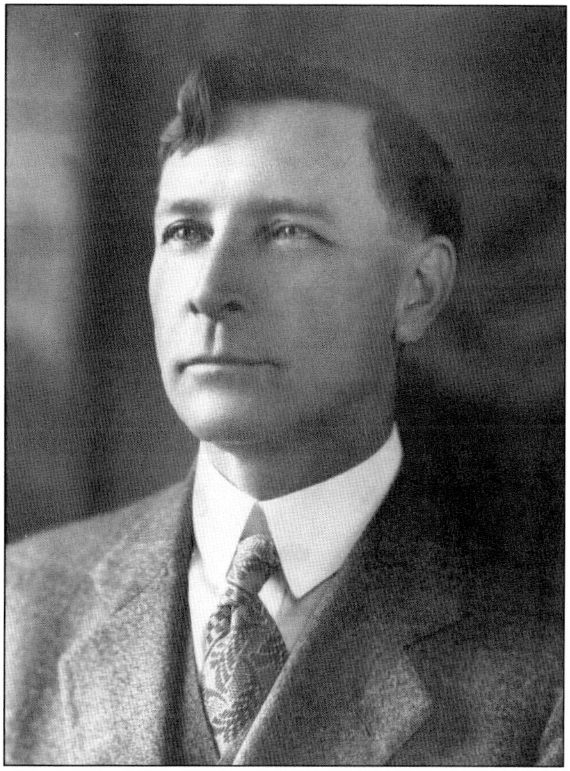

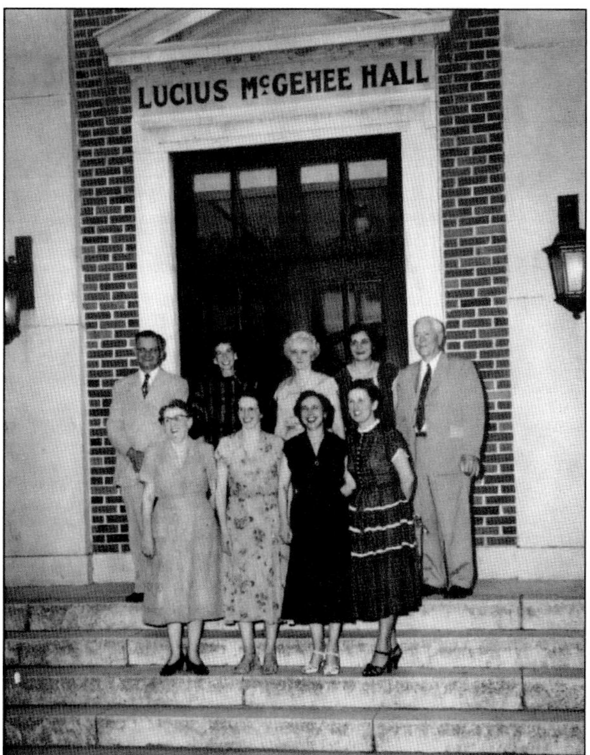

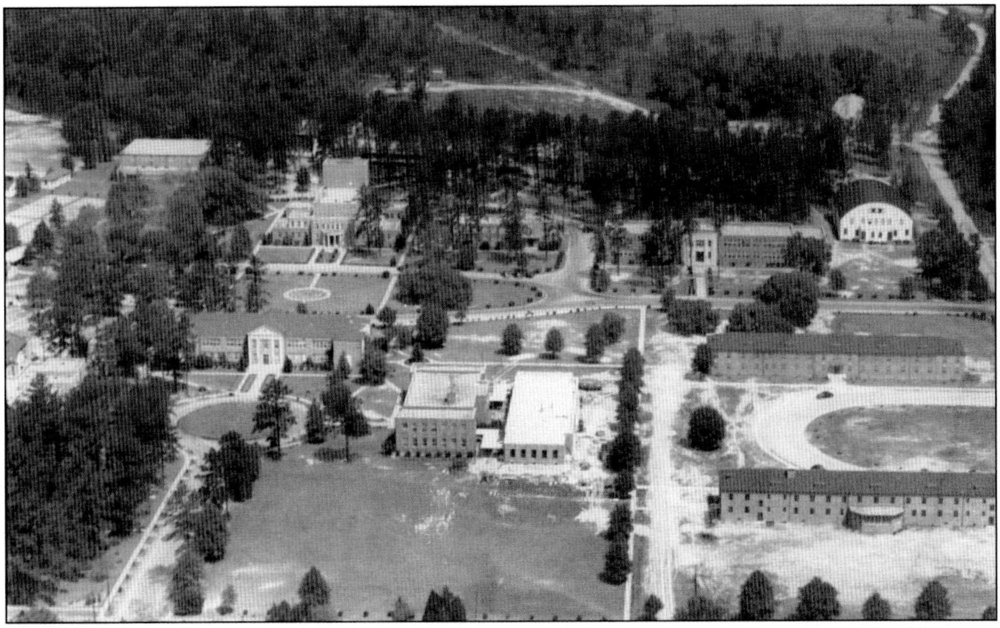

Hammond Junior College became Southeastern Louisiana College in 1928. Seven buildings in the Art Deco style were constructed between 1938 and 1940. This aerial view of the campus in the 1940s shows Pottle Hall to the rear of McGehee Hall on the left, Senior Hall behind the science buildings in the center, and the Teacher Training Building and the women's gym behind Mims and Southeastern Halls on the right.

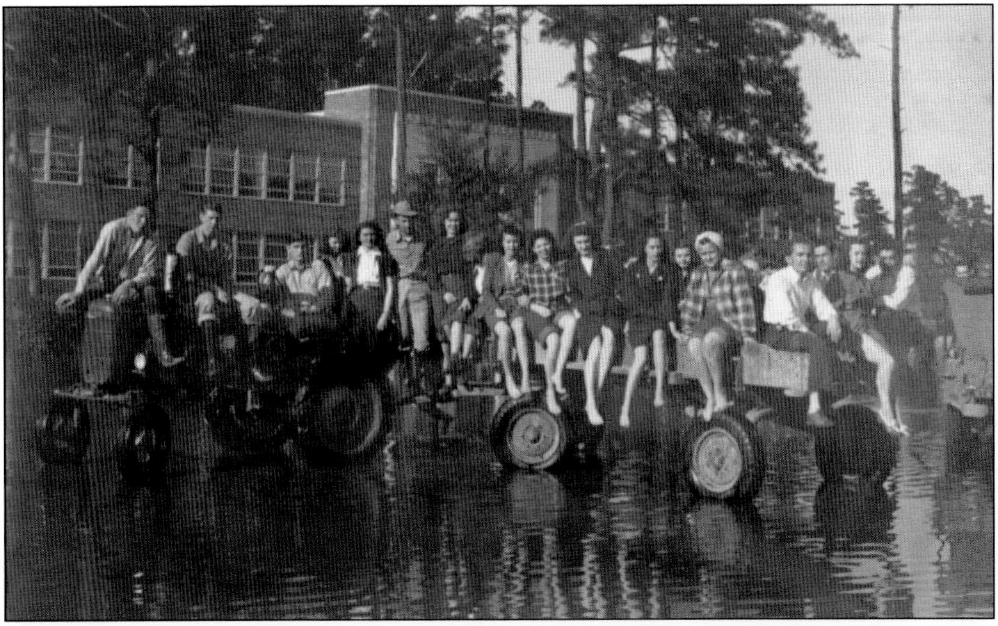

Southeastern students, seated on a tractor pulling a flatbed, brave the flooding of their campus in 1937 in front of the Teacher Training Building, later McClimans Hall. The building housed the Southeastern high school and elementary school until the early 1970s, when a new laboratory school was constructed on the other side of campus. Drainage was poor, and light flooding occurred with regularity, as documented in Southeastern's *Le Souvenir* yearbooks.

Four men demonstrate the typical dorm life at Southeastern Louisiana College in the men's dormitory at Strawberry Stadium. Completed in 1937, the stadium dormitories featured a cafeteria, post office, and social room. The men's dormitories were on the second floor of the east side, while the football players lived on the second floor of the west side.

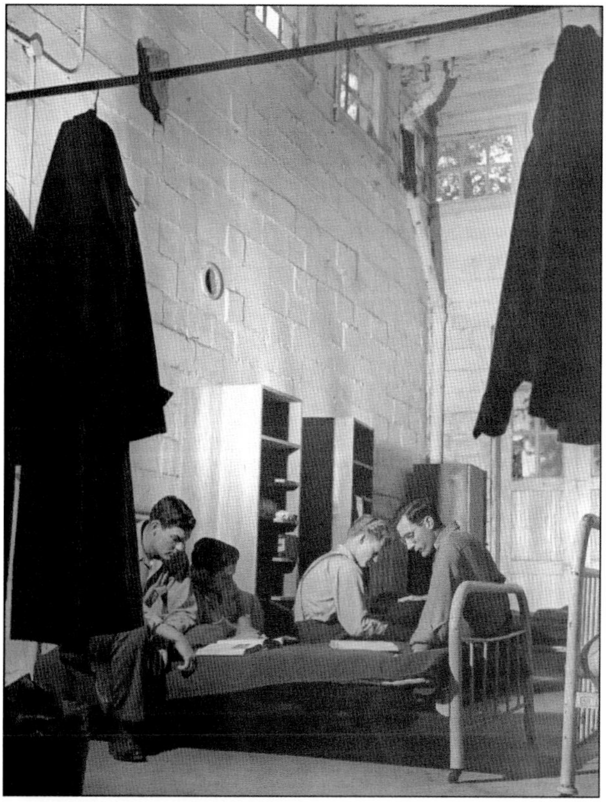

The dictionaries and typewriter on the desk suggest that this may be an English composition class in a room full of World War II veterans. Southeastern experienced a boom in enrollment after the war and had to depend on government "G" buildings to accommodate the effects of the G.I. Bill, which helped veterans access higher education. Northern colleges quickly filled, and Southeastern gladly absorbed the overflow.

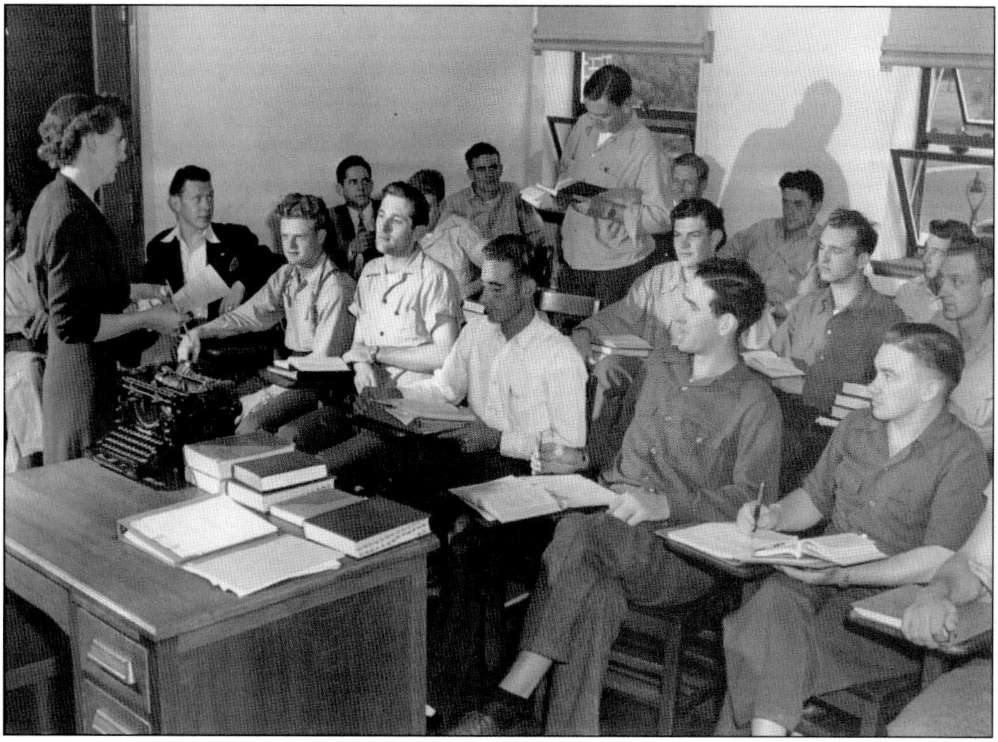

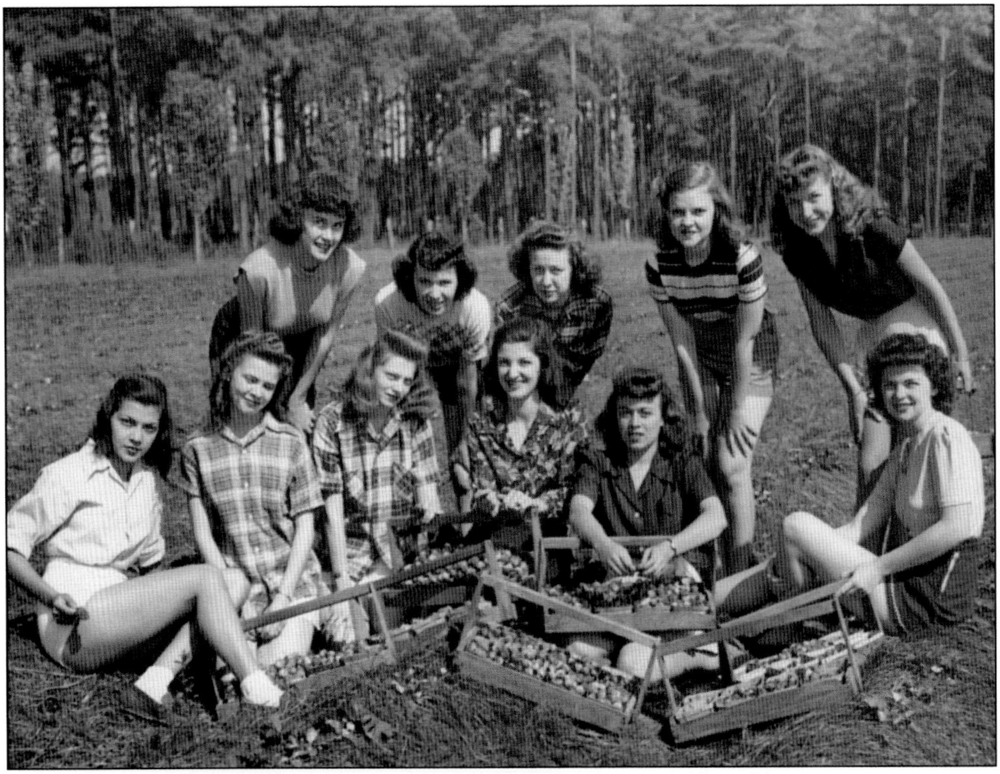

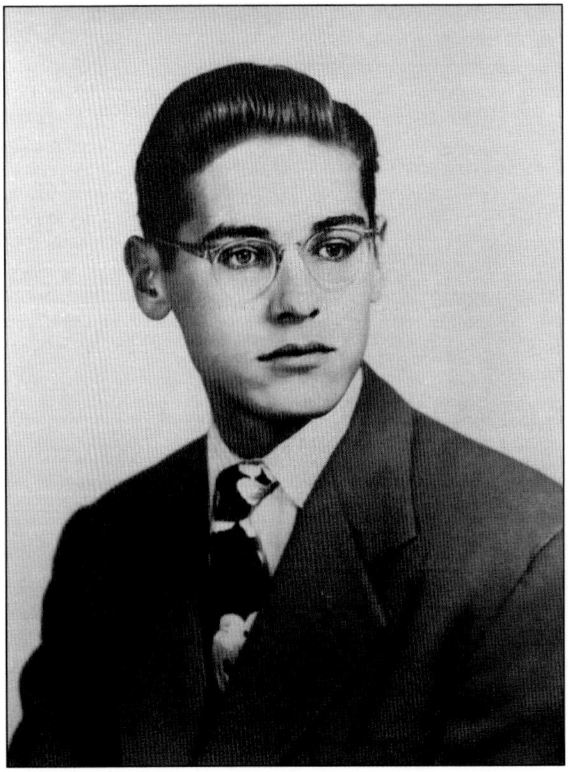

During World War II, men and women joined the war effort, and both industry and farming were affected by their absence. Southeastern enrollment declined by half from 1940 to 1944, but students who remained saved the strawberry crop of 1944 by working in the fields before classes. The college changed class schedules to accommodate the early work hours of student laborers.

One of the most notable Southeastern graduates was jazz pianist Bill Evans, who attended the school from 1946 through 1950 on a flute scholarship. He studied classical piano interpretation and composition, played with the college band, and cofounded a music fraternity. He later went on to form the Bill Evans Trio and become a renowned jazz artist, influencing countless other jazz musicians and winning a Grammy Lifetime Achievement Award.

Bibliography

Campbell, Edna. *Carving Charm with Hammer and Brush: Hammond's Historic District and Tangipahoa Parish Vignettes*. Hammond, LA: Edna Campbell, 1982.

———. *Our Cherished Roots: Hammond's Centennial Trail, 1889–1989*. Baton Rouge: Damon Press, 1987.

Citizens National Bank. *Tangipahoa Crossings: Excursions into Tangipahoa History*. Baton Rouge: Moran Publishing, 1979.

Couvillion, Vic. "James Renshaw's Hammond of 1893–1894." *Southeast Louisiana Historical Association Papers*, vol. 4, 1977.

Fontenot, Yves Leon. "Louisiana in the Spanish-American War." MA thesis, Louisiana State University, 1927.

Ford, Leon, III. *Hammond Army Air Field and Early Aviation in the Hammond Area*. Hammond, LA: Leon Ford, 1996.

Harris, Ronald. *We Hail Thee Now Southeastern: Remembering the First Seventy-Five Years of Southeastern Louisiana University*. Hammond, LA: Southeastern Development Foundation, 2000.

Nichols, C. Howard. *Centennial Souvenir: A Hammond History Source Book, 1889–1989*. Hammond, LA: Hammond Centennial Committee, 1989.

———. *Citizens Square: Recollections of Historic Hammond*. Hammond, LA: Citizens National Bank, 1984.

Perrin, James M. "A History of Education in Tangipahoa Parish, 1869–1979." MS thesis, Southeastern Louisiana University, 1980.

Romero, Ginger. *The Catholic Story in the Hammond Area of Louisiana: A Century of Action, 1890–1990*. Hammond, LA: Holy Ghost Catholic Church, 1993.

———. *The Louisiana Strawberry Story*. Natchitoches, LA: Northwestern State University Press, 1984.

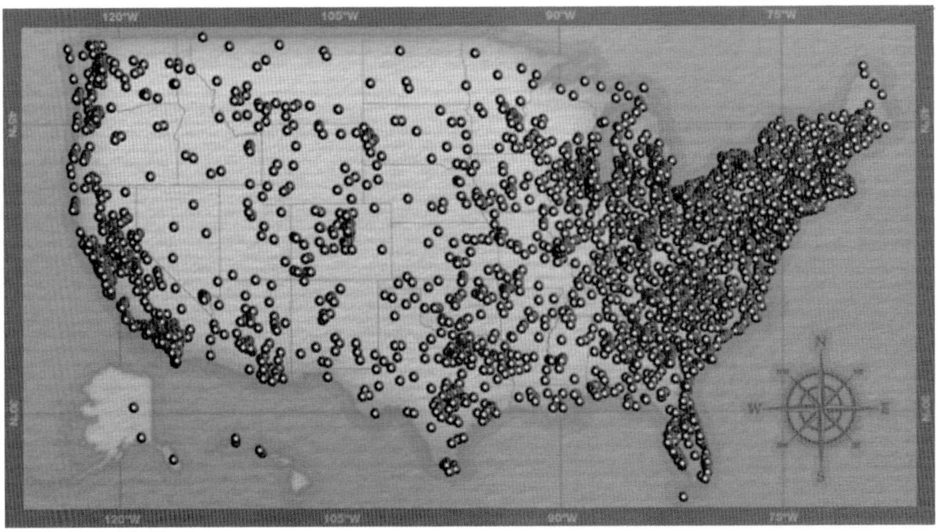